International Politics and Security in Korea

International Politics and Security in Korea

Jungsup Kim
Director, International Policy Division, Ministry of
National Defense, Republic of Korea

Edward Elgar
Cheltenham, UK · Northampton, MA, USA

Published by
Edward Elgar Publishing Limited
Glensanda House
Montpellier Parade
Cheltenham
Glos GL50 1UA
UK

Edward Elgar Publishing, Inc.
William Pratt House
9 Dewey Court
Northampton
Massachusetts 01060
USA

A catalogue record for this book
is available from the British Library

Library of Congress Control Number: 2006937959

ISBN 978 1 84720 029 7

Printed and bound in Great Britain by MPG Books Group of Companies

Contents

Acknowledgements

The completion of this book owes much to the support of many teachers and friends. My greatest debt is to my supervisors at Oxford University, Professor Rosemary Foot and Dr. Yuen F. Khong. Rosemary Foot has always provided detailed comments and constructive suggestions, challenging my arguments and helping to sharpen my thinking. I am deeply thankful for her care and attention to my work. I also wish to express my sincere appreciation to Yuen F. Khong for his wise counsel and constant encouragement. He gave valuable advice especially on US foreign policy and methodological issues in my writing. I also thank the examiners of my thesis, Professor Arthur Stockwin and Dr Aidan Foster-Carter, for their sincere interest in my work and kind suggestions.

I was also fortunate to have studied at Harvard University under two distinguished scholars: my adviser Professor Stephen Walt and Professor Ernest May. Their expert guidance was crucial to my development as a student of international relations and in helping me to pursue my doctoral studies at Oxford. I also owe much to the professors at Seoul National University where I spent four wonderful years as an undergraduate student, and especially thank Professor Park Chan Wook who encouraged me to study abroad.

I am indebted to many of the policy-makers who generously agreed to be interviewed: Ahn Kwang-chan; Chung Jong Wook; Han Yong-sup; Kim Chong Whi; Kim Sam Kon; Lee Bu-jik; Lee Sang-ok; Park Yong-ok; and Gary Samore. General Kim Kook-heun was also kind enough to permit me to have access to internal documents of his Bureau of the Arms Control of the ROK Defense Ministry. I thank General Hwang Eui-don as well for his help in arranging meetings with some of the above interviewees.

My studies at Oxford would have been impossible without the moral and material support from my parents and parents-in-law. Most of all, special gratitude goes to my wife, Kyuhee Cho. Despite her own professional responsibilities, she patiently endured some of the difficult times throughout my study abroad. This book is for her.

A note on romanisation

In romanizing Korean names, this thesis has generally followed the McCune-Reischauer system, retaining idiosyncratic spellings of names of well-known persons and places (for example, Seoul instead of Sŏul, Pyongyang instead of P'yŏngyang, and Kim Il Sung instead of Kim Il Sŏng). Korean surnames usually precede given names.

1. Introduction

1. Questions

Since the onset of the Korean War in 1950, scholars and policymakers alike have been concerned with the possibility of a second massive invasion of South Korea by the North. Indeed, North Korea appeared bent on communising the Korean peninsula by force, a prospect manifested through its repeated terrorist activities against South Korean leaders and civilians. From the attack on the South Korean presidential mansion in 1968 to the attempted assassination of South Korean president Park Chung-hee in 1974; from the killing of the Chun Doo-hwan cabinet members in Rangoon in 1983 to the bombing of a KAL airliner in 1987, North Korea terrorized the South in the hope of effecting the overthrow of its regime. However, all-out war did not break out during the Cold War, and, despite an uneasy standoff, the balance of power has been maintained. Relations between the United States and South Korea have acted as a deterrent against a North Korean attack, while North Korea's formidable military capabilities have kept the South from becoming too adventurous.

The end of the Cold War marked a major change in the balance of power between the two Koreas. Economically, South Korea's GNP rose to approximately ten times that of the North by the early 1990s. On the diplomatic front, South Korea established formal relations with the Soviet Union and China in 1990 and 1992 respectively, significantly weakening Pyongyang's position with Moscow and Beijing. Even the military balance on the peninsula seemed inclined towards the combined US and South Korean forces. In short, North Korea had become, vis-à-vis the South, economically weak, diplomatically isolated, and militarily disadvantaged. This shift in power put North Korea on the defensive.[1] Given this new political reality, one might have expected a more stable or manageable situation to have emerged on the peninsula.[2] Pyongyang might have been forced to abandon its long-time goal of unification by force and adopted in its place a more practical policy of economic reform and political reconciliation with the South. Indeed, instances of limited cooperation followed immediately after the end of the Cold War. The US and North Korea maintained a low-level direct dialogue in Beijing during 1989 and 1992, and Washington withdrew nuclear weapons from the South while cancelling the annual major US–South Korean joint military exercises called Team Spirit. Furthermore, prime ministers from both Koreas held meetings for the first time since the division of the peninsula, and produced a historic document on inter-Korean relations.

However, the Korean situation soon entered into a tense confrontation over the North's nuclear weapons programme. This dispute led to a serious crisis in 1994, stopping just short of war. Even after the nuclear crisis, Pyongyang continued to engage in various hostile activities against Seoul, including military clashes in the border area and the incursion of a North Korean submarine across the South's military demarcation line in 1996. Hence, the questions that this book employs are as follows: why is cooperation between the Koreas so difficult to attain and why does the Korean peninsula continue to endure high tension and crises even after the end of the Cold War? What has been the driving force in creating these tensions and crises? In order to answer these questions, the book examines major incidents in the Korean peninsula between 1988 and 1997. While the nuclear crisis has a prominent position, other issues, including diplomatic normalization, conventional arms control and Pyongyang's military provocations on the land and at sea in the midst of a food crisis will also be investigated in depth. Based on the analysis of the above cases, this thesis argues that the security dilemma in both Koreas along with Seoul's domestic politics has contributed to escalating or prolonging tensions, while American and Chinese intervention have tended to assist in resolving them.

An accurate understanding of the sources of the security problems is critical from the policy perspective. Analysts and policy-makers in Washington and Seoul have disagreed vehemently over the appropriate strategy for dealing with North Korea. An extreme, hard-line view sees no room for compromise and advocates isolation and containment, while a liberal position argues for unconditional engagement, viewing North Korea as essentially 'a victim of great-power politics.'[3] Although there are more moderate views on each side of the spectrum, this fundamental disagreement hampers the process of developing an appropriate policy towards the North. If this thesis succeeds in advancing a better understanding of Korean security problems through its analysis, then it might assist in facilitating productive policy debates and provide guidance as to an appropriate strategy towards North Korea.

2. Continuing Tensions and Crises on the Korean Peninsula: Previous Explanations

Various attempts have been made to explain why the Korean peninsula has experienced continuing or even more serious tensions after the end of the Cold War. Whereas one group of analysts blames the aggressive and irrational character of the North Korean regime, another stresses the mismanagement and aggressive behaviour of South Korea as a source of trouble. It has also been suggested that the domestic politics of North and South Korea have played a distorting role in inter-Korean relations. Finally, some scholars argue that US policy has to a large extent been responsible for shaping inter-Korean relations on the assumption that Washington's influence is dominant in Korean security issues. These different perspectives are outlined below.

A. North Korea's Aggressiveness and Irrational Leadership

One prominent view sees the North Korean regime as aggressive and dangerous. Scholars and policymakers holding these views argue: 'There exists no firm evidence that North Korea has completely abandoned its doctrine of forceful unification' in the period since it first invaded the South.[4] Sporadic spying activities, provocative infiltrations of border areas, and its nuclear weapons programmes are offered as proof of North Korea's offensive intentions.[5] According to this view, North Korea's assertive inclinations against South Korea are the main source of tensions on the peninsula. Moreover, some scholars in this group argue that Pyongyang's leadership is not only aggressive, but also irrational and unpredictable.[6] Focusing on the personalities of the absolute leaders of North Korea, Kim Il Sung and his son Kim Jong Il, and the North's national ideology of 'Juche'(Self-reliance) in explaining North Korean foreign policy, these scholars have described North Korea as 'erratic and periodically violent' and 'logic-defying.'[7] In short, Pyongyang's offensive motivations and irrational leadership are blamed for continuing to promote the tensions and crises on the peninsula, even in a changed international environment and with Pyongyang's weaker position with respect to Seoul.

Founded on this belief of North Korean aggression, scholarship about and policy towards North Korea since 1945 have been dominated by the logic of deterrence.[8] The central argument of deterrence theory is that 'great dangers arise if an aggressor believes that the status quo powers are weak in capability and resolve.'[9] In this light, it has been widely believed that any concessions on the part of South Korea and the United States are likely to cause North Korea to redouble its efforts to extract a further retreat rather than to respond in kind.

B. South Korean Mismanagement and Offensive Strategy

In contrast to the above view, some scholars have suggested that North Korea's sense of insecurity in a changed world is the real source of the insecurity on the peninsula.[10] This argument propounds that North Korea's military and security policlies are essentially based on fear or the necessity of survival. North Korea's nuclear programme, according to this view, was a logical and desperate response to the threat of US nuclear weapons, South Korea's increasing conventional military capability, and Pyongyang's loss of allied support at the end of the 1980s. This group of scholars is often critical of Washington and Seoul for failing to recognize the security fears of Pyongyang. The United States and South Korea, they argue, often exaggerate the hostility of North Korea and have made the situation worse by adopting policies insensitive to the North's security fears. The resumption of Team Spirit in 1993, for example, contributed to tensions by ignoring or underestimating North Korea's security concerns, despite repeated warnings from Pyongyang.[11]

Some scholars in this group go even further and argue that South Korea's offensive ambition has been the real obstacle to peace and cooperation on the peninsula. South Korean hard-liners are described as recognising the weakness of North Korea and pursuing 'a quick collapse and absorption of the North.'[12] In this view, behind Seoul's uncooperative policies–such as the reluctance to send food aid to Pyongyang and opposition to Pyongyang's normalization with Washington and Tokyo–are the intentions of right-wing factions in the South designed to isolate and weaken the North and ultimately to apply German-style unification to the peninsula. Hence, it is argued that Seoul's hostile attitude has exacerbated tensions by playing on Pyongyang's insecurities and thereby provoking desperate reactions. Additionally, whereas North Korea is described as being serious regarding arms control, South Korea is criticized as being passive and opposed to the North's proposals. Bluntly stated, this view posits that peace is not being achieved because hard-liners in the South do not want it.

C. Domestic Politics of North and South Korea

Other scholars, however, point to the domestic realm. They stress that inter–Korean relations are utilized for domestic political reasons in both North and South Korea, thus exacerbating tensions on the peninsula.[13] The North and South Korean public alike are vulnerable to their governments' political manipulation, as they have been conditioned by living under the threat of the other side for over half a century. Examples that illuminate possible links between inter-Korean matters and domestic politics are numerous. In October 1992, for example, the South Korean government's arrest of 95 North Korean spy agents cast doubt on the wisdom of cooperating with North Korea, and possibly contributed in shifting the course from reconciliation to confrontation. This spy-ring case, which had been announced just two months before a presidential election, was suspected to be a 'political conspiracy' designed to ensure the victory of a ruling party candidate.[14] Another example is the military clash in the border area in April 1996, involving a North Korean military demonstration and shooting exchanges between North and South Korean soldiers. This incident created a sense of crisis among the South Korean public and allegedly led to the defeat of the opposition party in the parliamentary election three weeks later.[15]

In a similar vein, many provocative actions of North Korea, such as infiltration attempts and the nuclear weapons programme, may have been pursued by Kim Il Sung and his son Kim Jong Il to tighten domestic control. The North's abrupt announcement of withdrawal from the Nuclear Non-Proliferation Treaty (NPT) in March 1993, in particular, has been speculated to be part of Kim Jong Il's strategy of preventing dissident voices from raising objections to his leadership during the power transition from his father.[16] Based on examples such as these, it has been argued that military tensions have often been created deliberately by leaders in both Pyongyang and Seoul for domestic political advantage.

D. Influence of the United States

Instead of focusing on the Koreas' strategic and domestic motives, some scholars put more weight on the role of external actors, the US in particular, in understanding security issues on the peninsula. Because of the dominant role that the US plays in Korean affairs, they argue that cooperation and confrontation on the peninsula have to a large extent been determined by differing political agendas in Washington.[17] This bureaucratic fighting in Washington is influenced by the actions and attitudes of the Koreas, as well as by the positions of the regional powers surrounding the peninsula. During the crisis over the North's nuclear programme, for example, Beijing's rejection of US sanctions against North Korea strengthened the position of the State Department advocating negotiation, while Seoul's opposition to a bilateral nuclear deal between the US and North Korea encouraged the voices of their opponents.[18] In this view, then, US policies have been informed through such dynamics, and those policies have had a dominant impact on the course of inter-Korean relations and the Korean security situation.

3. An Alternative Framework

While the arguments mentioned above satisfactorily explain certain aspects of the causes of the recurrent tensions on the peninsula, they also have weaknesses. The first two explanations, which stress the offensive strategies of North and South Korea as a source of tension, do not fully investigate the sense of insecurity that might have prompted the foreign policy of both nations. Given the bitter experience of the Korean War, the highly dangerous military standoff afterwards, and the fact that neither side can ever be completely secure until unified as one regime, the offensive behaviour of Pyongyang and Seoul may stem from a mutual apprehension. In other words, the policies of North and

South Korea may, in fact, be motivated by a mixture of fear and aggression. Furthermore, if North Korea has been so bent on pursuing the communization of the South, even after the end of the Cold War, these arguments fail to explain the period of cooperation between 1988 and 1992. During this time, North Korea responded in kind to initiatives by the US and South Korea. The mutual concessions and cooperative spirit exhibited appear to contradict deterrence logic's prediction that engagement would not yield cooperation from Pyongyang, but rather would embolden it to extract further concessions from the US and the South. In this light, this book examines the security dilemma–the idea that each party's efforts to increase its own security reduce the security of the other, as opposed to explanations based on the offensive intentions of those parties involved.[19]

In addition, the previous explanations, each focusing on only a single factor, do not fully take into account that various factors (security, domestic politics and international actors) have influenced the situation, though each may have a different relative importance depending on the circumstances. It would probably be too simplistic, for example, to argue for the overwhelmingly dominant role of the US in Korea, because the degree of American influence has varied, depending on the nature of the issues. Other explanations, based on security factors or domestic politics, seem to have a similar problem in that they do not take into full account the multi-dimensional character of Korean security problems. In other words, the previous explanations do not provide an adequate account of the conditions under which specific factors are more effective and how they are interrelated. This study attempts to account for inter-Korean relations through a set of factors rather than focusing on a specific one, aiming at a more balanced and in-depth understanding of the cause of Korean security problems.

As mentioned above, the security dilemma theory is employed to understand the security aspect of inter-Korean confrontation. States often do not recognize that this problem exists: they are often unaware that their own actions can be viewed as threatening to others, because they fail to see the world from their adversaries' point of view. Both North and South Korea, according to this theory, might be captives of this dilemma, and tensions and crises might be explained in this way. This book also looks at the role played by domestic politics, including the North Korean Juche (self-reliance) ideology, the participation of bureaucratic or factional interest groups and the manipulation of security issues by leaders for their own political purposes. Finally, the influence of external actors, not only the US but also China, Japan, Russia and the IAEA, is considered. In examining the role of external players, both the strategic environment of each country and its domestic political influences (e.g. elections and bureaucratic politics) has been taken into account in order to understand their behaviours.[20] Since these factors have often operated in a simultaneous and complementary way, efforts are made to understand how they are interrelated, and which of them matter most under different conditions.

A. Security Dilemma and Misperception

The security dilemma theory is a structural explanation, focusing on the systemic aspect of international politics. In this sense, it propounds that the imperatives of self-help in the anarchic international system have often forced both North and South Korea to adopt aggressive policies, even when there have been no offensive intentions. In other words, Seoul fears that the Pyongyang regime might undertake a surprise attack against the South, as it did in 1950. Similarly, Pyongyang seems to be apprehensive that South Korea and the US aim to attack or undermine the North by taking advantage of their superior economic and military powers. Under the pressure of such concerns, the security dilemma perspective posits that the actions taken by each Korea to strengthen its own security often threaten the other side's security and consequently provoke a hostile response.

In addition, this structural security dilemma might be compounded by psychological bias. As misperception theories generally point out, both North and South Korea might tend to interpret the actions of the other side as hostile and negative, even when they are neutral or friendly. The cognitive biases of both Pyongyang and Seoul towards each other could have increased the perceived intensity of this security dilemma, precluding a balanced analysis of the other side and multiplying the potential for conflict.

Systemic Factors
The security dilemma is particularly intense when two conditions hold:[21]

- First, when offensive and defensive military forces are more or less identical, states cannot signal a defensive intent. Then either side interpreting the signals must assume the worst because it cannot trust adversaries.
- Second, if offensive operations are more alternative than defensive operations, states will choose the offensive alternative if they wish to survive. This may encourage pre-emptive or preventive war because a defensive posture is ultimately deemed to be hopeless.

In the Korean context, the effects of these two conditions on the magnitude of the security dilemma are not entirely clear: while the first condition clearly seems to intensify the security dilemma because of the indistinguishability of offence and defence, the second condition (the relative effectiveness of offence vis-à-vis defence) appears ambiguous. It is extremely difficult to distinguish offensive and defensive policies in Korea, partly because many weapons held by both Koreas, whether conventional or non-conventional, can be used for both defensive and offensive purposes. Furthermore, massive military exercises and forward force deployment close to the DMZ can be interpreted as either offensive or defensive, depending on the initial assumption of the other's intentions.

Regarding the second of the above conditions, the relative effectiveness of offence versus defence is not clear, since the geographic implications of the peninsula do not entirely favour either the attacker or the defender. On the one hand, Korea's geography works against the aggressor, in part because of the creation of the DMZ, and in part because the natural geography of the peninsula provides only a few narrow corridors of attack for armoured and mechanized units.[22] Not only does a narrow front pose serious 'force-to-space constraints' by limiting the number of troops operating within a given space, but it also affords only a few predictable attack routes.[23] On the other hand, the small territory of the peninsula is to the aggressor's advantage. Since the length of South Korean territory is only about 700km, it took only seven days for North Korean troops to reach Pusan city, at the south-eastern end of South Korean territory, during the Korean War.[24] If a defender does not have deep rear territory, it does not enjoy much time to establish a second line of defence, and a blitzkrieg can be more effective and decisive. Regardless of the ambiguity created by the peninsula's geographic conditions, the overall balance between offensive and defensive effectiveness seems to favour the latter, due to additional factors operating in Korea. The presence of American forces in the South has made the North's offensive actions highly ineffective over the longer term, and at the same time, the potential of an elaborate military retaliation by the North has made pre–emptive offensive actions by Seoul unlikely.[25] In other words, significant retaliatory power on both sides has made offensive actions too risky, leaving the defensive mode as dominant.

North and South Korea, then, continue to live in a situation where offence and defence are virtually indistinguishable, but defence is more effective. This is an ameliorated security dilemma. In this situation, the security dilemma operates because offensive and defensive behaviours cannot be distinguished, but it does not operate as strongly as in a world where offence is dominant.[26] The emphasis on defence in this model may allow North and South Korea to react slowly and with restraint when they fear they are being menaced; although Pyongyang and Seoul can to some extent be threatening to the other side, that extent is limited. This might explain why North and South Korea have often adopted aggressive postures in the face of the other's offensive moves (indistinguishability of offence and defence), but ultimately extremely offensive actions that might trigger an all-out war have been contained (dominance of defence).

Psychological Bias

The incentives created by the international system are often not in and of themselves enough to explain the policies adopted by both countries. Furthermore, the issue of distinguishing offensive from defensive policies is primarily a question of perception. In order to explain the reactions of Seoul and Pyongyang to the systemic conditions described above, one must analyse their perceptions of those conditions. Drawing from the field of social psychology, the sub-field of attribution theory can provide some useful theoretical tools for analysing those perceptions. Attribution theory views individuals as 'naive scientists,' attempting to construct consistent explanations of the world around them, which can then serve as behavioural guides.[27] According to this theory, once a person develops an image of another, ambiguous and even discrepant information will be assimilated into that image. Thus, if one thinks that a state is hostile, behaviour that others might see as neutral or friendly will be ignored, distorted, or seen as attempted duplicity.[28] Following this line of analysis, this book examines the manner in which the psychological biases of both Pyongyang and Seoul have aggravated the security dilemma.

B. Domestic Politics and Ideology

Antagonistic Interdependence

As has been noted, there have been instances wherein leaders of both North and South Korea have reaped domestic political gains through tough actions towards the other. The political gains have varied, including victories in elections, enhancement of regime legitimacy, mobilization of the public and the securing of a power base, and improved political charisma during a period of power transition. Based on such cases, inter-Korean relations have often been described as 'antagonistic interdependence', meaning that, for various domestic political reasons, both the Pyongyang and Seoul regimes have needed tensions and confrontations to some extent, despite their public accusations against each other.[29] That is, the other side's hostility has not necessarily been a bad thing from the perspective of the leaders' domestic calculations, and each side has initiated hostile actions against the other and even welcomed and overreacted to the other's hostility.

In this sense, electoral politics in South Korea and succession politics in North Korea are carefully analysed in order to appreciate their impact on inter-Korean relations. With power in South Korea being transferred from military to civilian leaders during 1992 and 1993 for the first time since May 1961, democratization in Seoul may well have increased the importance of electoral politics on many issues. Although a direct connection between public opinion and foreign policy decision is not easily discernible, it has been noted that domestic structure is an important intervening variable in determining the influence of public opinion on foreign policy: the more society-dominated (the less state-dominated) a domestic structure, the stronger the correlation between public opinion and foreign policy.[30] In Pyongyang, on the other hand, the power transition from the absolute leader Kim Il Sung to his son Kim Jong Il was actively underway during the early 1990s. Although the North Korean regime had been carefully preparing for power succession from as early as 1972, it was only in 1990 that the military apparently came to accept Kim Jong Il, the most important task in the power transition process.[31] However hard the regime might have attempted to consolidate Kim Jong Il's power base, he lacked legitimacy and the necessary military background. Thus, the transition in this critical period may have affected Pyongyang's decisions.

Compartmentalized policy making

One of the puzzles of inter-Korean politics is that policies often seem irrational or inconsistent. When relations were improving rapidly in the fall of 1992, the South Korean intelligence agency announced the North Korean spy-ring case, creating much scepticism among the South Korean public about dialogue with the North. In this climate, President Roh was forced to cancel the scheduled visit of a deputy minister to Pyongyang to discuss joint economic development with the North, thus disrupting negotiations.[32] Incompatible behaviours are also found on the North Korean side. While Pyongyang was appealing to the world for food aid during the severe food crisis in the spring of 1996, North Korean armed soldiers were conducting military demonstrations close to the military demarcation line. This provocation, undertaken only a week after the North's appeal to the UN, evoked widespread condemnation from Washington and Seoul, and made urgently needed food for the North more difficult to obtain.

To understand such inconsistency and irrationality, the 'bureaucratic politics' model might be useful. In contrast to the 'rational actor' model that treats the nation-state as a unitary actor, the bureaucratic model assumes that various actors pursue their own purposes, promote their own power, and enhance their own position in the governmental hierarchy.[33] The policy consequences of this organizational decision-making approach could be political compromise among competing agents, foreign policy inertia and lack of innovation, or bureaucratic sabotage of presidential policy initiatives. Even without deliberate sabotage, presidential or a senior leader's directives may not be faithfully obeyed simply because of uncertainty about orders.[34] Orders may often be too general and unclear, leaving many of those responsible for implementing them uncertain as to what the president's or senior officials' decisions really are.

Juche ideology as a belief system[35]

Another perspective of the North's irrational behaviour–if indeed that behaviour is irrational–might be found in looking at North Koreans through their Juche (self-reliance) ideology, whose core meaning is a combination of national self–reliance and Korean nationalism.[36] Proclaimed by Kim Il Sung in December 1955, the ideology has always been consistent in promoting three related areas of self-reliance: 'independence in politics, self–sustenance in the economy and self-reliance in national defence.'[37] Unlike a typical political ideology such as Marxism, Juche has developed over the years, reflecting the leaders' goals in the context of changing international and domestic political situations.[38] It was first developed as anti-hegemonism designed to maximize the North's independence in the face of growing Sino-Soviet disputes, as well as the influence of the American military during the Cold War. Anti-hegemonism was also used in the late 1950s and the early 1960s to consolidate Kim Il Sung's political power by purging domestic rivals under the pretence that they were in collusion with Moscow or Beijing.[39] Later, the ideology grew to address other major issues, such as the legitimization of Kim's charismatic leadership, the justification of power transfer to his son, and the defence of North Korean socialism in the face of the collapse of the international communist bloc. The Juche ideology supposedly provides an unchallengeable guiding principle for virtually all fields of North Korean behaviour, including domestic and foreign policies. In that sense, North Korea's unitary ideology may have acted as a serious barrier to the pursuit of more pragmatic policies, as it can inhibit any rapid adjustment to changing realities.

On the other hand, Juche may be viewed as more of a comprehensive concept than just a player in the policy-making mechanism.[40] Partly because of the broadness of Juche and partly because of the leader's absolute authority to interpret it flexibly, Juche can be stretched to fit diverse situations. As suggested above, the historical evolution of Juche seems to represent that the ideology is an adaptable concept. One scholar states: 'The Juche's scheme is ... really a Gladstone bag for North Korea, flexible enough to accommodate all that North Korea pursues without tarnishing the integrity of the official ideology.'[41] This view suggests that it would be incorrect to assume a direct linkage between belief systems and actions in foreign policy, as many in the belief systems literature argue.[42] Therefore, the task of this study in relation to the Juche ideology is to determine to what extent the North's policy has been a pragmatic response to changing conditions, and to what extent policy has been dictated and distorted by ideology.

C. Influence of external actors

Relations between the North and South have not always remained strictly Korean, but have often had an international dimension, involving external players such as the US, China, the former Soviet Union/Russia and Japan. Among these actors, the US has undoubtedly been the dominant member on the peninsula, given its military alliance with South Korea and the hegemonic nature of its regional presence. US involvement has become even more pertinent since the end of the Cold War, as Pyongyang has put most of its national energy into dealing with Washington in an attempt to improve its deteriorating economic and diplomatic situation. Almost every demand from North Korea has been aimed at the US, and most of the issues in this research have something to do with the American factor.

In terms of influence on Korean issues since the end of the Cold War, China may be considered the second most important actor. From the time diplomatic relations were established in 1949, relations between China and North Korea have remained relatively cordial.[43] Although Beijing's traditional ties with Pyongyang have changed commensurate to its relations with Seoul, China has managed to maintain an even-handed policy towards the two Koreas, striking a balance between concerns for Pyongyang's stability and the benefits of economic relations with Seoul.[44] Behind this balanced approach has been Beijing's strong preference for a peaceful regional and international environment so that it could remain focused on its own efforts towards economic development and domestic stability. While some of Beijing's policies have been consistent with US interests, such as nuclear non-proliferation on the Korean peninsula, China has also insisted on a diplomatic approach towards North Korea in a manner that limits Washington's policy options including an UN-backed sanctions strategy against the North. To what extent Beijing has actually influenced the decisions of Pyongyang and Washington and on which issues needs further investigation.

Unlike China, the Soviet Union/Russia's influence on the peninsula has rapidly diminished since its humiliating abandonment of the North in 1990.[45] Moscow substantially curtailed its economic assistance, and, more importantly, suddenly established diplomatic relations with the South in 1990. The North's accelerated nuclear drive during the late 1980s and the early 1990s may also have been connected to its damaged relationship with the former Soviet Union. Although Russia began attempts to restore relations with North Korea in 1993, its active influence has not been apparent since the ending of the Cold War.[46] Thus, in contrast to Beijing, Moscow's role on the Korean peninsula seems often to have been indirect and limited.

As a result of North Korea's attempts to break out of its diplomatic isolation, Japan has become a more important partner for the North than it was during the Cold War. The two nations held official talks on normalization of ties for the first time in 1990, and unofficial contacts for resuming normalization talks followed in 1995. Given the huge importance of these discussions, the success of which might have substantially changed the strategic landscape of Northeast Asia, the process of and reasons for their failure are worthy of detailed analysis. It is argued that Japan's foreign policy has often been constrained by its tendency to follow America's position on security issues, as well as by unresolved animosity towards the South rooted in Japan's colonization of the peninsula.[47] Thus, the questions is to what extent pressure from Washington or Seoul shaped the course of the normalization talks, and to what degree Tokyo's internal decisions affected relations.

In addition to these nations, the International Atomic Energy Agency (IAEA) has also played an important role in the North's nuclear predicament. Although the IAEA may have had the same objective as the aforementioned individual countries (i.e. the prevention of the North from going nuclear), this international organization could well have had a different priority and approach to the issue. In fact, the IAEA maintained a tough position throughout negotiations, and its uncompromising stance may have further complicated Washington's efforts to resolve the nuclear standoff.[48] Therefore, it is necessary to examine the interactions between the IAEA, the US and North Korea, and to understand the relative importance and role the agency played in shaping the direction of the negotiations. In conclusion, examining the roles of these extra-Korean actors is aimed at understanding the international political context, which may have affected or determined competition and cooperation on the peninsula.

Through an exploration of the three explanatory factors mentioned above, this book argues that the security dilemma in both Koreas and domestic politics in the South were responsible for aggravating inter-Korean relations, while it is difficult to find a direct and significant correlation between the North's domestic politics and its external behaviour. This is contrast to previous explanations which stress North Korean aggressiveness or South Korean offensive strategy as the primary instigators. Furthermore, the lack of a direct link between the North's foreign policy and its domestic politics indicates that its leadership was more calculating and rational than it appeared to be. With respect to external actors, the US influence was most significant in shaping the situation, especially when the US was not preoccupied with other issues; China's balanced approach made it another important mediator. By contrast, Moscow's role was virtually invisible, and Japan showed a rather passive tendency to follow Washington. Beyond national politics, the IAEA complicated US-led nuclear diplomacy efforts with its strict position on inspections. Ultimately, however, difficulties tended to be resolved by US involvement and Chinese moderation.

4. Methodologies and Sources

The purpose of this study is to investigate the complexity of the post-Cold War security problems on the Korean peninsula. In each chapter, major cases are briefly described, and then analysed using the three different factors (security dilemma, domestic politics, and external actors). An assessment of the relative importance and interactions attached to each factor are then made.

Three methodological questions should be asked in relation to this task:

1. How can the three factors selected for possible explanations–the security dilemma, domestic politics, and the influence of external actors–be applied and tested?

First, what evidence would allow us to determine that the security dilemma is operating? The security dilemma arises when a defence-oriented policy threatens the other side and then triggers a counterproductive response. We can say that the security dilemma came into play in a specific chain of events only if defensive motivation was repeatedly expressed by key policymakers in adopting a certain policy, and the other side perceived it as a threat. Conversely, any counter-evidence demonstrating policymakers' motivations to be unrelated to security concerns, such as domestic political considerations, ideological constraints, and offensive intentions to exploit the other, would falsify the security dilemma arguments.

In a similar vein, a direct and positive influence of a government's actions on election results or the president's approval rating can be an indicator that domestic political factors were operating in South Korea. In addition, confusion, inconsistency, or compromise over policy may indicate the involvement of bureaucratic politics. In the case of North Korea, where it is more difficult to determine the effect of domestic political factors, the study investigates reasonable connections between the North's foreign policy and meaningful internal events, such as changes in the hierarchy of power, the differing stances among governmental agencies as demonstrated in the North Korean media, and Kim Jong Il's inheritance of power.

Finally, with respect to the influence of international actors, specific action or involvement should be provided as evidence of external intervention in order to determine the influence of foreign powers on the progress of the situation or the behaviours of the Koreas. For example, Washington's negative message to Tokyo vis-à-vis North Korean–Japanese normalization talks could be interpreted as evidence that American influence was an important factor in the failure of the negotiations. Likewise, as China has often played a prominent behind-the-scenes role in North Korean policies, this study accepts the influence of Beijing over Pyongyang when circumstantial evidence, such as a meaningful change in North Korean attitudes after contact between North Korean and Chinese officials, is found.

2. Once the relevant factors in explaining a given policy have been determined, it is necessary to assess the explanatory power of the factors. Hence, the second methodological task is to identify the more powerful causal relations between these factors and the policy choices of the decision-makers. When different factors are suggested in explaining a policy, how then can we find the most relevant factor among them? In a situation where information is restricted

and internal documents are rarely available, it is difficult to identify intentions clearly and to judge the relative explanatory power of the variables. Often the only possible option is to infer the most powerful causal link. Thus, by relying on 'causal inference', we check against spurious correlation by considering the persuasiveness of alternative explanations.[49]

It could be argued, for example, that the main impetus for Seoul's preference for rigorous inspections of the North's nuclear sites during the early 1990s was internal political motivations, on the grounds that South Korea's domestic political environment became more conservative prior to the upcoming presidential election. However, when we recognize that the South Korean government's position on the inspections had already been determined prior to these changes, it is perhaps more appropriate to consider an alternative explanation, such as the security dilemma. In other words, an explanation based on security motivations rather than domestic political factors may be more pertinent in interpreting this situation, given its stronger causal link.[50] In this manner, the study carries out a critical analysis of each case through a comprehensive review of the tenor of media coverage, reflecting the opinions of both the public and specialists at the time, as well as the position of government officials. In addition, we attempt to verify the primary motivations behind policy decisions by reviewing the memoirs of policy-makers and holding interviews with key decision-makers.

3. The third methodological question involves the psychological explanation of certain decisions made by North and South Koreans under the security dilemma. How do we know when certain decisions are biased, and under what criteria? How do we know, for example, that Seoul's decision to resume the Team Spirit military exercise in 1993 was mistaken? Unlike psychological experiments done in a laboratory, real foreign policy situations present ambiguous evidence and diverse judgments. Therefore, a rather weak and subjective criterion of bias is used for this study. A judgment will be deemed biased when it is held with a conviction stronger than is warranted by the available evidence. For example, if North Korean leaders seem convinced, without due reasonable evidence, that a joint US–South Korean military exercise would result in a pre-emptive attack on the North, it will be regarded as a biased belief. This standard is consistent with that used by other researchers.[51]

A methodological barrier to this research is asymmetric access to information about North and South Korea. Given the nature of security studies and the relatively recent period of this research, obtaining internal information has not been an easy task. Nonetheless, on the South Korean side, interviews with key decision-makers can to some extent compensate for the limitations in written information, and, in certain cases, leaks to the media offer additional information. By contrast, it is extremely difficult to acquire knowledge about decision-making in Pyongyang. Both the acquisition of written sources other than public propaganda and access to the decision-makers for interview are close to impossible. The lack of available sources on internal information is an intrinsic problem for all research on North Korea, especially regarding current security issues.[52] However, this problem need not be an insurmountable obstacle if the North's actions are carefully interpreted via consideration of its international and domestic situation. Although the internal decision-making of the North remains a black box for outside observers, it is granted that North Korean leaders must work within the constraints and incentives that the international and domestic systems place on them. Moreover, North Korean defectors, ranging from mid-level military officers to high-level party officials, provide some valuable inside information.[53] Verbal explanations from some North Korean officials about Pyongyang's intentions on major issues are also available, thanks to recent trips to the North by American officials and scholars.[54] Through such measures, the problem of limited access to internal information can to some degree be mitigated, and a reasonable, if not conclusive, interpretation of the North's behaviour is made possible.

Source material for this study includes primary sources and interview data, as well as secondary literature. Statements of various South Korean government institutions and the Defence Ministry's documents in particular have been collected and analysed. As noted earlier, interview data has also been collected from major decision-makers, including government officials, close aides to the presidents, and military officers of South Korea. This information has helped to identify how and on what basis South Korea has responded to or taken initiatives towards North Korea. Despite this advantage, however, interview data has a problem of verification, since interviewees might want to justify their actions or might experience difficulty in recollection. In order to mitigate this problem, the present study has checked the recollection of one interviewee against that of others, and has also attempted to supplement the information obtained by interview with written information from the public record.

For North Korea, various announcements and publications from Pyongyang–including announcements by the North Korean Foreign Ministry, statements by the People's Army Generals, and North Korea's newspaper, Rodong Sinmun–have been analysed in order to interpret its intentions, given that these are the official channels used by the North in expressing its ideas to the world. North Korean public statements are generally lengthy and detailed, and they may provide clues to understanding national decisions and intentions. However, it must be remembered that public statements serve many purposes, including propaganda and political agendas. Therefore, as has been stated, such statements have been used as evidence of Pyongyang's intentions only in combination with an objective analysis of its international and domestic situations.

5. Outline

This book is divided into seven chapters, including an introduction (Chapter 1) and conclusion (Chapter 7). Chapter 2 examines progress in relations between North Korea, South Korea, and foreign powers such as the US and Japan (1988.Jan.–1992.Oct.). More specifically, it deals with high-level US–North Korean contact and inter-Korean prime ministerial talks, emphasising the cooperative aspects rather than confrontation. Although our main purpose is to examine the causes of tension and crisis, it is deemed necessary, given the unprecedented positivism on the peninsula during the initial stages of the post-Cold War era, to explain fully how progress was made during that time. This chapter covers the same period as the following one (Chapter 3), which examines the limited nature of that progress. Through such a bipartite look at this period, Chapter 2 is able to stress the post-Cold War optimism on the peninsula, an optimism put to sharp contrast in the following chapters. The reader is thus afforded a relevant starting point from which to examine, in the following chapters, how the three explanatory factors have succeeded in halting or disrupting positive developments.

The next four chapters (3, 4, 5 and 6) investigate empirical cases to examine the source of tensions on the peninsula; this is accomplished through analysis via the three factors indicated above–the security dilemma, domestic politics and the role of external actors. Chapter 3 focuses on those cases limiting the progress described in Chapter 2, such as the failure to normalize US–North Korean and North Korean–Japanese relations, and the lack of progress in conventional arms control between the two Koreas. The primary concerns are why and how the new opportunities were not fully explored, leaving only limited progress and sowing the seed of future problems.

Chapter 4 traces the development of the nuclear crisis from the moderate cooperation of early 1992 to the mounting tension of spring 1993 (1992.Jan–1993.Mar.). The dispute over the 'challenge inspections' and the Team Spirit exercise, as well as the North's subsequent declaration of withdrawal from the NPT, is at the centre of the analysis. Chapter 5 covers the stalemate of the nuclear negotiations, the dangerous period of military standoff, and the dramatic ending of the nuclear crisis during 1994 (1993.Mar.–1994.Oct.).

Chapter 6 examines the continuing troubles after the nuclear crisis, including the North's food shortages, increased military tension at the DMZ, and North Korea's submarine infiltration incident (1994.Oct.–1997.Dec.). This chapter addresses the following specific questions: why did Pyongyang deliberately infiltrate the DMZ and the waters off South Korea's east coast (leading to serious tension on the peninsula), and why did Seoul react in a way which further destabilized the situation? Also, why did Seoul maintain a hard-line position towards the North's food shortage, and what was the character of the danger associated with such a position? At the same time, this chapter also looks at the role of international actors, the US in particular, to dampen the tensions. Thus, this chapter examines not only tensions but also their compromised resolutions. In this light, it has a different structure to the previous chapters which tend to outline only the breakdown of positive developments.

Finally, the closing chapter summarizes the findings obtained through the analyses of the cases and suggest their implications. Efforts have also been made to judge the relative importance of the three factors and their interactions in order to provide a balanced understanding of the complex nature of post-Cold War security problems on the peninsula.

The cases were selected on the basis of their importance in affecting the development of inter-Korean cooperation and confrontation. They encompass all the significant events or issues that appear to have determined the course of the situation for a particular period. Therefore, our aim of a balanced understanding of the sources of security problems on the Korean peninsula should be achieved, if significant episodes are not omitted in the selection of cases and they are properly analysed by the three major explanatory factors. Nevertheless, it should be noted that the intrinsic characteristics of the cases may well affect the role of these factors. Conventional arms control, for example, may exhibit the influence of the security dilemma more than it does domestic political factors. On the other hand, the normalization of diplomatic relations, by its nature, may have more to do with external actors than the other explanatory factors. Taking these points into account, we judge the relative importance of the three explanatory factors and their interactions in the concluding chapter.

Finally, it is necessary to explain why we centre on the period 1988–1997. First, all the basic security issues relevant to the post-Cold War period emerged during this period, driving the peninsula to great tensions and even to the brink of war. The main issues during the period of this study, such as the North's nuclear programme, conventional arms control, the armistice and new peace treaty between the US and North Korea, and normalization between Japan and the North, had not existed or emerged to any great degree before 1988, and continued to re-emerge after 1997. The situation since then appears, in a sense, to be a repetition of the same issues as those covered by this study (excepting the missile issue that surfaced in 1998), notwithstanding the changes in domestic and international settings. Therefore, an examination of this period may be deemed to provide relevant knowledge in understanding the current and future security situation of the peninsula. This will continue to be applicable until the situation changes fundamentally–a complete settlement of the nuclear issue, the normalization of Pyongyang's relations with Washington and Tokyo, and breakthroughs in conventional arms control.

Notes

1. North Korea has not attempted any terrorist activities since 1987, as South Korea's domestic situation has become more stable and legitimate. By the late 1980s, Pyongyang seemed to have realized that the South was not going to collapse from the internal chaos created by the North's aggression. See David Kang, 'Threatening, but Deterrence Works', in Victor D. Cha and David C. Kang, *Nuclear North Korea: A Debate on Engagement Strategies* (New York: Columbia University Press, 2003), pp. 61-3.
2. David Kang, 'North Korea's Military and Security Policy', in Samuel Kim ed., *North Korean Foreign Relations in the Post-Cold War Era*, (Oxford: Oxford University Press, 1998).
3. Victor D. Cha and David C. Kang, *Nuclear North Korea: A Debate on Engagement Strategies*, pp. 1-6.
4. Park Tong-whan, 'Issues of Arms Control Between the Two Koreas', *Asian Survey* 32, no. 4 (April 1992): p. 353.
5. William Taylor, Young-koo Cha and John Blodgett, eds, *The Korean Peninsula: Prospects for Arms Reduction under Global Détente* (Boulder: Westview, 1990); and Leonard Spector and Jacqueline Smith, 'North Korea: The Next Nuclear Nightmare?', *Arms Control Today* 21, no. 2 (March 1991).
6. Denny Roy, 'North Korea and Madman Theory', *Security Dialogue* 25, no. 3 (1994), pp. 307–16; and B.C. Koh, 'North Korea's Unification Policy after the Seoul Olympics', *Korea Observer* 19, no. 4 (Winter 1988), p. 384.
7. The citations are from William J. Taylor and Michael J Mazarr, 'US–Korean Security Relations: Post-Reunification'. *Korean Journal of Defence Analysis*, vol. 4, no. 1 (Summer 1992), p. 152; and Koh, 'North Korea's Unification Policy after the Seoul Olympics', p. 384.
8. On deterrence theory, see Thomas Schelling, *Arms and Influence* (New Haven: Yale University Press, 1966); Glenn Snyder, *Deterrence and Defence* (Princeton: Princeton University Press, 1960); John Mearsheimer, *Conventional Deterrence* (Ithaca, NY: Cornell University Press, 1983); and Jonathan Mercer, *Reputation and International Politics* (Ithaca, NY: Cornell University Press, 1996).
9. Deterrence theory, assuming that an opponent is 'greedy', calls for highly competitive policies and warns against the dangers of concessions. Any moderation and conciliation of status quo powers are apt to be taken for weakness by aggressive opponents. See Robert Jervis, *Perception and Misperception in International Politics* (Princeton: Princeton University Press, 1976).
10. Victor D. Cha, 'Engaging North Korea Credibly', *Survival* 42, no. 2 (Summer 2000); Leon Sigal, *Disarming Strangers: Nuclear Diplomacy with North Korea* (Princeton, NJ: Princeton University Press, 1998); David Kang, 'Preventive War and North Korea', *Security Studies* 4, no. 2 (Winter 1994/95); and Suh Dae-Sook, 'North Korea: The Present and the Future', *Korean Journal of Defence Analysis* 9, no. 2 (Winter 1998).
11. Sigal, *Disarming Strangers*; and Michael J. Mazarr, *North Korea and the Bomb: a Case Study in Non-proliferation* (Basingstoke: Macmillan, 1995).
12. Selig S. Harrison, 'US Policy Toward North Korea', in Suh Dae-Sook and Lee Chae-Jin eds, *North Korea After Kim Il Sung*, (London: Lynne Rienner, 1998).
13. Lee Jong-suk, *Pundansidaeŭi T'ong'ilhak [The Study of Reunification in the Divided Era]* (Seoul: Hanul, 1999), pp. 42-53; and Park Myong-lim, 'Pundan Chilsoŭi Kujowa Pyŏnhwa: Chŏktaewa Ŭichonŭi Taessangkwan'gyetonghak [Structure and Change of Division: Interface Dynamics of Hostility and Dependence]', *Kukka Chŏllyak [National Strategy]*, vol. 3, no. 1 (Spring/Summer 1997), p. 44.
14. *Dong-A Ilbo*, 9 December 1992.
15. *Chosun Ilbo*, 9 April 1996.

16. Intelligence officials in Washington and Seoul believed that Kim Jong Il was trying to impress his military by challenging the US and the IAEA. See David E. Sanger, 'Son of North Korean Leader May Be Succeeding to Power', *New York Times*, 25 March 1993, p. A10.

17. Lee Sam-sung, *Hanbando Haekmunjewa Migukyoekyo [The Nuclear Question and US Policy on the Korean Peninsula]* (Seoul: Hangil Publishing Company, 1994).

18. Chung Ok-nim, *Bukhaek 588il [588 days of North Korean nuclear bombs]*, (Seoul: Seoul Press, 1995).

19. For a thorough discussion of the basic workings of the security dilemma, see Robert Jervis, *Perception and Misperception in International Politics*, pp. 62-90; and 'Cooperation Under the Security Dilemma', *World Politics* 30 (January 1978). For earlier discussions of the security dilemma, see John H. Herz, 'Idealist Internationalism and the Security Dilemma', *World Politics* 2 (January 1950); Herbert Butterfield, *History and Human Relations* (London: Collins, 1951), and for a recent review of the theory, see Charles L. Glaser, 'The Security Dilemma Revisited', *World Politics* 50 (October 1997), pp. 171-201.

20. This book attempts to account for the causes of tensions and delays of cooperation in terms of a set of factors. In categorising the explanatory factors into three groups, the first two factors, the security dilemma and domestic politics, refer only to North and South Korean situations, and the security environment and domestic political situation surrounding external actors will be discussed in a section devoted to international contributors.

21. Jervis explains that the magnitude and nature of the security dilemma depend on two variables: the offence – defence balance and offence – defence differentiation. See Jervis, 'Cooperation Under the Security Dilemma', pp. 186-214

22. From the South's perspective, only three corridors (the East Coast, Munsan, and Chorwon corridors) are possible main routes for a North Korean attack. See Stuart K. Masaki, 'The Korean Question: Assessing the Military Balance', *Security Studies* 4, no. 2 (Winter 1994/95), pp. 369-71; and Michael O'Hanlon, 'Stopping a North Korean Invasion: Why Defending South Korea Is Easier than The Pentagon Thinks', *International Security*, vol. 22, no. 4 (Spring 1998), pp. 149-50.

23. John Mearsheimer calls this characteristic of terrain the 'length of the battlefront'. If the attacker is faced with a defender who is protecting a narrow front, it is more difficult for the attacker to penetrate the defensive lines than if the attacker can strike at a defender deployed across a broad front. See John J. Mearsheimer, *Conventional Deterrence* (Ithaca: Cornell University Press, 1983), pp. 44-5.

24. Mearsheimer refers to this as the 'depth of the battlefield', referring to the size of territory that a defender has behind his front-line forces. See Mearsheimer, *Conventional Deterrence*, pp. 44-5.

25. This is not to suggest that North Korea's military power is superior to that of the South, nor to assume that the South contemplates pre-emptive attacks against the North. Firstly, overall North Korean military capabilities clearly appear to be inferior vis-à-vis the combined forces of the South and the US. However, it is also true that even the superior US – South Korean forces are not capable of providing sufficient protection from North Korea's formidable firepower. With over 1000 170mm and 240mm long-range artillery deployed intensively along the 38th parallel, it is estimated that the North Korean forces are capable of firing approximately 15 000 rounds against the South within 30 minutes, destroying over 20 per cent of the Seoul area. Secondly, South Korea has an obvious self-interest in maintaining peace, and would thus be far from contemplating pre-emptive attacks. Moreover, Washington would exercise its restraining power against Seoul if the South did attempt to be militarily adventurous. However, in a crisis, it is impossible to rule out South Korea or the US wishing to launch a pre-emptive strike against North Korea. In fact, the Clinton administration seriously considered the surgical strike option against the North during the nuclear confrontation in 1994. However, the high cost of such military actions because of the North's retaliatory power was one of the main reasons that

Washington dropped the plan. On the cost of military conflict amid the nuclear standoff in May 1994 (US estimates), see Don Oberdorfer, *The Two Koreas, A Contemporary History* (New York: Addison-Wesley, 1998), pp. 314-5.

26. With the combination of the two variables, Jervis envisages four possible worlds. The first world is a doubly dangerous one, in which offence and defence are indistinguishable and at the same time offence is dominant. The second world is an ameliorated security dilemma situation like the Korean case. The third world (offence and defence are distinguishable, but offence is dominant) is not a security dilemma situation, but security problems exist because aggression is possible and easy. The fourth world (the two conditions can be distinguished and defence is dominant) is doubly stable. See Robert Jervis, 'Offence, Defence, and the Security Dilemma', in Robert J. Art and Robert Jervis, *International Politics: Enduring Concepts and Contemporary Issues*, 3rd edition (New York: HarperCollins Publishers, 1992), pp. 146-69.

27. Richard Nisbett and Lee Ross, *Human Inference: Strategies and Shortcomings of Social Judgment* (Englewood Cliffs, New Jersey: Prentice-Hall, 1980).

28. Good examples of works which apply the concepts of attribution theory to foreign policy problems are Robert Jervis, 'Hypotheses on Misperception', *World Politics* vol. 20, no. 3 (April 1968); Jervis, *Perception and Misperception,* and Deborah Welch Larson, *Origins of Containment: A Psychological Explanation* (Princeton: Princeton University Press, 1985). For the role of historical analogies in foreign policy decision-making, see Yuen Foong Khong, *Analogies At War: Korea, Munich, Dien Bien Phu, and the Vietnam Decision of 1965* (Princeton: Princeton University Press, 1992).

29. Lee Jong-suk, *Hyondae Pukhanŭi Yihae [Understanding of Modern North Korea]* (Seoul: Yoksapipyongsa, 2000), p. 31. A similar concept to this 'asymmetric interdependence' is Park Myong-lim's 'interface dynamics'. See Park'. Pundan Chilsoŭi Kujowa Pyŏnhwa: Chŏktaewa Ŭichonŭi Taessangkwan'gyetonghak [Structure and Change of Division: Interface Dynamics of Hostility and Dependence]', *Kukka Chŏllyak [National Strategy],* vol. 3, no. 1 (Spring/Summer 1997), p. 44.

30. Thomas Risse-Kappen, 'Public Opinion, Domestic Structures, and Foreign Policy in Liberal Democracies', *World Politics*, vol. 43, no. 4 (July 1991), pp. 479-512.

31. Kongdan Oh and Ralph C. Hassig, *North Korea Through the Looking Glass* (Washington, DC: Brookings Institution Press, 2000), pp. 85-9.

32. BBC Monitoring Reports, *Summary of World Broadcasts,* Far East, No. 1507 (8 October 1992), A1/3, hereafter cited as *BBC Summary* with the number of the monitoring report and the actual date of the news item. See also *Korea Newsreview*, 17 October 1992, p. 9.

33. On general discussions of bureaucratic politics, see Graham Allison, *Essence of Decision: Explaining the Cuban Missile Crisis* (Boston: Little Brown, 1971); Morton H. Halperin, *Bureaucratic Politics and Foreign Policy* (Washington, DC: The Brookings Institution, 1974); and Roger Hilsman, *The Politics of Policy Making in Defense and Foreign Affairs: Conceptual Models and Bureaucratic Politics* (Englewood Cliffs, NJ: Prentice-Hall, 1990). For a critique, see Stephen D. Krasner, 'Are Bureaucracies Important? A Re-examination of Accounts of the Cuban Missile Crisis', in Charles W. Kegley, Jr. and Eugene R. Wittkopf eds., *The Domestic Sources of American Foreign Policy: Insights and Evidence* (New York: St. Martin's, 1988).

34. According to the testimonies of former North Korean diplomats, communication among bureaucratic organizations is very poor, although Kim Il Sung and Kim Jong Il have been in firm control of the government. This lack of horizontal cooperation may have led to confusion or inconsistency in implementing Kim's directives.

35. The notion of a 'belief system' is used here as a general term, interchangeable with other similar concepts such as 'the image', 'operational code', and 'cognitive map', all of which basically refer to the same factor: the nature of the filtering device for existing beliefs about empirical and normative issues. For development of the study of belief systems in international

relations and differences between these concepts, see Steve Smith, 'Belief Systems and the Study of International Relations', in Richard Little and Steve Smith eds, *Belief Systems and International Relations* (Oxford: Basil Blackwells, 1988), pp. 11-36.

36. While the previously discussed misperception approach (in relation to the security dilemma) focuses on the psychological accounts of why individuals in general interpret the world the way that they do, the analysis of ideology here is focused more on a named individual or group with the question of how specific individuals see the world. For a different focus between the work of belief systems and the psychological literature on international relations, see Smith, 'Belief Systems and the Study of International Relations', pp. 12-13.

37. See Park Han S., 'The Nature and Evolution of Juche', in Kim Ilpyong ed., *Two Koreas In Transition: Implication for US Policy* (Maryland: InDepth Books), pp. 33-44.

38. Park Han S., *North Korea: The Politics of Unconventional Wisdom* (Boulder, Co.: Lynne Reiner, 2002), p. 20.

39. *Ibid.*, p. 22.

40. Kongdan Oh and Ralph C. Hassig, *North Korea Through the Looking Glass* (Washington, DC: Brookings Institution Press, 2000).

41. Quoted in *ibid.*, p. 175.

42. Ole R. Holsti, for example, has noted that 'The role that belief systems may play in policy making is much more subtle and less direct'. See Holsti, 'Foreign policy formation viewed cognitively', in R. Axelrod ed., *Structure of Decision* (Princeton, NJ: Princeton University Press, 1976), pp. 18-54.

43. But relations are not free from troubles. For example, relations cooled during the Chinese Cultural Revolution in the late 1960s and the Sino-American rapprochement of 1972. For a historical review of Sino-North Korean relations, see Lee Jong-suk, *Pukhan-Chungguk Kwan'gye [North Korea − China Relations: 1945 − 2000]* (Seoul: Chungsim, 2000).

44. Kim Ilpyong J., 'China in North Korean Foreign Policy', in Samuel S. Kim ed., *North Korean Foreign Relations in the Post-Cold War Era* (Oxford: Oxford University Press, 1998), pp. 94-113; and Samuel S. Kim, 'The Making of China's Korea Policy in the Era of Reform', in David M. Lampton, ed., *The Making of Chinese Foreign and Security Policy in the Era of Reform, 1978 − 2000* (Stanford: Stanford University Press, 2001), pp. 371-408.

45. David Reese, *The Prospects for North Korea's Survival* (Oxford: Oxford University Press, 1998), pp. 77-9.

46. Jane Shapiro Zacek, 'Russia in North Korean Foreign Policy', in Samuel S. Kim ed., *North Korean Foreign Relations in the Post-Cold War Era* (Oxford: Oxford University Press, 1998), pp. 75-90.

47. For the origins and general tendency of Japan's post-war foreign policy, see Kent Calder, 'The Reactive State: Japanese Foreign Policy', *World Politics,* vol. 40, no. 4 (July 1989); Michael J. Green, *Japan's Reluctant Realism: foreign policy challenges in an era of uncertain power* (New York: Palgrave, 2003); Christopher W. Hughes, *Japan's Security Agenda: military, economic, and environmental dimensions* (Boulder: Lynne Rienner Publishers, 2004); and Glenn D. Hook et al., *Japan's International Relations: politics, economics, and security* (London: Routledge, 2001). For a comprehensive analysis of Japan's politics in its institutional, historical and cultural context, see also J.A.A. Stockwin, *Governing Japan: Divided Politics in a Major Economy* (Malden, MA - Blackwell Publishers, 1999).

48. Sigal, *Disarming Strangers*, pp. 95-108.

49. Judith Goldstein and Robert Keohane, 'Ideas and Foreign Policy', in Judith Goldstein and Robert Keohane eds, *Ideas and Foreign Policy: Beliefs, Institutions, and Political Change* (Ithaca and London: Cornell University Press, 1993), p. 29.

50. Another example is that Seoul's tough reaction to the North's provocations in the DMZ in 1996 may have stemmed from its security concerns, such as fear of a rift in the ROK − US alliance

and the ramifications of nullification of the armistice regime. However, the explanatory power of this security factor-based account can be limited, if it is decided that Seoul overreacted, not proportional to the seriousness of the situation. Thus, other factors, such as Seoul's domestic political motivation, may have been operative and should be considered as an alternative explanation.

51. Nancy Kanwisher, 'Cognitive Heuristics and American Security Policy', *Journal of Conflict Resolution* vol. 33 (December 1989): 653; and Nisbett and Ross, *Human Inference*, pp. 13-4.

52. In that sense, it has been said that research about North Korea has remained at a level of deciphering, and is far from achieving the descriptive or explanatory stage.

53. Hwang Jang Yop, Secretary of the Workers Party for International Affairs, and Koh Young-hwan, a mid-level diplomat and former interpreter for Kim Il Sung, are examples of North Korean defectors who have published books on North Korea. See Hwang Jang Yop, *Nanŭn Yŏksaŭi Chilli rul Poattda [I have Witnessed Historical Truth]* (Seoul: Hanul, 1999); and Koh Young-hwan, *Pyongyang Yisibosi [Pyongyang's Twenty Five Hours].* (Seoul: Kyoryuone, 1992).

54. For example, Selig Harrison, American expert on North Korea, and C. Kenneth Quinones, Korean desk officer at the State Department during the Clinton administration, offer vivid descriptions of North Korean intentions by citing key North Korean officials. See, for example, Selig S. Harrison, 'Promoting a Soft Landing in Korea', *Foreign Policy,* no. 106 (Spring 1997), pp. 70-2.

2. Challenges and Opportunities in the post-Cold War era: 1988–1992

In the first few years after the Cold War's end, newfound evidence of the North's nuclear programme posed a great challenge to the nuclear non-proliferation regime. Nevertheless, significant progress was made during this time, including a series of American diplomatic initiatives and inter-Korean prime ministerial talks. This chapter will examine the causes of such progress. A brief overview of the events during this period will be offered first, followed by an examination of the various international and domestic elements which caused or facilitated the progress. As was suggested in the introduction, however, the mood of cooperation gradually diminished, and a period of recurrent tension and crisis followed. Because the issues explored in this chapter, North Korea's nuclear problem in particular, continue to re-emerge, an understanding of the international and domestic settings surrounding the two Koreas during this period will provide a valuable context in which to understand the tensions and crises to be examined later.

1. Diplomatic Progress on the Korean peninsula in the midst of Nuclear Challenge

Washington began to have suspicions about a North Korean nuclear programme in March 1984, when a US surveillance satellite detected what appeared to be the construction of a nuclear reactor at Yongbyon, 60 miles north of Pyongyang.[1] Although the reactor was not conclusive proof of a nuclear weapons programme, Washington was highly suspicious and sought Moscow's support in urging non-proliferation. Sharing American interests, Moscow encouraged the North to sign the Nuclear Non-Proliferation Treaty (NPT) by offering to supply four 440 MW nuclear reactors.[2] On 12 December 1985, North Korean Party Secretary Kang Song San signed the NPT in Moscow, and American concerns over Pyongyang's nuclear intentions were temporarily allayed.[3]

In the following years, however, US suspicion was renewed as more troubling evidence emerged. Another and much larger reactor was detected under construction at Yongbyon in June 1988. At that time, North Korea had not signed a safeguards agreement with the IAEA to monitor its facilities, despite its obligation as a member state of the NPT.[4] The following year, satellite photos first detected what appeared to be a nuclear reprocessing plant capable of extracting plutonium from spent reactor fuel, and the Central Intelligence Agency (CIA) came to believe that North Korea was unloading weapons-grade plutonium from the reactor.[5] In May 1989, convinced that Pyongyang's nuclear weapons programme was serious, Washington informed the South Korean government of its intelligence findings.

Following the US intelligence briefing to South Korea in spring 1989, the two nations began to implement a series of diplomatic measures intent on persuading Pyongyang to accept IAEA inspections.[6] The first was the withdrawal of American nuclear weapons from South Korea.[7] In the face of North Korean accusations, officials in Washington came to recognize that little progress would be made as long as American nuclear weapons were in place on the divided peninsula.[8] It was in this context that President Bush announced, on 27 September 1991, that all US ground- and sea-based tactical nuclear weapons would be removed throughout the world.[9]

The second measure taken was the cancellation of the Team Spirit military exercises. Harshly condemned by North Korea, these joint exercises, held every year since 1976 by the American and South Korean armed forces and involving more than 100 000 troops, had been a symbol of the alliance and were intended to deter a North Korean military attack.[10] Held about 50 kilometres south of the DMZ, the demonstrations generally involved amphibious landings, airdrops, manoeuvre warfare and exhibitions of chemical and nuclear prowess.[11] On 7 January 1992, in order to induce Pyongyang's cooperation, the South Korean Defence Ministry, in consultation with the US, announced the suspension of the 1992 Team Spirit exercise.

A final measure of diplomacy was the holding of direct and high-level talks with Pyongyang. With the expectation that an American overture towards improved diplomatic relations could act as a significant incentive for Pyongyang to cooperate on the nuclear issue, a high-level talk took place on 22 January 1992, in New York.[12] Representing the United States was Arnold Kanter, Undersecretary of State for political affairs, and the DPRK delegation was headed by Kim Yong Sun, Secretary for International Affairs of the Korean Workers' Party. This was the highest-level contact between the two governments since 1953.

Pyongyang's response to the US initiatives was positive. On 7 January 1992, a North Korean Foreign Ministry spokesman issued a statement that his country had 'decided to sign the nuclear safeguards accord in the near future', and on 30 January, just over a week after the New York talks, North Korea kept its word.[13] Although many obstacles remained before inspections could begin, North Korea was now officially committed to the inspection process, an objective long demanded by the United States and South Korea.

At the same time, significant progress was also made in inter-Korean relations. Through more than thirty meetings from September 1990 to February 1992, the two prime ministers managed to produce two important accords. The 'Basic Agreement' adopted on 13 December 1991, declared that both sides would respect the other's political and social system and not interfere in each other's internal affairs.[14] Both sides also pledged not to use armed forces against the other. On 31 December 1991, two weeks after the signing of the Basic Agreement, North and South Korea reached another agreement on a nuclear accord, the 'Joint Declaration on the Denuclearization of the Korean Peninsula', in which both nations vowed not to 'test, manufacture, produce, receive, possess, store, deploy or use nuclear weapons.'[15] In addition, some basic principles and items on confidential building measures (CBMs) were adopted, including (1) an agreement to refrain from the use of force against one other, (2) the use of dialogue to settle disputes, (3) the designation of a demarcation line and (4) the installation of a military hot-line.

Pyongyang and Tokyo also made efforts to normalize their relations. Momentum towards normalization was created in September 1990 when a large number of Japanese delegates visited Pyongyang. This Japanese delegation, consisting of Japanese Diet members, Foreign Ministry officials, and journalists, attracted attention, especially because it was led by a top leader of Japan's ruling party, Shin Kanemaru. During three face-to-face meetings with Kanemaru, Kim Il Sung made a surprise proposal for early normalization with Japan. The North Koreans also wanted to settle the matter of compensation for Japan's colonial rule of Korea as quickly as possible, even proposing that some of the reparations money be paid before diplomatic relations were established.[16] The visit concluded with a joint declaration signed by the Japanese delegation and the North Korean Workers Party, stating: 'Negotiations between governments toward normalising diplomatic relations would begin in November.'[17] On the basis of this statement, Pyongyang and Tokyo held eight rounds of normalization talks between January 1991 and November 1992.

2. Explanations

The progress on both the inter-Korean and nuclear fronts seems remarkable even by post-Cold War standards. How can this new level of cooperation on the peninsula be explained, particularly in the midst of challenges posed by North Korea's nuclear programme? The role of outside actors, security logic in the North and South, and the domestic settings of both Koreas will be explored as progenitors of an environment wherein such progress was able to occur.

A. International setting: US global strategy and China's pragmatism

American attention was heavily distracted away from Asia during the late 1980s and early 1990s, as Washington became preoccupied with more pressing developments in Europe and the Middle East, including the sudden collapse of the Berlin wall, events in Eastern Europe, the reunification of Germany and the mounting crisis in the Persian Gulf.[18] With the Cold War's sudden end, a 'peace dividend' became one of the dominant issues in the US, and voices for reduced defence spending increased.[19] Despite this waning in American attention to Asian security issues, non-proliferation established the Korean peninsula at the top of Washington's foreign policy agenda. Although the term 'proliferation' had been in use since the 1960s, its importance and high stakes were only recognized with the passing of the Cold War and the onset of the Gulf conflict of 1990–91, at which point policy makers began to strengthen non-proliferation policies.[20] The five permanent members of the UN Security Council issued a communique at the conclusion of their January 1992 summit, in which they declared the proliferation of unconventional weapons a threat to international peace and security, and committed themselves to concerted follow-up actions aimed at strengthening non-proliferation approaches.[21] In the United States, this renewed commitment to non-proliferation began with the Bush administration and was accelerated under Clinton.

As we have seen, this changing international environment and the emerging evidence of a North Korean interest in acquiring nuclear weapons led Washington to undertake a series of diplomatic initiatives. In the context of the peninsula, there were strategic considerations which justified US nuclear withdrawal. The weapons positioned in the South, which had once acted as a central component of the deterrent posture, were no longer considered effective deterrence tools by some American military officers. William J. Crowe, former chairman of the Joint Chiefs of Staff, called on Washington to consider linking the resolution of Pyongyang's nuclear programme with the removal of American nuclear weapons from the South, arguing 'the actual presence of any nuclear weapons in South Korea is not necessary to maintain a nuclear umbrella over the ROK.'[22] Furthermore, the Gulf War had cogently illustrated that the increased effectiveness of high-tech conventional weapons had left the presence of nuclear devices on Korean soil much less important than in previous years.[23]

Washington's decision was also made with an eye on events beyond the Korean context. As instability in the Soviet Union grew following the attempted coup against President Mikhail Gorbachev in August 1991, new concerns about Russia's ability to control their nuclear arsenals emerged in Washington. Faced with this new concern over 'loose nukes' in former Soviet republics, President Bush announced a unilateral decision to withdraw all US tactical nuclear weapons abroad on 27 September 1991, expecting a reciprocal move by

Gorbachev.[24] Thus, Washington's nuclear initiative was primarily designed to demobilize tactical nuclear weapons in the former Soviet republics, and this unrelated event in Moscow provided the critically needed impetus for diplomatic progress on the Korean peninsula.

The decision to cancel the Team Spirit exercise was also initiated and pressed forward by Washington after bureaucratic debate, and in spite of Seoul's opposition.[25] The exercises' provocative nature had been noted by some American officials, including Ambassador Donald Gregg, while the usefulness of the drill had also been questioned. A senior military officer with command experience in Korea said: 'With the advent of computer simulation, you could train the same without all the great expense and wasted effort of putting all these people in the field.'[26] In 1991, the US Department of State led the initiative to reconsider the exercises, as the likelihood of North Korean military adventurism had abated parallel to its declining relations with Moscow.[27] Not all US government agencies were in favour of cancellation, however. The Joint Chiefs of Staff, for example, opposed it, arguing that the North's demand for the cancellation was 'an unbalanced proposal', while it remained free to run its own exercises.[28] Nonetheless, the exercise was too costly for Washington given the softening of the Soviet threat and growing budget problems at home. The Team Spirit was one of the largest and most costly US field training with an ally during the 1980s, at roughly $150 million per year.[29] Thus, Defense Secretary Cheney favoured cancellation, and Washington decided to suspend the exercise, persuading the reluctant South Korean government to do so as well.[30]

China also seems to have had a role in Pyongyang's decision to cooperate with Washington and Seoul. Beijing furtively pressured North Korea to sign the IAEA safeguards agreement, while stressing publicly that peaceful dialogue, not pressure, should be the way to deal with the North Korean nuclear issue. In May 1991, Premier Li Peng visited Pyongyang and reportedly urged the North to sign a safeguards agreement. Pyongyang's stance on the safeguards agreement then began to change.[31] Pyongyang's position on the North–South prime ministerial talks also changed immediately after Kim Il Sung's trip to China in September 1990, during which Chinese leaders, including Vice Premier Deng Xiaoping and President Jiang Zemin, reportedly exhorted Kim to embark on high-level talks with Seoul. Upon his return, Kim Il Sung is said to have told members of his politburo that he had 'no choice but to meet Roh Tae Woo.'[32] More apparent was Beijing's role in North Korea's change of policy towards a joint North and South Korea UN membership. In his visit to Pyongyang in May 1991, Premier Li Peng made it clear that China would no longer veto South Korea's admission to the United Nations.[33] In order to avoid a situation where South Korea entered the UN alone with Chinese support or abstention, North Korea decided to join at the same time. Pyongyang announced that it had 'no alternative but to enter the United Nations at the present stage.'[34]

What made Beijing adopt this positive role and how can its influence over Pyongyang be explained? The answer seems to lie in the international and domestic environment surrounding Beijing and its pragmatic foreign policies towards the US and the two Koreas. By the early 1990s, China loomed as an emerging power in Asia. Many western analysts noted its tremendous economic and military potential.[35] Already by 1992, the Chinese economy had become the third largest in the world in absolute terms. On the other hand, the post-Cold War era posed new problems. In the aftermath of the Tiananmen Square bloodshed in 1989, which demonstrated the presence of social forces for political liberalization after a decade of economic reform, the regime in Beijing faced the possibility of severe domestic instability.[36] Moreover, China was under increasing US pressure in the areas of human rights, arms sales and the trade imbalance, leading Beijing increasingly to view the US as a potential rival in the region.[37] This resulted in a foreign policy objective aimed at a stable external environment, wherein it could focus its energies on economic development while maintaining political stability at home.[38]

Under these circumstances, Beijing pressed the North into cooperating with the US on the nuclear issue not only because the stability of the region and non–proliferation regime were at stake, but also because it saw economic benefits in having closer ties with South Korea. China, however, consistently refused Washington's insistence on public pressure. In November 1991, when US Secretary of State James Baker sought support for economic sanctions against North Korea, Foreign Minister Qian Qichen responded that 'dialogue, not pressure', should be the way to deal with Pyongyang.[39] Fearful of the repercussions if the North Korean regime should collapse–a massive influx of North Korean refugees into China and US forces on the Chinese border–Beijing did not want to abandon its long-standing relationship with North Korea too quickly.[40]

As China's growing ties with South Korea resulted in a cooling of relations between Beijing and Pyongyang, Chinese leverage over Pyongyang has often been questioned. However, unlike the Soviet Union, whose influence was minimized through its abandonment of Pyongyang in an abrupt and humiliating way, Beijing succeeded in keeping relations largely intact thanks to a cautious and patient approach towards the Korean peninsula. While China's rapprochement with Seoul was against Pyongyang's wishes, it also took a number of steps to reassure the North and to prepare it for the eventual normalization of ties between China and the South. For example, in September 1990 when Kim Il Sung met with Deng Xiaoping in Shenyang, northern China, Deng reassured Kim of continued support.[41] Moreover, North Korea's dependence on China deepened with the drastic decline in trade with the former Soviet Union.[42] Although China demanded payment for crude oil in hard currency, it continued to play a crucial role in North Korea's economic survival, providing food grain, coal, electrical appliances, rubber products, soap, sugar, and many other items.[43] By contrast, North Korean–Soviet Union trade began to plummet in the early 1990s. During the 1980s, the USSR had been North Korea's main trading partner, providing half of North Korea's total foreign economic assistance. In 1990, however, bilateral trade between the two countries dropped to less than half of the amount of 1989. Beginning in 1991, China replaced the Soviet Union as North Korea's primary trading partner.[44] The loss of Moscow's prestige on the peninsula also meant that Pyongyang could no longer play Moscow off against Beijing. It thus seems likely that Chinese advice may have actually influenced Pyongyang's decisions.

Japanese efforts to initiate normalization talks with North Korea can be understood in the context of Tokyo's various interests in forming closer ties with Pyongyang.[45] Economically, North Korea's abundance of raw materials and inexpensive labour attracted Japanese businesses. Politically, there were no less than 250 000 pro-Pyongyang supporters in Japan, including 'the Association of Korean Residents in Japan', who continued to maintain informal contact with North Korea and sent as much as $600 million a year to Pyongyang.[46] Moreover, Japan might have believed that closer economic and diplomatic relations with Pyongyang would help lessen anti-Japanese feeling and aid in constructing an amicable environment for a growing Japanese role in the region. In particular, the Socialist Party argued that Japan should overcome the burden of history and smooth relations with North Korea by reaching agreement on compensation, as it had done when it normalized relations with the South.[47] The personal ambition of conservative politicians to boost their political status through successful normalization, including Kanemaru, former Foreign Minister Watanabe Michio, and Chief Cabinet Secretary Kato Koichi, was another driving force behind Tokyo's approach.[48]

B. Security logic of both Koreas

North Korea's sense of insecurity and strategic decision to cooperate
Although some scholars and analysts have described North Korea as intrinsically 'violent' and 'logic-defying', its behaviour during this period appeared rather defensive. Despite its provocative rhetoric and worrisome nuclear programme, the North, in the end, responded in kind to Washington's nuclear diplomacy by signing the safeguards agreement. Pyongyang also participated in prime ministerial talks with Seoul and agreed on the two important documents. Behind this cooperative behaviour seemed to be a compelling pressure to improve diplomatic and military conditions.

First, with the end of the Cold War, Moscow and Beijing established diplomatic relations with Seoul, leaving Pyongyang virtually alone in international politics. Furthermore, the successive collapse of the Eastern

European communist states, particularly the internal insurrection in Romania, must have been a considerable shock to Kim Il Sung. Pyongyang's insecurity was well displayed in the warning that North Korean foreign minister Kim Young Nam made to the Soviet Union's foreign minister, Shevardnadze, upon his visit to Pyongyang with news of Moscow's decision to establish diplomatic ties with Seoul. The Moscow decision 'will leave us no other choice but to take measures to provide for ourselves some weapons for which we have so far relied on the Soviet Union', said Kim in anger.[49] Faced with diplomatic isolation, North Korean leaders appeared concerned about the danger of unification through absorption by the South. In a secret memorandum delivered to the Soviet foreign minister, on 2 July 1990, North Korea opposed Moscow's move towards normalization with Seoul on the grounds that such a move would 'encourage the arrogant South Korean authority to apply German style unification on the peninsula.'[50] In his 1991 New Year's address, Kim Il Sung also said: 'Given the situation that two different systems exist in the North and South, ... two governments should be respected under the principle that any side should not attempt to eat the other side.'[51] Hence, Pyongyang's concessionary moves, including the signing of the safeguards, the adoption of the Basic Agreement, and normalization talks with Japan, appear to have been made in an effort to address the North's diplomatic isolation and its fear of absorption by the South.[52] Through the prime ministerial talks and the Basic Agreement, the Pyongyang regime was accepted by the South as a 'legitimate system' whose internal affairs would be respected. A high-level contact with Washington and normalization talks with Tokyo could also be a North Korean attempt to tackle its diplomatic isolation.[53]

Pyongyang's next calculation behind the conciliatory moves seems to have been related to its sense of military insecurity. What Pyongyang tried to accomplish was a US nuclear withdrawal and the cancellation of the Team Spirit exercises, both of which were described as a 'great victory.'[54] It should be remembered that North Korea had been under an American nuclear threat through most of its history. During the Korean War, for example, president Dwight D. Eisenhower hinted that the US would use the bomb in an effort to end the war quickly, and he and his Secretary of State John Foster Dulles later claimed that the nuclear threat had played a major role in breaking the deadlock in the truce negotiations.[55] Even after the Korean War, the United States continued to make a series of implied and direct nuclear threats to deter another North Korean invasion.[56] Faced with these threats, North Korean leaders did not hide their sense of nuclear vulnerability. 'The entire nation must be made into a fortress. We do not have an atomic bomb. Therefore we must dig ourselves into the ground to protect against the threat of atomic bombs', said Kim Il Sung.[57] There is no evidence that Washington or Seoul actually intended to use nuclear weapons pre-emptively to attack North Korea.[58] Nonetheless, the defensive nature of American-South Korean intentions may not have been so obvious to Pyongyang. Isolated from the outside world and faced with serious military confrontations with the US, North Korea might have believed that the US would attack using nuclear weapons.[59]

On 12 November 1991, the North Korean Foreign Ministry spokesman issued a statement, saying 'if the USA actually withdrew nuclear weapons from South Korea, it will allow for our signing of the nuclear safeguards agreement.'[60] Similar statements followed, which stressed the linkage between US nuclear withdrawal and the North's signing of the safeguards agreement.[61] Even so, North Korea was not completely satisfied with the US nuclear initiative because an American nuclear umbrella would continue to remain over South Korea. Pyongyang demanded the elimination of air-launched nuclear arms as well, complaining that the US proposal 'is not a comprehensive withdrawal but a partial and selected one. It means the nuclear threat to the DPRK and the danger of a nuclear war on the peninsula will still exist.'[62] Nonetheless, Pyongyang finally dropped its demand for the elimination of the US nuclear umbrella as a condition for the signing of the safeguards agreement, probably under the belief that the removal of the weapons from the actual peninsula was in itself a substantial achievement.[63] Additionally, as will be seen later, Pyongyang's desperate need for economic assistance through improved relations with Washington and Seoul might have led the North to accept this partial solution of the American nuclear threat.

As has been said, the US–South Korea joint military exercise called the Team Spirit was another security concern for Pyongyang. The exercises were among the largest American field training exercises with an ally during the 1980s, and the 1982 US AirLand Battle Doctrine–an offensive strategy designed for an early deep-strike into enemy territory with manoeuvring conventional and nuclear capabilities–probably made the exercise more formidable and threatening.[64] North Korea continually reacted with anger, describing the display in 1989 as a 'virtual declaration of war.' It also responded by conducting joint military exercises with the Soviet Union between 1986 and 1989.[65] Some American officials understood the North Koreans' fear. Ambassador Donald Gregg said: 'Whenever we ran it, they would go to a higher state of alert. It was an absolutely Pavlovian reaction.'[66]

The North's fear of Team Spirit may have become more acute in the face of its deteriorating relations with the Soviet Union. After 1990, it became unclear whether 'the North Korean–Soviet Treaty of Friendship, Co-operation and Mutual Assistance', signed in 1961, actually remained in force. The two nations ended annual joint naval exercises in 1990 and never resumed them. In January 1992, Soviet Deputy Foreign Minister Igor Rogachev flew to Pyongyang and proposed a revision of the treaty, which would eliminate automatic military support in the event of a threat to the other side[67] North Korea's loss of a military ally was compounded by its observance of the virtually unchecked power and reach of US diplomacy and military technology during the Gulf War in January 1991.[68]

The link between Team Spirit and nuclear policies was made clearer on 7 January 1992, when the ROK Defence Ministry finally announced the suspension of Team Spirit. A DPRK Foreign Ministry spokesman announced on the same day its intention to sign a safeguards agreement with the IAEA.[69] Three days later, claiming victory in the cancellation of the Team Spirit, Pyongyang announced: 'with a climate and conditions created for the solution of signing the nuclear safeguards accord, we decided to sign the accord and accept a nuclear inspection.'[70] In sum, Pyongyang's concession seems to have been motivated by defensive considerations aimed at the regime's survival in a changed international environment.[71]

South Korea's security concerns about concessions towards the North
In the wake of diplomatic progress between the US and North Korea, it should be noted that South Korea often resisted US-led diplomatic initiatives, thereby limiting the progress during this period to some extent. The American nuclear initiatives were, after all, substantial concessions with serious implications for South Korean security. When US officials hinted in June 1991 that Washington was willing to consider nuclear withdrawal from South Korea, Seoul voiced strong opposition.[72] Hyun Hong-choo, South Korea's ambassador to the US, made it clear that the South Korean government would oppose withdrawal, saying, 'If we allow this, we can expect that many other unreasonable demands [by the North] may follow.'[73] Chung Eui-young, spokesman for the Foreign Ministry, also argued that the issue of American nuclear warheads should not be linked with the North's obligation to sign the IAEA safeguard.[74] This view was endorsed by various South Korean media, including the Korea Herald, which claimed that Pyongyang's campaign for the denuclearization of the Korean peninsula 'implies North Korea's plot to remove US forces from Korea' in order for it to 'communize' the peninsula.[75] Although Washington's position that a link existed between the North's nuclear weapons and US warheads on the peninsula eventually prevailed, this was only after concerted American efforts to reassure its ally that the US nuclear umbrella for South Korea would remain in place. On 7–8 August 1991, US Undersecretary of Defence Paul Wolfowitz met South Korean National Security Adviser Kim Chong Whi to ensure that South Koreans would accept a US nuclear withdrawal. Some Korean participants opposed the removal on the grounds that it could be used as a bargaining chip, but they were eventually persuaded otherwise.[76] Finally, before announcing the withdrawal of all American ground- and sea-based tactical nuclear weapons throughout the world in September 1991, President Bush privately informed President Roh in a meeting at the United Nations that the US would continue to provide a nuclear

umbrella for South Korea.[77]

South Korea also opposed the American decision to suspend the Team Spirit exercise. Like the US withdrawal issue, the Roh administration saw the exercise as a useful bargaining tool, and advocated its use in pressuring North Korea into nuclear inspections. Moreover, many officials were concerned that this might be viewed by Pyongyang as a sign of a weakened US commitment to Seoul. In response to such trepidation, Washington took measures designed to address Seoul's security concerns. On 11 November 1991, the two nations agreed to postpone a scheduled withdrawal of seven thousand US troops from the South 'until the danger and uncertainties surrounding the North Korean nuclear programme and security in the region have been thoroughly addressed.'[78] Secretary Cheney also promised that other joint military exercises would be extended to make up for the Team Spirit.[79] Placated by Washington's measures, South Korea began to soften its position, suggesting that it would reconsider the 1992 Team Spirit exercise if progress were made on the nuclear issue.[80] Finally, on 7 January 1992, the ROK Defence Ministry announced the suspension of Team Spirit, but made it clear that 'whether to stage the Team Spirit in the future will depend on North Korea's attitude.'[81]

The South Korean government also disliked Washington's initiation of high–level talks with North Korea. In his discussions with US State Department officials, Kim Chong Whi, President Roh's National Security Adviser, approved the talks only with the explicit condition that they be limited to a one-time meeting.[82] Having conceded to this demand, US chief negotiator Kanter rejected the North's appeals for another meeting, and the talks held in New York on 22 January 1992 ended without further arrangements. In addition to Seoul's resistance, Washington was not ready to upgrade its relations with Pyongyang. Although it decided to hold a high-level talk to induce cooperation on the nuclear issue, the Bush administration was divided on how to deal with North Korea. Strong opposition within the administration constrained Kanter, prohibiting him from conducting a serious diplomatic dialogue with his counterpart.[83] Thus, this divided and constrained position and Seoul's insistence on limiting talks to the New York meeting complicated the US–DPRK dialogue.

In sum, South Korea resisted American diplomatic concessions, especially in the case of the nuclear withdrawal from South Korea and the suspension of the Team Spirit exercise, which it thought might have substantial negative implications for the security of the country, while progress was made rather easily on symbolic and nominal issues, such as the holding of prime ministerial talks.

C. Domestic setting of both Koreas

While conciliatory moves during this period were made in response to international pressure, they also occurred because of various domestic factors present in both Koreas.

North Korea: economic imperative and power succession

In the early 1980s, the North Korean economy began to show weakness, and with the substantial reduction or cessation of economic aid from China and the Soviet Union, it continued its drastic contraction to the point of economic collapse. In September 1990, Soviet Foreign Minister Shevardnadze officially informed Pyongyang that Moscow would suspend further large-scale Soviet investments in North Korea and cut military aid, additionally demanding that further oil purchases be made in hard currency. The result was a sharp reduction in North Korea–Soviet Union trade. That year, bilateral trade dropped to 1.1 billion US dollars, less than half of the 1989 amount,[84] and in 1991, with hard currency required for most payments, trade turnover further dropped to $364 million. In 1993, Beijing followed Moscow by demanding payment for crude oil in hard currency, thus ending the 'friendship price.'[85] As a result, North Korea's GDP continued to decline sharply, making it less than a tenth of South Korea's by 1993.[86]

Faced with these economic troubles, the North Korean regime began to place its emphasis on pragmatic change rather than dogmatic adherence to past policies. In an effort to attract foreign investment, Pyongyang opened its doors to foreigners, and in 1984 adopted many joint-venture laws, providing preferential treatment for some foreign investors.[87] More significantly, in December 1991, the North set up its first Free Economic Trade Zone (FETZ) in the Najin-Sonbong district to solicit foreign investments.[88] Private ownership of stores by Koreans was permitted in the zone, and various other preferential measures were undertaken, including a tariff-free environment for products passing through the zone.[89]

Pyongyang's interest in economic reform was also demonstrated by Kim Il Sung's trip to China in October 1991. Although Kim had made as many as 39 official and unofficial visits to China before, this unusually long trip of 14 days was special in that most of the places Kim visited were industrial sites undergoing Chinese economic reforms.[90] Kim said after the trip that he was impressed by the developments in China.[91] In his 1992 New Year's address, Kim Il Sung also acknowledged the difficult living conditions in the North for the first time, saying 'in order to solve the problem of providing the population with food, clothing and housing ..., great efforts must be continuously put into agriculture and light industry.'[92] A severe energy shortage was also acknowledged: 'The most important and urgent task to be fulfilled in socialist economic construction this year is to increase the production of electricity and coal.' Kim's reference to 1991 as 'a year of severe trials' was in stark contrast to previous addresses, which had unflinchingly lauded the achievements of his socialist regime. Many commentators in both South Korea and Japan read it as a virtual acknowledgement of socialism's defeat.[93]

During this period, relatively reform-minded people came to prominence in North Korean politics. Premier Yon Hyong-muk, known as one of the few North Korean officials with whom South Korean counterparts could do business, was personally involved in a high-level dialogue with Seoul for almost two years. During Yon's administration–from his appointment as Premier in December 1988 to his removal from office in December 1992–there is no doubt that North Korea was taking a more conciliatory approach towards other nations.[94] In July 1992, Deputy Premier Kim Tal-hyon, who also showed serious interest in economic cooperation with the South, visited South Korea for seven days, making an extensive tour of industrial sites.[95] Moreover, it was reported in September 1991 that the Secretary of the Korean Workers Party in charge of international affairs, Kim Yong Sun, had been promoted to third ranking official in North Korea, below only Kim Il Sung and Kim Jong Il. This decision was described as one of the most noteworthy changes to have occurred in the North Korean power structure in years.[96] Kim Yong Sun was known as a central figure in the North's efforts to improve diplomatic relations with the outside world.

The rise of more moderate figures in North Korean politics and the regime's emphasis on economic reforms suggested that pragmatism was beginning to prevail in Pyongyang. On 26 December 1991, at the joint meeting of the Central People's Committee and the Standing Committee of the Supreme People's Assembly, the Basic Agreement was praised as 'a historic document of epoch-making significance', and no criticisms of South Korea or the United States were made in a subsequent public report.[97] More importantly, the nineteenth plenary meeting of the sixth Korean Workers Party (KWP) Committee on 24 December 1991 gave party clearance for international inspection of the nuclear programme and for a bilateral nuclear accord with Seoul.[98] As has been observed, this could not have taken place without the approval of Kim Il Sung and his son Kim Jong Il and the acquiescence of the armed forces.[99] Such reasoning has led Selig Harrison to argue that the meeting marked a conditional victory for pragmatists advocating international negotiations.[100]

As was the case with North Korea's newfound pragmatism vis-à-vis economic imperatives, the succession from Kim Il Sung to his son Kim Jong Il may have been a domestic basis for more conciliatory policies. It has been speculated that the political campaign aimed at making Kim Jong Il his father's successor began as early as 1972, when his name was proposed by two of his father's comrades at a closed session of the Korean Workers Party (KWP)'s Central Committee meeting at the Sixth Plenum of the Fifth Congress.[101] Kim Jong Il was subsequently appointed to the Secretariat and the Political Committee in 1973 and 1974, respectively. However, it was only in October 1980, at the Sixth Congress of the KWP, that Kim Jong Il was first introduced as an important officer of the party and publicly designated as successor. He was elected to the Party Secretariat, ranking second only to his father, and listed as fourth in the Presidium of the Politburo (or Standing Committee). He was also appointed to the Military Commission of the party, ranking third behind Kim Il Sung and O Chin-u. No one else had been elected to all three committees except his father, and this was a clear indication that Kim Jong Il had won party approval.[102]

Nevertheless, succession was far from complete, as the military, North Korea's most powerful organization, still remained outside Kim Jong Il's control. Only in 1990 was he appointed vice chairman of the National Defence Commission (NDC), the supreme state military organization.[103] The following year, he became supreme commander of the Korean People's Army, and was finally named chairman of the NDC in 1993. The late 1980s to early 1990s, then, was a very important period in affording closure on the issue of succession. This crucial task meant that Kim Il Sung and Kim Jong Il would have to be more devoted to maintaining a stable international environment than they otherwise might have been, for fear that confrontation with Washington or Seoul might complicate the transition of power.

South Korea: democratization and rising aspiration for inter-Korean reconciliation

In South Korea, on the other hand, democratization and the public's growing demand for inter-Korean reconciliation served as the basis for the Roh administration's conciliatory policy towards Pyongyang. President Roh's election in 1987 was the first direct popular vote since 1972, and acted as a meaningful transition towards democracy. Roh, however, had only won 36.6 per cent of the vote, and his victory was due more to division among opposition candidates than public approval.[104] There was deep suspicion that Roh would continue to take a tough stance on domestic and inter-Korean issues alike, swayed by both the military and his predecessor Chun Doo Hwan. Because of his unpopularity, Roh had even pledged during the presidential campaign to hold a national referendum at the midterm of his tenure, promising to resign if he received a no-confidence vote.

One of the salient characteristics of the South Korean government under Roh was that the ruling party no longer dominated national politics. The defeat of Roh's party in the April 1988 parliamentary election marked the first time that the ruling party had failed to secure a majority position in parliament. Moreover, the so-called 'jaeya' sectors (consisting of the forces that had opposed the military dictatorships of Park Chung-hee and Chun Doo-whan) and the public at large had gained in confidence after their success in forcing the Chun government to accept the democratic presidential election of 1987. The 'jaeya' forces, in particular, no longer had to worry about operating underground.[105] The

Roh administration could not suppress, dominate, or intimidate the people in the name of national security, and in the wake of democratization, the public increasingly called for more information and greater access to the government's policy towards North Korea. The expectation of a new relationship with the North was growing.[106]

The Roh regime yielded. The government made available more information about North Korea, and in selected locations, the South Korean public was allowed access to Rodong Shinmun, North Korea's major newspaper.[107] The major television networks began showing films about North Korea and other communist countries. School textbooks were revised to dilute their anti-communist agendas.[108]

Seoul's efforts to improve inter-Korean relations through prime ministerial talks were also made within this democratising political setting. President Roh was desperate to show the public that he was sincere in his quest for reunification and democratization. This dramatic policy initiative was needed to pre-empt the radical opposition's demand for prompt reunification. Research on the impact of democratization on foreign policy has concluded that an insecure central authority during democratization tends to mobilize popular support through nationalist appeals.[109] The bold diplomatic initiative towards the North was, in this sense, a prestige strategy adopted by the insecure Roh regime at a time of Korean democratization.[110] Managing to produce two important documents with the North, President Roh boosted his image as a true democratic leader and secured domestic support for his weak regime.

To explain the progress on the peninsula from 1988 to 1992, three explanations have been suggested. Despite the different weights that should be accorded these three factors, they appear complementary to each other, contributing to an understanding of the full picture of this period.[111] US diplomatic initiatives and Chinese pragmatic foreign policy born of their global, regional and domestic motivations played a major role in inducing the North's cooperation. At the same time, Pyongyang's attempts to improve security amidst an adversarial post-Cold War environment made this unusually positive diplomatic progress possible. In addition, political pressure in a democratising Seoul for inter-Korean reconciliation, and the necessity of internal stability in Pyongyang during a time of economic hardship and impending power succession were the domestic bases for this progress. On the other hand, the limited nature of this progress was glimpsed in Seoul's opposition to American concessions to North Korea. The next chapter will detail more fundamental shortcomings associated with this period of apparent progress.

Notes

1. US intelligence about the North's nuclear programme in this section is largely based on Don Oberdorfer, *The Two Koreas, A Contemporary History* (New York: Addison-Wesley, 1998); and Michael J. Mazarr, *North Korea and the Bomb: a Case Study in Non-proliferation* (Basingstoke: Macmillan, 1995), pp. 39-46.
2. In 1991, however, Moscow insisted on hard currency payment for the reactors, as the Soviet economy and its relations with Pyongyang had deteriorated. As a result, the promised reactors were not delivered to the North.
3. Although North Korea joined the NPT under pressure from Moscow, it is not clear whether Pyongyang intended to comply with IAEA safeguards requirements at that time. Pyongyang had no experience in dealing with the IAEA, and, prior to the 1990 Gulf War, it had little reason to suspect IAEA pressure.
4. Under the NPT, a member-state has 18 months to conclude a safeguards agreement with the IAEA. But North Korea was given extra time because of the IAEA's mistake of sending the wrong kind of safeguards agreement to North Korea. Nonetheless, the new deadline for a North Korean response – December 1988 – passed without Pyongyang taking any action to comply.
5. Furthermore, it was believed by 1990 that North Korea was testing bomb components in an effort to develop the sophisticated explosive casings for nuclear weapons. Son Sung Young, 'The Korean Nuclear Issue', *Korea and World Affairs*, vol. 15, no. 3 (Fall 1991), p. 477.
6. On a detailed account of US diplomacy over the North's nuclear issue, see Leon Sigal, *Disarming Strangers: Nuclear Diplomacy with North Korea* (Princeton, NJ: Princeton University Press, 1998). For a critical response, see Aidan Foster-Carter, 'Dove Myths: No Better Than Hawk Myths', *Nautilus Institute Policy Forum Online (PFO)* 01-02D (7 March 2001) at http://www.nautilus.org/fora/security/0102D_Foster-Carter.html.
7. Since President Eisenhower had authorized the deployment of nuclear warheads on Honest John nuclear missiles in December 1957, the US continued to deploy nuclear weapons systems to South Korea. For a detailed history of American nuclear deployments and strategy in Korea, See Peter Hayes, *Pacific Powderkeg: American Nuclear Dilemmas in Korea* (Lexington: Lexington Books, 1991), pp. 34-5, 48-9; and Bruce Cumings, 'Nuclear Imbalance of Terror: The American Surveillance Regime and North Korea's Nuclear Programme', in Raju G.C. Thomas ed., *The Nuclear Non-Proliferation Regime: Prospects for the 21st Century* (London: Macmillan Press, 1998), pp. 215-6.
8. Oberdorfer, *The Two Koreas,* p. 257.
9. *Korea Newsreview*, 5 October 1991, pp. 4-5.
10. In the mid–1970s, the threat of war from North Korea escalated in the wake of South Vietnam's collapse. Against this background, the Team Spirit exercise was initiated in June 1976, designed to deter the aggression of North Korea. See Hayes, *Pacific Powderkeg*, p 93; and *Korea Newsreview*, 11 January 1992, p. 4.
11. Hayes, *Pacific Powderkeg*, p. 93.
12. In announcing the US – DPRK talks in New York, the State Department spokesman Richard Boucher said: 'We are prepared to improve our relations with North Korea in the context of their addressing a number of concerns, most immediately the nuclear issue...', See *Chicago Tribune*, 18 January 1992, p. C13.
13. *BBC Summary,* Far East, No. 1271 (7 January 1992), A3/1.
14. For the full text of the Basic Agreement, see *BBC Summary,* Far East, No. 1255 (13 December 1991).
15. For the full text of the Joint Declaration on the Denuclearization of the Korean Peninsula see *BBC summary,* Far East, No. 1284 (21 January 1992).

16. *Joong-Ang Ilbo*, 29 September 1990. It was reported that Kanemaru offered to pay Pyongyang the equivalent of what had been paid to Seoul in 1965 for normalization, which would have ranged from $4~10 US billion in 1990.

17. Richard Halloran, 'North Korean Relations with Japan', in Suh Dae-Sook and Lee Chae-Jin ed., *North Korea After Kim Il Sung* (London: Lynne Rienner Publisher, 1998), p. 216.

18. Paul H. Kreisberg, 'The US and Asia in 1990', *Asian Survey*, vol. 31, no. 1 (January 1991), p. 1.

19. The Gramm – Rudman – Hollings Act obliged the Bush administration to cut the federal budget deficit to $100 billion in FY 1990, to $64 billion in FY 1991, and to $28 billion in 1992. The defence budget was trimmed due to President Bush's continued insistence that he would not increase taxes, a position he maintained until June 1990. See *Asian Security 1990~91: annual report of Research Institute for Peace and Security* (London: Brassey's, 1990), p. 45.

20. Brad Roberts, 'From Nonproliferation to Antiproliferation', *International Security*, vol. **18**, no. 1 (Summer 1993), pp. 139-173.

21. See the statement read by British Prime Minister John Major on behalf of the summit participants at 31 January 1992, in UN document S/PV, 3046.

22. William J. Crowe, Jr. and Alan D. Romberg, 'Rethinking Security in the Pacific', *Foreign Affairs*, vol. 70, no. 2 (Spring 1991), p. 134.

23. Don Oberdorfer, 'US Decides to Withdraw A-Weapons From S.Korea', *Washington Post*, 19 October 1991, A1.

24. Because of the rather peaceful revolutions in Eastern Europe and Germany, the Bush administration had originally considered withdrawing some US land-based tactical nuclear warheads from Europe in 1990. This nuclear initiative, however, was shelved when Iraq invaded Kuwait. See Sigal, *Disarming Strangers*, pp. 27-28.

25. Seoul's resistance to the cancellation will be discussed later in detail.

26. Sigal, *Disarming Strangers*, p. 31.

27. Mazarr, *North Korea and the Bomb*, p. 67.

28. Sigal, *Disarming Strangers*, p.31.

29. See Hayes, *Pacific Powderkeg*, p. 93; and Mazarr, *North Korea and the Bomb*, p. 67.

30. Sigal, *Disarming Strangers*, p.31.

31. Adrian Buzo, *The Guerrilla Dynasty: Politics and Leadership in North Korea* (Boulder, CO.: Westview Press, 1999), p. 195.

32. *Dong-A Ilbo*, 27 October 1990.

33. *Chosun Ilbo*, 26 May 1991.

34. T.R. Reid, 'N. Korea Seeks Separate UN Membership', New York Times, 29 May 1991, p. A21.

35. On China's growing power, see Nicholas D. Kristof, 'The Rise of China', *Foreign Affairs*, vol. 72, no. 5 (1993), pp. 59-74. For a critical view of China's potential, see Gerald Segal, 'Does China Matter?' *Foreign Affairs*, vol. 78, no. 5 (1999), pp. 24-36. See also Michael E. Brown et al. eds, *The Rise of China* (Cambridge: MIT Press, 2000).

36. David Shambaugh, 'China in 1991: Living Cautiously', *Asian Survey*, vol. 32, no. 1 (January 1992), pp. 19-31.

37. Jianwei Wang and Zhimin Lin, 'Chinese Perceptions in the Post-Cold War Era: Three Images of the United States', *Asian Survey*, vol. 32, no. 10 (October 1992), pp. 902-17. See also Rosemary J. Foot, *The Practice of Power: US Relations with China since 1949* (Oxford: Oxford University Press, 1995), pp. 242-57.

38. Nicholas Eberstadt and Richard J. Ellings, 'Assessing Interests and Objectives of Major Actors in the Korean Drama', in Eberstadt and Ellings, eds, *Korea's Future and the Great Powers* (Seattle: University of Washington Press, 2001), pp. 332-3.

39. *Joong-Ang Ilbo*, 15 November 1991.

40. Robert A. Scalapino, 'China and Korean Reunification – A Neighbor's Concerns', in Eberstadt and Ellings, eds, *Korea's Future and the Great Powers*, pp. 118-20.

41. *Joong-Ang Ilbo*, 27 October 1990. China's official newspaper, *Renmin Ribao*, also urged a close relationship between Pyongyang and Beijing, calling the North a 'revolutionary comrade with blood bond', during the establishment of full diplomatic ties with Seoul. See *Dong-A Ilbo*, 19 April 1992.

42. China's share in North Korea's total foreign trade increased from 24per cent in 1991 to 28per cent in 1992 and 34per cent in 1993. See Kim Ilpyong J., 'China in North Korean Foreign Policy', in Samuel S. Kim, ed., *North Korean Foreign Relations In the Post-Cold War Era*, p. 107.

43. Kim, 'China in North Korean Foreign Policy', p. 108.

44. By 1995, Russia had dropped to fifth place in a listing of North Korea's main trading partners, behind China, Japan, South Korea, and India. See Kim, *North Korean Foreign Relations in the Post-Cold War Era*, pp. 82-3.

45. For Japan's political and economic interests in the North, see George O. Totten, 'Japan's Policy Toward North Korea', *Korea Observer*, vol. 16, no. 2 (Summer 1985), pp. 134-48.

46. David E. Sanger, 'North Korea Is Collecting Millions From Koreans Who Live in Japan', *New York Times*, 1 November 1993, p. A1. For detailed information about this pro-Pyongyang organization in Japan, see 'The Lurid 50~year History of Chochongnyon', *NKnet* at http://www.nknet.org/en/keys/lastkeys/2001/4/04.php.

47. *Dong-A Ilbo*, 12 October 1990.

48. Jin Chang Soo, 'Pukil Kwan'gye: Kukkyo Sulibŭi Chŏngch'ichŏk Yoin [North Korea – Japan Relations: political factors of normalization]', in Park Hak Soon and Jin Chang Soo, eds, *Pukhanmunjeui Kukchechŏk Chengchŏm [International Ramifications of the North Korean Problem]* (Seoul: Sejong Institute, 1999), p. 278.

49. Quoted in Spector and Smith, 'North Korea: the Next Nuclear Nightmare?' p.13.

50. This memorandum was made public on 19 July 1990 – an unusual occurrence – by one of the North Korean official media, *Minju Chosun*, one month after former Soviet President Mikhail Gorbachev and South Korean President Roh Tae-woo held a historic meeting in San Francisco. For the whole text of the memorandum, see *Dong-A Ilbo*, 20 September 1990.

51. *BBC Summary*, Far East, No. 0654 (5 January 1991).

52. Other behaviour, such as the threat to develop nuclear weapons, also seems to be related to diplomatic isolation.

53. Pyongyang's approach to Tokyo was also motivated by economic reasons. In 1983, 20 per cent of North Korea's external trade was already with Japan, and further investment was anticipated after normalization. Financial aid in the form of colonial-era reparations was another incentive for Pyongyang. See Denny Roy, 'North Korea's Relations with Japan: The Legacy of War', *Asian Survey*, vol. 28, no. 12 (December 1988), pp. 1284-7.

54. *BBC Summary*, Far East, no. 1275 (10 January 1992).

55. For the question of the efficacy of the nuclear threat and alternative explanations for the Korean War's conclusion, see Rosemary J. Foot, 'Nuclear Coercion and the Ending of the Korean Conflict', *International Security* 13, no. 3 (Winter 1988/89), pp. 92-112

56. In June 1975, Secretary of Defence James Schlesinger publicly threatened North Korea with a nuclear attack in retaliation for aggression. 'If circumstances were to require the use of tactical nuclear weapons…I think that would be carefully considered', said Schlesinger. See AP, 'Schlesinger Warns N. Korea US May Use Nuclear Arms', *St. Louis Post Despatch*, 21 June 1975, cited in Hayes, *Pacific Powderkeg*, p. 60.

57. Bermudez Jr. 'North Korea's Nuclear Arsenal', p. 5.

58. The rationale for US nuclear weapons in South Korea was to deter a North Korean attack or defend the South in the event of North Korean aggression, 'provid[ing] additional security to' South Korea. This point had been expressed explicitly alongside every American nuclear threat. See Bermudez Jr. 'North Korea's Nuclear Arsenal', p. 5.

59. Peter Hayes argues that American military moves in South Korea after the end of the Vietnam War, such as the revision of operational aspects of nuclear strategy in the peninsula, may have heightened the North Korean concern about a possible US nuclear attack. See Hayes, *Pacific Powderkeg*, p. 129.

60. *BBC Summary,* Far East, No. 1230 (12 November 1991).

61. *BBC Summary,* Far East, No. 1240 (25 November 1991); *BBC Summary,* No. 1247 (3 December 1991); *BBC Summary,* No. 1258 (17 December 1991); *BBC Summary,* No. 1263 (22 December 1991).

62. *BBC Summary,* Far East, No. 1206 (16 October 1991). North Korean Premier Yon Hyong Muk demanded a complete renunciation of the US nuclear umbrella as a condition for allowing inspections. See Steven Weisman, 'North Korea Adds Barriers to A-Plant Inspections', *New York Times,* 24 October 1991, p. 11.

63. On 3 December 1991, Kim Pyong-hong, vice-director of North Korea's Research Institute of Disarmament and Peace, said that North Korea would no longer demand the elimination of the US nuclear umbrella, as long as the withdrawal of US weapons could be verified. See *BBC Summary,* Far East, No. 1247 (3 December 1991).

64. Since the adoption of the AirLand battle doctrine, the Team Spirit exercises had been used as opportunities for testing it on the peninsula. See W. Livsey, 'US and ROK Readiness', *Asia — Pacific Defence Forum,* vol. 10, no. 1 (Summer 1985), p. 43.

65. *Korea Newsreview,* 11 January 1992, p. 4.

66. Sigal, *Disarming Strangers,* pp. 30~1.

67. Under a revised treaty proposed by Moscow, Russian military support would be provided only in the event that North Korea was attacked without provocation. Jane Shapiro Zacek, 'Russia in North Korean Foreign Policy', in Samuel Kim, ed., *North Korean Foreign Relations In the Post-Cold War Era,* p. 85.

68. According to one diplomat in Pyongyang, the Gulf War 'was a nasty shock for the leadership in Pyongyang'. See John Ridding, 'Gulf war result jolts N Korean thinking', *Financial Times (London),* 13 March 1991, p. 3.

69. *BBC Summary,* Far East, No. 1271 (7 January 1992). In fact, Seoul and Pyongyang agreed to exchange the Team Spirit cancellation and signing of a safeguards agreement, and announced the news simultaneously, according to the South Korean director of arms control division of Defence Ministry, Han Yong-sup, who was involved in North-South talks during the period. Interview with Han, 9 September 2002.

70. *BBC Summary,* Far East, No. 1275 (10 January 1992).

71. Domestic political factors behind the North's concession will be examined in the next section.

72. Jim Mann, 'US Weighing Deal to End A-Arms in Korea', *Los Angeles Times,* 9 June, 1991, p. 1.

73. *Ibid.*

74. 'US Mulls Deal for N-Free Korea', *Korea Newsreview,* 15 June 1991, pp. 4-5. Both remarks show the 'deterrence logic' that South Korean officials had in mind towards North Korea: concessions would make Pyongyang redouble its efforts to extract further changes from Seoul and Washington, and hence showing only firm resolve could 'deter' the North's aggressiveness.

75. Cited from *Korea Newsreview,* 17 August 1991.

76. See *Korea Newsreview,* 17 August 1991, p. 6; and 'US — South Korean Security Consultation in Honolulu Confirmed', *Central News Agency (Taiwan),* 9 August 1991.

77. *Korea Newsreview,* 5 October 1991, pp. 4-5.

78. Joint Communiqué of the 23rd ROK—US Security Consultative Meeting, Seoul, 20~2 November 1991.

79. Sigal, *Disarming Strangers,* p. 31.

80. On 16 December 1991, Deputy Prime Minister Choe Ho Chung said: 'The government has not yet made a decision to stop or scale down the drill. Such a decision could be made if the [inter-

Korean] contacts relating to nuclear issues progress'. See *BBC Summary, Far East,* No. 1258 (16 December 1991). However, opposition to the cancellation among hard-liners in Seoul continued. For instance, it was suspected that the opposition of Defence Minister Lee Jong Koo was a factor in his replacement in December 1991. See Don Oberdorfer, 'US Welcomes Korea's Nuclear Accord', *Washington Post,* 1 January 1992, p. A1.

81. *BBC Summary,* Far East, No. 1271 (7 January 1992).
82. Interview with Kim Chong Whi, 26 August 2002.
83. Bureaucratic politics in Washington and its negative effects on the high-level talk in New York will be discussed in more detail in the next chapter.
84. Zacek, 'Russia in North Korean Foreign Policy', p. 82.
85. Kim Ilpyong J., 'China in North Korean Foreign Policy', in Samuel S. Kim, ed., *North Korean Foreign Relations In the Post-Cold War Era,* p. 107.
86. See Mack, 'A Nuclear North Korea', p.27.
87. However, due to various limitations, such as strict regulations of the foreign firms' activities and an uncertain business environment in the North, a total of only US $150 million was put into the investment in 140 joint ventures from 1984 to 1992. See *North Korea News,* 2 November 1992, pp. 2-3.
88. Najin-Sonbong is located in the northeast corner of the country
89. North Korea proposed an ambitious three-stage investment plan in 1992, in which $3.3 US billion would be invested in that area by 2010. For an historical analysis of North Korea's economic reforms, see Sin Ji-Ho, *Pukhanŭi Kaehyok Kaebang: Kwagŏ, Hyŏnhwang, Chŏnmang [North Korea's Reform and Open-Door Policy: past, present, and the prospect]* (Seoul: Hanul Academy, 2000), pp. 82-124.
90. The Huafei Colour Display System Co Ltd in Nanjing, for example, was the largest joint-venture in Jiangsu Province, and the Yizheng Chemical Fibre Corporation in Yangzhou was China's largest producer of chemical fibres, built at the suggestion of Deng Xiaoping. *Xinhua News Agency* in Beijing reported that Kim Il Sung showed interest in funding and the loan repayments. See *BBC Summary,* Far East, No. 1202 (14 October 1991), A3/1.
91. *Dong-A Ilbo,* 26 October 1991.
92. For the Text of the recording of Kim Il Sung's New Year address, delivered at a joint meeting of the Central Committee of the Korean Workers' Party, the Central People's Committee and the State Administration Council at Kumsusan Assembly Hall on 31st December, see *BBC Summary,* Far East, No. 1269 (4 January 1992), C/1.
93. *Joong-Ang Ilbo,* 3 January 1992.
94. Suh Dae-Sook 'North Korea: The Present and the Future', *Korean Journal of Defense Analysis* vol. 9, no. 2 (Winter 1998), pp. 63-4.
95. In discussions with South Korean businessmen and economic officials, Kim proposed joint ventures, stressing the marriage of North Korea's labour force with South Korean expertise. See *BBC Summary,* Far East, No. 1442 (25 July 1992).
96. *Dong-A Ilbo,* September 4, 1991.
97. *BBC Summary,* Far East, No. 1265 (26 December 1991).
98. *BBC Summary,* Far East, No. 1264 (28 December 1991).
99. Oberdorfer, *The Two Koreas,* p. 263.
100. *Ibid.*
101. On power succession in North Korea, see Suh Dae-Sook, 'Kim Jong Il and New Leadership in North Korea', in Suh Dae-Sook and Lee Chae-Jin ed., *North Korea After Kim Il Sung* (London: Lynne Rienner Publisher, 1998), pp. 24-5; and Kongdan Oh and Ralph C. Hassig, *North Korea Through the Looking Glass* (Washington, DC: Brookings Institution Press, 2000), pp. 85-9. For more detailed history of power transition in Korean, see Lee Jong-suk, *Hyŏndae*

Pukhanŭi Yihae [Understanding of Modern North Korea] (Seoul: Yoksapipyongsa, 2000), pp. 395-529.

102. Kim Il and O Chin-u, for example, ranked higher than Kim Jong Il in the Politburo, but neither one had served on the Secretariat.
103. *Chosun Ilbo*, 25 May 1990.
104. On domestic political conditions during the Roh administration, see Lee Manwoo, *The Odyssey of Korean Democracy: Korean Politics, 1987–1990* (New York: Praeger Publisher, 1990), pp. 107-38.
105. Almost 1000 *jaeya* people, who had previously operated underground, joined the opposition party led by Kim Dae-Jung and openly raised their radical voices. See *Chosun Ilbo*, 2 February 1988.
106. *Chosun Ilbo*, 10 June 1988.
107. *Chosun Ilbo*, 1 November 1988.
108. *Chosun Ilbo*, 10 August 1989.
109. Edward Mansfield and Jack Snyder, 'Democratization and the Danger of War', *International Security*, vol. 20, no. 1 (Summer 1995), pp. 26-31.
110. Mansfield and Snyder argue that, through the domestic mobilization tactics of insecure elites, democratization tends to lead to aggressive foreign policy, and consequently increases the proclivity for war. However, this was not found to be the case vis-à-vis South Korea, as here nationalist appeals called for reconciliation rather than confrontation.
111. In examining the causes of tension, greater attention will be paid to the different weights of the three factors in the next chapter.

3. Limitations and Shortcomings: 1988–1991

Despite the apparent progress detailed in the previous chapter, there were some limitations in inter-Korean relations and asymmetries in their external relations. In their talks, both Koreas failed to address fundamental issues, most notably arms control. Additionally, unlike South Korea and its relations with China and the former Soviet Union, the North failed to achieve closer ties with the US and Japan, deepening Pyongyang's isolation and stymieing the aforementioned progress. This chapter covers the same period as the previous one. However, while the previous chapter largely focused on progress, this chapter will examine the limited nature of the cooperation between the two Koreas and with the external actors. Moreover, in contrast to the previous chapter, this section will attempt to understand the relative importance of all factors and their interrelationships.

1. Limited progress

Two critical limitations need to be emphasized in the development of relations between the two Koreas and relevant external players. On the inter-Korean front, the Basic Agreement that was signed was not a peace agreement in itself, but rather 'a time-limit agreement applicable only to the initial stage of reconciliation and cooperation.'[1] Critical issues including the termination of the 'Armistice Agreement'[2] and adoption of a 'Peace Agreement' still needed to be tackled, as the Basic Agreement stated only that a peace agreement and an armistice agreement should coexist 'until a state of peace has been realized.'[3] The unresolved armistice issue became a source of tension in 1994.[4] More importantly, the gap over important conventional arms control issues had not been narrowed and key proposals from both sides were dropped in the final agreement.[5] Faced with opposition from the North, for example, South Korean proposals, such as the exchange of military information and personnel, a notification of military movements and the reduction of offensive military capabilities, were deferred to future 'Military Sub-Committee' talks.[6] Phased disarmament and other proposals of the North were also dropped in the agreement. Consequently, when compared with the ambitious proposals suggesting comprehensive operational arms control measures and massive arms reductions,[7] what was actually adopted by the Koreas were rudimentary confidence-building measures–a very modest success at best.

On the other hand, the late 1980s and the early 1990s saw attempts at establishing diplomatic cross-recognition, whereby previous enemies would normalize relations with each other. This involved South Korea attempting normalization with the Soviet Union and China, while North Korea would work to normalize ties with the US and Japan. These new diplomatic dynamics were instigated by the South Korean government's new foreign policy initiative known as Nordpolitik, which proposed cross-recognition by each Korea's allies. In a special declaration on 7 July 1988, President Roh Tae Woo declared 'cooperation with Pyongyang in its efforts to improve ties with the US and Japan, and, in parallel, the seeking of improved ties with the Soviet Union and China.'[8] Following the announcement of Nordpolitik, South Korea successfully established diplomatic relations with former communist countries, including the Soviet Union in 1990 and China in 1992.[9]

The North's initiatives towards the US and Japan, on the other hand, turned out to be unsuccessful. Encouraged by President Roh, Washington adopted a so-called 'modest initiative' towards Pyongyang, allowing substantive discussion between the Americans and North Koreans, unofficial visits to the US, and the easing of US financial regulations and commercial exports to Pyongyang.[10] In response to this 'modest initiative', Pyongyang asked for a bilateral meeting with the United States. With Washington's approval, meetings began on 5 December 1988 in Beijing at the political counsellors' level, and continued to take place until September 1993. The 'Beijing talks' were a great achievement for Pyongyang, affording the North a direct channel to the United States in which to address compelling North Korean issues. Nonetheless, the Beijing talks failed to produce any significant diplomatic progress between the two nations, as the US insisted that the North Korean nuclear issue be resolved first. A more significant and higher level contact between Pyongyang and Washington was the Kanter–Kim Young Sun meeting in New York on 22 January 1992. This meeting, however, was not productive enough to enable the discussion of normalized relations, and it ended without producing any progress in their bilateral affairs.[11]

North Korea's approach to Tokyo also resulted in failure. Although momentum towards normalization was created by Kanemaru's visit to Pyongyang in September 1990, the two sides failed to narrow the gap on a number of thorny issues during the eight rounds of normalization talks held between January 1991 and November 1992. Firstly, Tokyo rejected Pyongyang's demand of compensation for Japan's actions during the colonial period and the years of 'abnormal relations' after the Second World War.[12] A second dispute arose over the North's nuclear programme. While Japan urged North Korea to accept international inspections, Pyongyang rejected the request as irrelevant to normalization talks. A final major obstacle was the alleged abduction of a

Japanese woman called Li Un Hye.[13] Pyongyang denounced the allegation, contending that it had been fabricated. In the midst of this deadlock, the talks finally ended on 5 November, 1992 without any agreement.

In sum, while progress was made during the early post-Cold War period, it was limited. Because of the stasis in arms control negotiations, the danger of military confrontation between the two Koreas remained essentially the same, and Pyongyang's isolation deepened as a result of its failure to normalize relations with Japan and the US. The failure of cross-recognition can be seen as critical, as the tensions of the following years, including the nuclear dispute and disagreements over the Armistice Agreement, appear to have been closely related to North Korea's diplomatic isolation. At the same time, the dangerous conventional arms standoff and the lack of progress in arms control talks meant that such tensions could develop into a catastrophic military clash if disputes were mismanaged.

2. Explanations

This segment will examine the limitations of the progress just described, including the ineffectual nature of the inter-Korean talks and the failure of Pyongyang's attempts to normalize relations with the US and Japan. More specifically, it will attempt to explain the failure in achieving cross-recognition and the lack of progress in arms control talks through the use of the three different perspectives detailed in chapter one. While the 'external actors' exponent will focus on the international environment and the strategic and domestic calculations of big powers surrounding the Koreas, the security dilemma portion will stresses the security concerns of Koreans and thus their security-driven behaviours. In addition, domestic politics of both Koreas will be explored in order to understand the internal constraints imposed on their foreign policy decisions.

(1) Failure of the Cross-Recognition
The cooperative mood outlined in Chapter 2 did not extend to the establishment of better North Korean diplomatic relations with either the US or Japan. This section will examine three factors: domestic and international factors pertaining to the US and Japan, the security fears of South Korea, and South Korean domestic politics.

A. External Actors: The US and Japan

Unprepared Washington
As mentioned earlier, pressing developments in Europe and the Persian Gulf region attracted most of America's attention and diplomatic energy during the

late 1980s and the early 1990s, leading to the dropping of Asian security issues, excepting non-proliferation, from the top of the US foreign policy agenda. In addition, after the Gulf War, calls within the US to prioritize domestic issues, especially economic ones, gradually strengthened.[14] Vis-à-vis Asia, the mounting trade imbalance with Asian countries, including Japan, China and South Korea, pushed economic issues to the forefront of American foreign policy.[15] Moreover, faced with the pressure of the federal budget deficit and 'peace dividend' in the wake of the Cold War's end, the early 1990s saw a reduction in American forces stationed in Asia, despite President Bush's 1989 reassertion that the US must remain a 'Pacific power.'[16]

In this fluid situation, the US was faced with a decision as to how it should respond to the issue of normalizing ties with North Korea. Although Washington had opened talks with the North, it soon became apparent that its interests in or ability to upgrade relations was far below Pyongyang's. In the Beijing talks, initiated in December 1988, the US continually rejected Pyongyang's repeated proposals to upgrade this counsellor-level contact to an ambassadorial-level meeting, insisting that the North Korean nuclear issue should be resolved first.[17] One State Department official involved in Washington's decision said: 'We put in an awful lot of time convincing some members of the administration that we were doing the right thing. The big issue was whether we on the US side would make any unconditional moves of good faith. Especially because of the Republicans in the Senate, we were worried that moving too quickly would erode our support at home', suggesting that the consensus on the talks within the US government was weak and fragile.[18]

With the high-level New York talks of 22 January 1992, Pyongyang appeared to have a better chance of establishing closer ties with Washington, but strong opposition from within the US government ensured again that talks would not go far enough to achieve normalized relations. The idea of direct talks with North Korea ran into fierce resistance from National Security Adviser Brent Scowcroft, Director of Central Intelligence Robert Gates, and from Undersecretary of Defense Paul Wolfowitz.[19] Sceptical about the North's intentions, they argued that engaging in direct talks would be regarded as a sign of weakness. A divided administration resulted in 'a classic bureaucratic compromise': holding the talks but prohibiting the participants from conducting a serious diplomatic dialogue.[20] Constrained by this situation, the American participants were required to take a tough and strict line. Kanter had 'talking points' that he virtually had to read, which were reviewed and approved in advance by an interagency group.[21] Additionally, while the benefits of cooperation were implied, they were sketched out in very vague terms only.[22]

In sum, the US policy approach towards North Korea was mainly reactive and incremental. Washington's apparent lack of direction in Asian policy and the resulting bureaucratic battle over how to conduct US foreign policy at the start of the post-Cold War period seem to account, to a large extent, for the failure to improve relations with North Korea. In addition, the US was alarmed by Iraq's nuclear potential after the Gulf War, and was increasingly concerned about non–proliferation during this period.[23] Furthermore, it seems difficult to have anticipated a bold US foreign policy move during an election year, especially as President Bush was under criticism for having ignored domestic issues and having spent too much time on foreign affairs.[24] In this light, the US was not prepared to consider establishing diplomatic ties with North Korea, as the North's nuclear programme remained a troubling issue. In other words, the North's worrisome nuclear weapons programme, at this time of seeming confusion in US foreign policy, seems to have further discouraged Washington from taking the bold diplomatic initiative of upgrading relations with a potential nuclear proliferator.

Japan's passive foreign policy
Unlike US–North Korean relations, interest in rapid normalization between Japan and North Korea was initially strong on the part of both Pyongyang and Tokyo. As was noted in the previous chapter, each had its own motives to form closer ties. In the end, however, the gap was not narrowed. Unlike those politicians in favour of rapid normalization, the Japanese Foreign Ministry, in particular, maintained a firm stance on the issues that divided the two governments.[25] Regarding compensation, for example, the Foreign Ministry was resolved that the issue should be treated as claims on Japan for property damages before 1945 only, criticising the joint communiqué of the Kanemaru delegates and North Korea in September 1990 for its promise of covering losses incurred after World War II.[26] The alleged abduction of a Japanese national was also troublesome. This issue was raised at a third round of meetings on 20–22 May 1991, and it twice caused the suspension of meetings.[27] While perhaps relatively minor in comparison with compensation and non-proliferation, this matter raised a number of other issues, including Pyongyang's record of terrorist support and Japanese perceptions of human rights in North Korea.[28] Kanemaru's involvement in a financial scandal in late 1992 and his subsequent loss of influence in Japanese national politics further affected normalization talks.[29]

Alongside these domestic obstacles in Japan, Washington's influence over Japanese foreign policy contributed to the deadlock. Washington was not happy with the joint communiqué issued on 28 September 1990 at the end of the Japanese delegates' visits. Concerned that Pyongyang's improved relations with Japan might hamper American efforts to resolve the North's nuclear issue, the US government urged that inspection of North Korean nuclear facilities be conducted before normalization talks commenced.[30] On 9 October 1990, Michael Armacost, US ambassador to Japan, met Kanemaru and expressed Washington's concern over the nuclear issue.[31] Washington also sent intelligence officials to Tokyo and provided additional information about the North's nuclear programme.[32] Ceding to US demands, the Japanese government began to insist that the nuclear issue be an agenda item after the third round of preliminary talks, which took place on 15–16 December 1990.[33] In the following nine governmental meetings, the nuclear issue served as one of the major obstacles to progress.

In view of growing American pressure with regard to the North's nuclear status and a hardening in the Japanese public's mood towards Pyongyang over the abduction dispute, it was in Japan's interest to slow the pace of negotiations.[34] Foreign Ministry officials especially preferred this approach, believing that Japan had little to lose in slowing the pace, while a rapid breakthrough was urgent for the North.[35] The Foreign Ministry believed that Tokyo-Pyongyang normalization should be made consistent with the US grand strategy in Asia, and it was deemed necessary for Japan to wait until uncertainties between Washington and Pyongyang had been cleared up.[36] In May 1991, Vice Foreign Minister Kuriyama Takakazu stressed 'policy coordination between Japan and the US' in order to cope with the 'instabilities and uncertainties as the primary challenge in the post-Cold War era.'[37] 'The ongoing talks with North Korea over the normalization of diplomatic ties have been made as part of such efforts', added the Minister. It was amid this stalemate that North Korea walked out of the meeting at the eighth round of talks held in November 1992, probably concluding that normalization talks with Japan would get nowhere without first satisfying the US demand for nuclear inspection.[38]

Although the abduction, compensation, and the nuclear matter all contributed to a deadlock in the negotiations, Japanese officials seem to have viewed the nuclear issue as a more central obstacle than the other two. In September 1991, the chief Japanese negotiator, Nakahira Noboru suggested in an interview with *the Japan Times* that the abduction issue might be overlooked for the sake of progress.[39] Three weeks before this statement, it was reported that Japan and North Korea had almost resolved their differences over the scope of compensation.[40] When President Bush declared the withdrawal of US tactical nuclear weapons throughout the world, Prime Minister Miyazawa Kiichi said on 18 October 1991, 'with the US decision to withdraw its nuclear weapons, North Korea is expected to change its position on the nuclear issue. Thus, the Japanese government will do its best for normalization talks.'[41] Foreign Minister Nakayama Taro also said in a press interview on October 31: 'Japan's talks with North Korea will accelerate if the issue of suspected US nuclear weapons in South Korea is solved in line with the proposal Mr. Bush made.'[42] These remarks made by key decision-makers in Japan show how much the fate of the normalization talks hinged on the nuclear issue and the American pressure associated with it.

B. Seoul's security fear of the North's diplomatic gains

The previous chapter showed that South Korea strongly expressed its security concerns over the US diplomatic initiatives towards the North even in the midst of progress on the nuclear and inter-Korean issues. Its concerns seem more apparent when one looks at Seoul's hardening position on North Korean talks with Washington and Tokyo. Despite its pledge in the 1988 *Nordpolitik* declaration to help Pyongyang form closer ties with western countries, the Roh administration attempted to prevent such events from occurring. First, with Pyongyang's increasing attempts at a direct deal with the US by route of its nuclear card, the South Korean government opposed the normalization of Washington and Pyongyang relations.[43] Seoul's dislike of improved relations between Pyongyang and Washington became more apparent in the fall of 1991, when Washington explored the idea of high-level talks with North Korea as a part of its nuclear diplomacy. As has been noted, the South Korean government tried to hinder progress towards normalization by prohibiting follow-up meetings after the talk.[44]

South Korea was also unhappy with the Tokyo–Pyongyang normalization talks, and this position affected Japanese negotiations with the North. During summit talks between Japanese Prime Minister Kaifu Toshiki and President Roh in January 1991, South Korea issued five demands as the basis for Pyongyang–Tokyo normalization talks: 1) North Korea should sign the IAEA safeguard; 2) Japan should not offer compensation money to the North until relations were fully normalized, and the money should not be used to build up the North's military power; 3) Seoul and Tokyo should maintain close consultation over the matter; 4) Japan should take account of meaningful progress in the inter-Korean dialogue; and 5) North Korea should emerge from isolation and pursue reforms.[45] Japan accepted all the five conditions. In April 1992, South Korea again urged Japanese prudence in upgrading relations with North Korea until Pyongyang's acceptance of inter-Korean nuclear inspection. As a result, the chief Japanese negotiator Noboru Hahira found it difficult to contemplate normalising diplomatic ties with North Korea until Pyongyang had dispelled all nuclear suspicions.[46] Considering the strong anti-Japanese sentiments of many South Koreans and the broad sensitivities related to the Japanese colonization of Korea, Tokyo may well have found it difficult to ignore Seoul's objections on the Korean issue.

Given this inconsistency between declaration and action, therefore, the Roh administration's intentions and sincerity concerning *Nordpolitik* have been questioned. Some analysts argue that *Nordpolitik* was an aggressive foreign policy designed to speed the collapse of the Pyongyang regime by seeking further isolation of the North, despite its rhetoric of peaceful co-existence.[47] These scholars contend that the Roh administration was seeking supremacy over the North, based on the then-prevalent assumption that North Korea, like other failed communist countries, would not last long.[48] Indeed, that was exactly how North Korea perceived Roh's *Nordpolitik*.[49]

The engagement policy implemented by the Roh administration after the 1988 *Nordpolitik* declaration, however, casts doubt on this perspective. Overall, the

South Korean government accepted the North as a 'legitimate political and social system' as demonstrated by the 1991 Basic Agreement, and pledged to provide economic assistance at a time when Pyongyang was suffering enormous diplomatic setbacks and economic troubles. In addition, the opening of North Korean dialogue with the US and Japan was initiated and encouraged by Seoul. When Roh announced *Nordpolitik* in 1988 without prior consultation with Washington,[50] the US government publicly praised Roh's initiative as 'positive and constructive', and in an internal State Department document called the policy 'a major–indeed historic–reversal of traditional ROKG [South Korean government] policy.'[51] Since the central barrier to American overtures towards Pyongyang had been South Korean opposition, Roh's initiative now enabled Washington to review the delicate question of direct talks with Pyongyang and to adopt the so-called 'modest initiative' which led to the opening of the Beijing talks.[52] The momentum for Japanese–North Korean talks was also created by President Roh's special declaration in July 1988 and his ensuing policies. In September 1988, the South Korean government announced that it was willing to help North Korea resolve the pending issues with Japan, and Japan announced the lifting of sanctions imposed on Pyongyang since the bombing of a Korean Airline aircraft in 1987 by North Korean terrorists.[53] The following month, Prime Minister Takeshita Noboru expressed Japan's interests in improving relations with North Korea, and, as noted earlier, Kanemaru led a large number of Japanese delegates to Pyongyang in September 1990.[54]

So what, then, accounts for Seoul's policy shift from encouragement to obstruction regarding Pyongyang's pursuit of diplomatic improvement? Two important changes on the Korean peninsula after 1988 awakened the South's sense of insecurity. First, in April 1989, Washington informed the Roh administration about the North Korean nuclear weapons programme. Faced with this growing concern, Seoul became anxious about dramatic strategic changes, including normalization between the North, the US, and Japan. As was seen earlier, a key subsequent precondition from Seoul for Pyongyang's normalized relations with Washington and Tokyo was the resolution of the nuclear issue.[55] Seoul's alarm was further intensified by Kanemaru's promise of compensation, as Japan's reparations money could be used to improve North Korea's military capabilities, particularly in the nuclear realm.[56] Out of such fear, South Korea insisted that any economic assistance to North Korea should be made on the condition of satisfactory progress in international inspection of the North's nuclear facilities.

A second change that may have affected Seoul's sense of security was the withdrawal of American troops from South Korea. With the Soviet threat assuaged and amidst growing budget problems at home, the US had reduced its forces in Europe. A similar reduction of forces in Asia, and particularly in South Korea, had been under consideration by the US Congress since 1989. On 2 June 1989, Senator Carl Levin proposed that approximately 10 000 of the 43 000 US troops in Korea be withdrawn in phases over a period of five years, and on 23 June, Senator Dale Bumpers and others tabled a resolution calling for a withdrawal of the same number over the next three years.[57] Although the Bush administration's initial response to these proposals was a reiteration of its intent to maintain troops in South Korea, the troop numbers were in question throughout 1989.

Seoul's response was absolutely negative. A month after Senator Bumpers' proposal, South Korean Defence Minister Lee Sang Hoon stressed in his meeting with US Defence Secretary Dick Cheney that any withdrawal of American forces would be premature unless it followed a comprehensive peace settlement between the Koreas.[58] In his address to a joint meeting of the US Congress on 18 October 1989, President Roh also warned that any sudden cutback of US military forces in South Korea would bring about 'tragic' results, arguing that a 'lessening of the US military presence might cause North Korea to misjudge the US commitment to peace in the region.'[59] Nonetheless, constrained by budget cuts, the US Defense Department began to propose cutbacks in late January 1990, including the withdrawal of 2000 Air Force support personnel, and finally on 15 February, Secretary Cheney and Defence Minister Lee agreed that 7000 non-combat troops would withdraw over the next three years.[60] During this process, South Koreans were 'very upset' and 'horrified' according to a senior US aide who travelled to Seoul with Cheney.[61] Seoul was given only one week's notice, after months of speculation about possible troop cuts had been dismissed by US officials with the reassurance that there would be no change without full consultation between the two governments. 'They [South Korean officials] have a fear...that any withdrawal means the beginning of the plug being pulled, that the American security blanket is gone', a senior US official said.[62] Despite growing economic and military capabilities vis-à-vis the North, the South Koreans' sense of insecurity and a psychological dependency on the US seemed hard to shake.[63]

This fear of American military withdrawal, coupled with new concerns about the North's nuclear weapons programme, seems to have awakened a sense of insecurity among the South Koreans, and Pyongyang's diplomatic achievements would make Seoul all the more uncomfortable. In other words, uncertainties surrounding the North's nuclear capability and American commitment left Seoul reluctant to allow Pyongyang the increase in its economic and strategic resources that closer ties with Washington and Tokyo would afford. The North's nuclear weapons programme, then, while stemming from a desire to enhance security and procure diplomatic leverage and economic concessions from the US, had a negative impact on the South's sense of security, and thereby encouraged counter-actions obstructing North Korean access to Washington and Tokyo.[64] The North's nuclear weapons programme was, thus, counterproductive vis-à-vis security between 1988 and 1992, although the ultimate outcome of nuclear diplomacy between Washington and Pyongyang remains to be seen.

In conclusion, security-driven actions by both North and South Korea constrained progress and cooperation, as is predicted by the security dilemma model. This is not to suggest that all their actions were motivated entirely by security concerns. Intentions to exploit the other in the minds of the politicians may well have been responsible. Pyongyang's attempt to acquire nuclear weapons, for example, may have been informed by an ultimate goal of communizing the Korean peninsula by force, should a more favourable situation arise in the future. Similarly, Seoul's attempts to block Pyongyang's diplomatic gains may have been motivated by a desire to maintain the upper hand. With the continued isolation of the North, Seoul could continue to operate from a position of advantage. In this regard, defensive and offensive (exploitative) motives were both present, and the situation was not purely rooted in security concerns. Nevertheless, it can still be said that the security dilemma was operating to the extent that 'security fears' were responsible for the limits in diplomatic progress. Moreover, it should be noted that offensive motives have been intertwined with or rooted in Korean security fears since the beginning, as neither party can ever ultimately be secure as long as the other side exists.

C. Rightward shift of the political mood in Seoul

As was previously indicated, President Roh was desperate to impress on the public that he was sincere in his quest for inter-Korean reconciliation and reunification. Seoul's active engagement in inter-Korean prime ministerial talks was pursued in that context. *Nordpolitik,* hurriedly devised and announced without prior consultation with Washington, was designed to cope with the public's growing demand for reconciliation with North Korea in the wake of democratization.[65] Given its roots in such a domestic political climate, the degree to which *Nordpolitik* was implemented out of sincere interest in and commitment to a peaceful coexistence on the peninsula is brought into question. It follows, then, that President Roh's promise to help Pyongyang transcend its diplomatic isolation was likely to alter because it was intimately related to the state of South Korean politics.

Beginning in early 1989, as the Left grew in influence, conservatives and the public in general came to have second thoughts about Roh's manner of accommodating the *Jaeya* forces. Radical students were trying to overthrow the government and attempted a march to the North to participate in North Korea's 'World Festival of Youths and Students', scheduled for 1 July 1989. Despite the government's disapproval, one of the student leaders, Lim Soo-kyong, and a dissident clergyman, Moon Ik Hwan, managed to reach Pyongyang in March 1989, and received a rousing welcome from North Koreans.[66] Students continued to hold violent demonstrations throughout the nation, using the issue of the unification to undermine the Roh regime. President Roh, then, was viewed as suspect by both the Right and Left. While the Left doubted Roh's sincerity, the

Right believed that he was playing a dangerous game.[67] In March 1989, Kim Yong-gap, the minister of government administration, for example, resigned after insisting that the country was in danger of leftist control.[68]

In this unstable political environment, President Roh indefinitely postponed in March 1989 a referendum on support for his rule which he had proposed during the presidential campaign in 1987.[69] Not confident that he could get through a referendum, Roh reneged on his promise to hold an interim appraisal of his leadership, and did so with tacit support from opposition leaders who feared that a referendum could plunge the nation into chaos.[70] Once the issue was out of the way, Roh began to crack down on the Left (*jaeya* forces) in an effort to placate the right-wing, one of his key political support bases.[71] His government jailed all those prominent dissidents who tried to contact North Korea without government authorization, including Lee Young-hee, an editor of the leftist paper *Hangyore Shinmun*, Paik Nak-chung, an English professor, and Koh Un, an outspoken poet.[72] All police forces were mobilized to counter the violent leftist demonstrations with authorization to fire if necessary.

Another, probably more significant, event that strengthened the Roh administration's shift to a hard-line anticommunist stance was the formation of the conservative ruling party. On 22 January 1990, President Roh and the two opposition leaders, Kim Young Sam and Kim Jong Pil, jointly announced that their parties would merge into a grand conservative majority party, thus leaving the largest opposition party, led by Kim Dae Jung, in isolation.[73] The purpose was to break the political deadlock that had resulted from a four-party system in which no party enjoyed a majority. South Korea's political landscape changed overnight, and Roh seemed guaranteed of three years in office. With less concern about negative domestic feedback, the Roh administration was now able to accelerate its approach towards former communist countries.[74] In doing so, however, the South Korean government was little constrained by domestic criticism regarding the North's deepening isolation, and took an aggressive and rigid stance on Pyongyang's diplomatic gains.

While this rightward political shift offered a permissive environment for Seoul's tough policy, what actually prompted the South Korean government to deny Pyongyang's diplomatic improvements was yet another political calculation. Pyongyang's improved relations with Washington and Tokyo were predicted to impact negatively the improving inter-Korean relations, since the political and economic benefits that would come from closer ties with the US and Japan would make Seoul less attractive to Pyongyang as a dialogue partner.[75] In a situation where the Roh administration could claim the improvements in inter-Korean relations as one of its few achievements, the prospect of losing control of the issue would have caused unbearable political damage to the government. In this regard, Seoul continued to insist throughout 1990 and 1992 that Pyongyang's approach towards Washington and Tokyo be conducted in accordance with an improvement of inter-Korean relations, fearing that the North would take less interest in improving relations with the South if it had closer ties with the US and Japan. For example, in summit talks with Japanese Prime Minister Kaifu Toshiki in January 1991, President Roh urged Japan to 'take account of meaningful progress in the inter-Korean dialogue' in its normalization talks with Pyongyang, and insisted that 'Seoul and Tokyo should maintain close consultation over the matter'.[76] Some South Koreans even suspected that Japan's move was motivated by a desire to keep the Korean peninsula divided.[77] Although this claim was unsubstantiated, historically deep–rooted resentment against Japan made it emotionally appealing to many South Koreans.[78] Seoul's dislike of the rapidly improving nature of Pyongyang's relations with Washington and Tokyo can, therefore, be understood in the context of South Korean sensitivity concerning any external influence on *Korean* issues and the Roh administration's political preoccupation with achievements on inter-Korean issues.

(2) Lack of Breakthrough in Conventional Arms Control

Two explanations seem relevant for the failure of meaningful progress in conventional arms control talks. One explanation is based on the security fears of both sides regarding the proposals, and the other stresses the strong military–industrial complex as an obstacle. This section does not deal with external actors, as their role or influence on inter-Korean arms control talks during this period was not found to be strong.[79]

A. Seoul and Pyongyang's fears of being exploited

The security dilemma appears to have been responsible, to some extent, for the failure of any breakthrough in arms control talks in that each side's proposal was designed to enhance its own security at the expense of the other. Before looking at the negotiations, it might be useful to examine the military balance at the time of the talks, as the complexities inherent in each side's proposals should be seen in the context of their relative military strengths and weaknesses. It is difficult to judge whether the military balance on the Korean peninsula was in favour of North or South in the early 1990s. When we compare the two in terms of weaponry and troop numbers, North Korea retained a fairly substantial advantage.[80] Table 3.1 compares the major weapon systems of both Koreas, and shows that the North enjoyed a numerical superiority in almost every category. Based on this 'bean count' approach, some have argued not only that the military balance favoured the North, but also that by the 1990s South Korea had not yet caught up.[81]

However, many analysts have also conceded that this numerical advantage can be misleading. Given the increasing qualitative edge that Seoul maintained over Pyongyang, the actual war-fighting capabilities of many of the North Korean forces would be much lower than is suggested by the numbers.[82] This advantage is borne out by a look at the Koreas' respective air power. While most of the North's combat aircraft were 1950s and 1960s vintage, replete with 'very poor radar, high vulnerability and low ammunition capacity',[83] South Korean aircraft, such as the F-16s, was widely regarded as the most capable aircraft of its kind and as far superior to anything possessed by the North at the time.[84]

With regard to the navy, while most North Korean vessels were small, patrol–sized craft unable to operate over 50 nautical miles at a time[85] and were regarded by experts as 'primitive and crude', the South Korean navy was evaluated as being 'a decade ahead' of the North's in terms of combat capability.[86] The qualitative advantage of South Korea was not as clear vis-à-vis ground forces, since much of the North's forces were mechanized and its artillery was long-range and powerful. Nonetheless, the South did have the upper hand in certain key areas, including tanks and armoured vehicles.[87] Another gap was the ability to command, control, communicate and provide intelligence (C3I) to combat units. Whereas South Korea had access to the American C3I technology that had demonstrated its effectiveness during the Gulf War, North Korea did not have communication satellites, sophisticated reconnaissance aircraft or modern communication systems.

Taking these qualitative and quantitative factors together, then, it is hard to judge decisively which side enjoyed military superiority: the North was quantitatively dominant, but this numerical advantage was offset by the South's qualitative edge. What was clear, however, was that the balance was shifting in favour of the South, and the trend appeared more permanent than temporary.[88] The gross national product of North Korea had dropped from a quarter of the South's GNP in 1980 to a tenth in 1990, and, with this increasing gap in national wealth, South Korea had begun to surpass Pyongyang in overall military spending by 1974. South Korea reached 1.4 times the North's military expenditure by 1980, 2 times by 1990, and 2.7 times by 1995.[89]

With this background in mind, it is now possible to investigate the lack of progress on the arms control front. From Seoul's perspective, the North's proposal for deep manpower reductions could not guarantee increased security against a surprise attack, because it would leave North Korea with its offensive armaments intact. Moreover, Pyongyang rejected the dispersal of its troops and weapons near the DMZ to rear areas, as this would leave Seoul less vulnerable. Finally, once the Koreas had both completed their troop reduction, the North would be free to exploit its character as an authoritarian and military-centric regime and its superior mobilization capabilities, and easily restore its manpower strength.[90] The North's proposal for a suspension of qualitative innovation vis-à-vis military equipment was also unacceptable, as the South saw its qualitative edge as compensating for the North's quantitative advantage. In this sense, Seoul criticized the North's proposals as an attempt to 'create favourable conditions for communizing the entire peninsula.'[91]

On the other hand, the reduction in armaments proposed by the South contained a number of features unacceptable to North Korea. Traditionally, the North Korean military had relied on numerical superiority to offset its technological inferiority. The South Korean arms control proposals would undermine this advantage, while leaving Seoul unconstrained and free to exploit its greater economic wealth and closer contacts with the US for continuing modernization of its weapons systems. Such an arrangement would inevitably lead to the military superiority of the South Korean armed forces, a condition obviously unacceptable to North Korea. Other operational arms control measures advocated by the South, such as the exchanges of military information and personnel and invitations to observe notified military training exercises, were also hard to accept for the North. Given that the military balance was shifting in South Korea's favour, Pyongyang may have had little confidence in sharing military information, fearing that such measures would reveal the weakness of its military capabilities. It thus seems that the proposals of both Seoul and Pyongyang were designed to tackle each side's respective security concerns, all the while reducing the other side's security through unfavourable changes in the military balance.[92] These gaps were consequently difficult to overcome.

A psychological perspective might also prove helpful in understanding the lack of substantial progress in arms control talks. Numerous psychological experiments have indicated that human beings have a tendency to make a 'fundamental attribution error', meaning that people tend to explain the behaviour of others as the result of their innate character, failing to notice the impact of other situational factors.[93] Attribution theory also propounds that people are inclined to believe that their own actions are compelled by circumstance.[94] This error might have taken place in Korean arms control talks. The South interpreted the North's arms reduction proposal as 'nothing but a propaganda ploy, not worthy of serious consideration.'[95] Most South Korean analysts argued that they were motivated by 'the projection of the image of a peace-oriented North Korea, the weakening and division of South Korea's domestic consensus on defence issues, politicization of the issue of the US military presence in South Korea, and the maintenance of its superior military power.'[96] However, few noted Pyongyang's situational constraints, including its poor economy, diplomatic isolation, and growing military disadvantage, which might well have affected its proposals. In other words, South Korean observers might have overestimated the aggressive and opportunistic traits of the Pyongyang regime, while underrating the effects of its environment. Through the tragedy of the Korean War and its subsequent confrontation, Seoul had established its perception of the North Korean regime as offensive and intrinsically dangerous, probably leaving it psychologically difficult for South Koreans to find explanations contrary to their existing image of Kim Il Sung's regime.[97] In a similar vein, North Korea did not show any sympathy towards Seoul's fear of surprise attacks and its appeal for confidence building measures

Table 3.1 The Military Balance: North and South Korea (1988)

Force/Weapon Category	North Korea		South Korea	
Army		1 000 000		650 000
Personnel	T-34/54/55/62	3300	M-47	350
Tank	T-59	175	M-48A5	950
			Type 88	250
Armoured Fighting	MICV	150	MICV	200
Vehicle	APC	4000	APC	1550
	RECEE	140		
Artillery	Towed artillery	2500	Towed artillery	4000
	SP artillery	3300	SP artillery	some
	MRL	2300	MRL	140
	SSM: Scud	15	SSM: Honest John	12
	SSM: FROG-5/7	54		
Anti-Tank	SU-76/100	800	M-18/36	58
	RCL: 82-107mm	some	RCL: 57/106mm	some
	ATGW	some	ATGW: TOW	some
Air Defence	23-100mm	8000	20-40mm	600
	SAM: SA-7	some	SAM: HAWK	110
			Nike Hercules	200
Navy				
Personnel		41 000	60 000(incl 25 000 marines)	
Submarines		24		3
Destroyers		0		9
Frigates		3		25
Missile Craft		34		11
Torpedo Craft		173		
Patrol		154		81
Amphibious		craft only		15
Air Force				
Personnel		70 000		40 000
Bomber	Il-28	80		
Fighting Aircraft	MiG-15/17/19	430	F-5A/B/E/F	204
	MiG-21	120	F-4D/E	128
	MiG-23	46	F-16 C/D	48
	iG-29	30		
Transport		280		
				36

Source: International Institute for Strategic Studies, *The Military Balance 1990–91* (London: IISS, 1991), pp. 166–69

(CBMs). Thus, this lack of understanding about Seoul's situational pressure could represent Pyongyang's cognitive bias.

B. Interests of military-industry complex in both North and South Korea

The above explanation assumes that Pyongyang and Seoul were interested in arms control talks, but they simply could not achieve much due to negative strategic implications inherent in the other side's proposals. However, it is also possible that either or both of them were not serious about bold arms control measures in the first place, and this lack of interest may have inhibited progress. This hypothesis is founded on the high level of power and autonomy enjoyed by the military in both Koreas during the early 1990s, though this was to different degrees.

In the wake of democratization, the South Korean armed forces began to lose their unchallenged status. Prior to the Roh administration, the military sector had always enjoyed a privileged position in the government's resource allocation, and most budgetary demands of the Defence Ministry were accommodated by the Economic Planning Board. However, democratic changes exposed the defence sector to rigorous public screening, and its expenditure, which had made up nearly 30 per cent of the national budget, became the target of other ministries.[98] As a result, the defence budget decreased from 4.7 per cent of the GNP during the Chun regime to 4.0 per cent during the Roh administration. Social welfare spending surpassed defence spending in 1989 for the first time, and has maintained an edge since then. This shifting resource allocation suggests the decreasing power of the armed forces in South Korean politics.

Nonetheless, having enjoyed a 30 year rule after the 1961 coup, the South Korean armed forces remained an influential group. Although the Roh regime had grown in legitimacy, its status was still fragile and questionable, as Roh had been handpicked as successor by the former president. In Roh's cabinet and the military, there remained many rightist officials and generals closely affiliated with former president Chun Doo Whan. Dissatisfied with the government's conciliatory policies towards the Left and North Korea, these hard-liners often defied the President. As early as August 1988, unhappy with the rising demands of radical left-wing groups and Roh's indecisive governing style, the Home Minister circulated to government employees a book entitled *Is the Right-Wing Dead?*[99] As has been noted, another of Roh's cabinet members resigned in protest that the government was not effectively dealing with the liberal offensive. On 21 March 1989, at the graduation ceremony at the Korean Military Academy, General Min Byung-don, the head of the Academy, criticized Roh's *Nordpolitik,* even refusing to salute the President during the ceremony.[100] Under these circumstances, Roh had little political incentive to fight against the institutional interest of the armed forces, unless there were compelling reasons to do so. As Morton Halperin has pointed out, Presidents and their advisers are very careful to choose the issues on which they will fight hard against sustained domestic opposition.[101] Roh, then, had few reasons to accept the radical arms reduction proposed by the North, fearing it would invite fierce resistance from the military and alienate the bulk of his own constituency.

Furthermore, the strong defence industry in the South would have opposed structural arms controls. By the late 1980s, the South Korean military-industrial sector satisfied most of the domestic needs for a conventional weapons system, and as of 1988, there were 82 defence contractors designated by the government.[102] While the majority of these were medium-sized companies specialising in basic weapons and ammunition, larger items, such as aircraft, missiles, and naval vessels, were produced by a handful of big conglomerates with strong lobbying power over the government.[103] In the 1980s, as defence procurement began to decline amidst increasing competition for arms exports to the Third World, most firms engaged military-industrial products were facing over-capacity and suffering serious financial difficulties.[104] From 1980 to 1986, nine defence contractors went bankrupt, and many other firms were on the verge of collapse when arms control talks began with Pyongyang.[105] Financial rescue packages, not arms reduction, were now the defence industry's demand on the Roh administration. Based on such reasoning, Western observers such as Selig Harrison argue that a powerful military-industrial complex and hard-liners in the South have been major obstacles to meaningful force reductions.[106] In this view, entrenched vested interests in the South were responsible for resistance to the North's proposals.

Given the privileged status of the armed forces in the North, Pyongyang probably had even greater difficulty in pursuing arms control policies. This was further complicated by the power succession process from Kim Il Sung to Kim Jong Il, during which military positions began to be given to the younger Kim. As he was collecting his military titles, including that of vice chairman of the National Defence Commission (NDC) in 1990 and supreme commander of the Korean People's Army in 1991, Kim began to make mass promotions in order to install a new generation of military leaders.[107] In an attempt to show his control over the military, Kim Jong Il also received letters pledging support from the military officers.[108] Although it appeared that the military was firmly under Kim Il Sung's control, there were some signs that internal frictions existed. In February 1991, Pyongyang radio made the unprecedented announcement that 'opportunists' existed, who 'betrayed the principle of revolution, denied the leadership of Kim Il Sung and the Party, and attempted to disrupt the Party's leading role over the military.'[109] There was also the rumour of a military coup attempt in 1992, which has not been verified but is frequently cited in the West.[110] The story goes that a group of officers who were trained in the Soviet Union plotted to kill an assemblage of North Korean officials, and upon discovery, the participants were executed and approximately 600 officers trained in the Soviet Union during the 1980s were purged. In this important succession period, it is hard to imagine that Kim Il Sung and his son would adopt any arms control measures with Seoul that would threaten their efforts to get the military firmly behind Kim Jong Il.

3. Conclusion

Compared with the instances of cooperation examined in the previous chapter, in which three different explanations proved complementary to each other in elucidating the events of this period, understanding the limitations needs a more careful examination. The three perspectives stress various aspects of the issues that have been examined and provide different, if not conflicting, answers to the cause of the limitations placed on the level of cooperation.

On the failure of the Japan–North Korean normalization talks, the external actor approach suggests American pressure for a slow down and the hard-line stance of the Japanese government as major reasons for the breakdown of the talks, while the security dilemma approach stresses the South Korean government's fear that Japanese reparations money could be used to improve North Korea's military and nuclear capabilities. On the other hand, the domestic politics approach emphasizes Roh's concern that improved relations between Pyongyang and Tokyo would have a negative impact on inter-Korean relations, thus undermining efforts to boost his image and popularity.

In the case of the Tokyo–Pyongyang talks, US pressure and South Korean opposition seem to have served as major stumbling blocks. After the US had pressed Japan to link normalization talks with the issue of the North's nuclear programme, the Japanese government's position became hardened and uncompromising. Although it was also reluctant to concede on compensation and the matter of Li Un Hye's abduction, there seems to have been some possibility that talks would have proceeded more positively without American pressure over the nuclear issue. There were two main political groups which presented different ideas with respect to the normalization talks: one, including businessmen, the Socialist Party, and conservative politicians like Kanemaru, advocated rapid normalization, while the other group led by the Foreign Ministry was more cautious. One analyst has argued that Japan's adoption of a 'slow down' approach was a victory for the Japanese Foreign Ministry, as it successfully took advantage of American pressure to strengthen its case against rapid normalization.[111] In that sense, the absence of US pressure would have shifted the fighting within the Japanese government in favour of the rapid normalization group.

Alongside American pressure, South Korean opposition was another factor that obstructed the normalization talks between Pyongyang and Tokyo. Unlike the US–North Korean talks, here Seoul's opposition seems to have stemmed more from domestic political motivation than from security fears. While Seoul may have had legitimate security concerns that Japanese reparation money could be used to improve the North's military capabilities, the Roh administration had itself offered a large amount of economic aid to the North even after having learned of the existence of the North's nuclear weapons programme.[112] Therefore, it seems reasonable to conclude that what really bothered Seoul was not so much its security, but the understanding that Japan–North Korea normalization would hurt inter-Korean relations and thereby damage Roh's popularity. North Korean normalization with Japan and its attendant economic aid would reduce the value of the political and economic partnership with the South. For the Roh administration, closer ties between Pyongyang and Tokyo were not to be welcomed.

On the failure of diplomatic progress between Washington and Pyongyang, the three approaches also provide different explanations. The 'external explanation' stresses the US preoccupation with Europe and the Middle East and bureaucratic politics in Washington. On the other hand, 'the security dilemma' suggests that because of security concerns, South Korea inhibited further diplomatic improvements between the US and North Korea. Finally, the 'domestic politics' approach contends that Seoul's opposition to the US–North Korean ties may be seen to represent the Roh administration's preoccupation with improving inter-Korean relations and a rightward political shift in the South.

It is difficult to weigh the relative importance of one factor vis-à-vis the others in the US–DPRK talks, since each factor alone seems to explain sufficiently the limited progress. Washington's lack of interest and ability to bring about a major diplomatic breakthrough would likely have led to almost the same consequences even without the South's opposition. Given the US preoccupation with other pressing international issues and its growing concern about the North's nuclear ambitions, it is doubtful that Seoul would have affected the internal debate in Washington and its final policy outcome. Conversely, an American attempt to improve relations with Pyongyang would nonetheless have encountered a major obstacle in the form of South Korean opposition. US officials had made it clear from the beginning of their modest initiatives towards North Korea that they would walk 'in step with, but not in advance of, the ROKG.'[113] Unlike the Japanese–North Korean talks, the source of Seoul's opposition seems to have stemmed from both domestic political reasons and security concerns. In a situation where the North's nuclear ambitions were emerging on the one hand, and US military commitment to the South was increasingly under question on the other, closer ties between Pyongyang and Washington aggravated Seoul's sense of insecurity. Consequently, any of these three factors–the US's lack of interest and ability to upgrade diplomatic ties with Pyongyang, South Korea's security-driven resistance to Pyongyang's diplomatic gains, or domestic political opposition to improved US–North Korean ties–would sufficiently explain the failure of advancement in US–North Korean relations.

Finally, two explanations compete in attempting to understand the lack of meaningful progress in conventional arms control. One is the security dilemma perspective, which notes the intrinsic problems of the proposals: each side intended to increase its own security without addressing the other side's security concerns. The other explanation takes into account the strong influence demonstrated by the military in both Koreas, and questions the interests and devoutness of the political leaders in adopting substantial arms control measures. Although the two perspectives are not necessarily contradictory to each other, a closer examination is needed to understand the extent to which each can explain the outcome of the arms control negotiations.

In the case of South Korea, both the security dilemma and domestic politics seem to provide satisfactory answers as to the lack of progress in arms control. Given the influential position of the military and conservative political atmosphere during the arms control talks, the Roh administration did not have authority or pressing reasons to go against the military–industrial complex and hard-liners. At the same time, an analysis of arms control proposals suggests that the difficulty in finding a common ground for arms control between the North and South would not have lessened even without the military's influence. Most conservative scholars reasoned at the time that the South Korean government would not give preference to arms control, because the arms race was a more concrete measure of deterrence against the superior North Korean military.[114]

On the other hand, the explanatory power of the security dilemma seems more powerful than that of the domestic political approach in the case of North Korea. There is little doubt that the armed forces enjoyed a privileged status in North Korea, making it difficult for even absolute leader Kim Il Sung to pursue policies against the military's interests. Nonetheless, Kim Il Sung was under pressure to take some substantial arms control measures in order to lessen the North's economic troubles. As has been seen, the reduction in economic and military assistance from the Soviet Union and China left an already struggling North Korean economy in a critical situation. In 1990, the North Korean economy recorded a negative economic growth of 3.7 per cent, which doubled to reach a negative growth of 7.6 per cent by 1992. Oil shortages, in particular, caused serious problems for the North Korean forces, restricting their mechanized training.[115] It was reported that pilots were being limited to less than 30 hours' flying time a year.[116] Artillery and mechanized forces were reported to have faced similar constraints on their exercises. In short, North Korean forces were too large and costly for its struggling economy, making arms reductions imperative. Moreover, the shift in military balance towards Seoul beginning in the 1980s may have pressed Pyongyang into becoming more serious about arms control talks. North Korea's wish to avoid a disadvantageous arms race was well expressed in its repeated proposals during the negotiations with the South. Despite these strong economic imperatives, North Korea could not sustain the negotiating momentum.

Although it remains unclear whether the pressure for arms control was strong enough to risk military interests, the outcome of the talks seems to have more to do with North Korean security concerns than with the institutional interests of the military. Among the South's proposals rejected by the North, only the reduction in offensive military capabilities would harm their military interests because of an affect on the military budget and organization. The other issues–exchanges of military information and personnel, notification of military movement, and redeployment of forward-based forces into rear areas–would not have had a direct impact on the organizational interests of the armed forces. Rather, the refusal lies in security implications vis-à-vis the South. In a situation where the military balance was shifting in favour of the South, North Korea maintained a 'strategy of ambiguity' about its military capability; thus sharing military information with the South would undermine this strategy. Also, given that forward deployment was designed to maximize the effect of its current forces, signalling that the North maintained sufficient second-strike capabilities against the US and South Korea,

Redeployment of forces into rear areas would weaken this deterrent strategy.[117] In other words, while the security dilemma perspective provides a satisfactory account for all aspects of the outcome, the domestic political approach exhibits a weakness in its explanation of why North Korea opposed certain proposals that were not critical for the organizational interests of the military.

In conclusion, the unproductive nature of the diplomatic talks between North Korea, the US and Japan shows that American involvement and the South Korean political factor played major roles. The conventional arms control talks, on the other hand, betray the presence of the security dilemma factor, while the role of international players is not conspicuously detectable.[118]

Notes

1. Lim Dong Won, 'Inter-Korean Relations Oriented Toward Reconciliation and Cooperation', in James Cotton ed., *Korea under Roh Tae-Woo: Democratization, Northern Policy and Inter-Korean Relations* (Allen & Unwin, 1993), p. 270.
2. Formally ending the Korean War, the United Nations Command (UNC) signed the armistice agreement with the North Korean Army and the Chinese People's Volunteer forces on 27 July 1953. The agreement carried phrases regarding the Demilitarized Zone (DMZ) that was established between the opposing forces as a buffer zone.
3. See the Basic Agreement, article 5.
4. Dispute and military tensions over the armistice issue will be dealt with in a following chapter. The Basic Agreement consists of three chapters; 'reconciliation' governing political relations, 'exchanges and cooperation', and 'Non-aggression' focusing on the conventional arms control measures. For the full text of the Agreement, see *BBC Summary*, Far East, no. 1255 (14 December 1991), A3/1.
5. The major difference was that South Korea focused on a gradual approach through confidence-building measures, while North Korea advocated comprehensive disarmament measures. Vis-à-vis the structural arms control issue, the South placed its first priority on the reduction of offensive weapons, whereas the North placed more importance on troop reductions, offering a four-step plan to reduce troop strength to a ceiling of 100 000 for each side over a ten-year period. North Korea also wanted cessation of qualitative innovation of armed forces while South Korea was silent on this.
6. The Military Sub-Committee was held eight times between March 1992 and September 1992, but those disputed issues were never resolved.
7. The initial positions of North and South Korea were well expressed in the first Prime Ministerial talks on 5–6 September 1990. See keynote speeches by South Korean Prime Minister Kang Yong-hun and North Korean Prime Minister Yon Hyong-muk in BBC Summary, Far East, No. 0863 (5 September 1990), A3/2, and no. 0864 (8 September 1990), A3/1-5.
8. For the full text of the Roh's special declaration, see Korea Newsreview, 9 July 1988, pp. 4-5.
9. 'Northern Policy' had also been adopted by the administration of Park Chung Hee and Chun Doo Hwan administrations in 1972 and 1983, respectively, and its basic policy goal of improving relations with the Soviet Union and China was similar to Roh's Nordpolitik. Roh's policy, however, was a clear departure from those of his predecessors, because his administration was the first to accept a principle of cross-recognition. Even by the time of the Chun administration, South Korea was still reluctant to accept Pyongyang's diplomatic ties with the West. In June 1983, Chun's Foreign Minister, Lee Bum-suk, who had made the first use of the term 'Northern Policy', said: 'We [South Korea] will selectively block or allow North Korea's advance into the international community…' For historical development of *Nordpolitik*, see Kim Hak-Joon, 'The Republic of Korea's Northern Policy: Origin, Development, and Prospects', in James Cotton ed., Korea under Roh Tae-Woo, pp. 245-66; and Lho Cholsoo, The Transformation of South Korea's Foreign Policy 1988 – 1993: Nordpolitik, Moscow and the Road to Pyongyang, D.Phil Thesis (Oxford University, 1999).
10. US Department of State, DOS cable, 'Policy/Regulation Changes Regarding North Korea: Informing Seoul, Tokyo, Moscow and Beijing', 28 October 1988, confidential (declassified 1995). Cited in Oberdorfer, The Two Koreas, pp. 194-5.
11. The American participants took a tough and strict line, avoiding serious discussion about normalized relations. See Oberdorfer, The Two Koreas, p. 266-7.
12. The Japanese Foreign Ministry maintained that Pyongyang's demand should be treated as claims on Japan for property damages in the only pre-1945 period, thus avoiding the issue of apology and compensation for losses incurred afterwards. See Dong-A Ilbo, 1 October 1990.
13. The abduction issue became another major thorny point during the third round of normalization talks. Kim Hyun Hee, a former North Korean agent, revealed that she had received Japanese-

language training in North Korea from a Japanese woman, Li Un Hye, in preparation for her special mission in Japan. See Joong-*Ang Ilbo*, 16 May 1991.

14. *Asian Security* 1991–1992, pp. 39-43.
15. Paul H. Kreisberg, 'The US and Asia in 1989: Mounting Dilemmas', *Asian Survey,* vol. 30, no. 1 (January 1990), pp. 13-24.
16. Gerald M. Boyd, 'Bush Restates US Determination To Remain a Power in the Pacific', *New York Times*, 23 February 1989, p. A10. US force reductions in Asia will be discussed later in detail.
17. On 7 June 1990, for example, Richard Solomon, Assistant Secretary of State for East Asian and Pacific Affairs said: 'The US is ready to expand the channel... [but] the most important task North Korea is facing is to join the safeguards regulations of the IAEA'. See *Korea Newsreview*, 16 June 1990, pp. 6-7.
18. Quoted in Lho, 'The Transformation of South Korea's Foreign Policy 1988–1993', p. 265.
19. Sigal, *Disarming Strangers*, p. 34.
20. *Ibid., p. 35.*
21. Oberdorfer, *The Two Koreas*, p. 266.
22. In particular, Kanter was specifically forbidden to mention the word *normalization* in connection with US-North Korean relations. See Oberdorfer, *The Two Koreas*, p. 266.
23. Ashton B. Carter and William J. Perry, *Preventive Defense: A New Security Strategy for America* (Washington, DC: Brookings Institution Press, 1999), p. 134.
24. John E. Yang, 'Bush's Year Begins in Australia; President Focusing On Trouble at Home', *Washington Post*, 1 January 1992, A23.
25. For a detailed analysis of the major issues in the normalization talks, see Lee Kyo-duk, *Pukilsukyowa Nampukhan Kwan'gye [North Korea-Japan normalization and Inter-Korean Relations]* (Seoul: Minjokt'ong'il Yonguwon, 1997), pp. 5-20.
26. *Dong-A Ilbo*, 1 October 1990.
27. *Chosun Ilbo*, 23 May 1991.
28. Adrian Buzo, *The Guerrilla Dynasty: Politics and Leadership in North Korea* (Boulder, CO.: Westview Press, 1999), p. 193.
29. *Chosun Ilbo*, 23 October 1992.
30. Jin, 'North Korea – Japan Relations: political factors of normalization', pp. 276-77.
31. 'Kanemaru briefs Armacost on Pyongyang visit', *Japan Economic Newswire*, 9 October 1990.
32. Masao Okonogi, 'Japan – North Korean Negotiations for Normalization: An Overview', in Manwoo Lee and Richard W. Mansbach, eds, *The Changing Order in Northeast Asia and the Korean Peninsula* (Seoul: Institute for Far Eastern Studies, Kyungnam University, 1993), pp. 204-5.
33. 'Little Progress seen in Japan-N. Korea Nuclear Dispute Talks', *Asahi News Service*, 21 May 1991.
34. Buzo, *The Guerrilla Dynasty*, p. 193.
35. Jin, 'North Korea – Japan Relations: political factors of normalization', p. 278.
36. It was unusual in the first place for Japan to undertake such a wide-ranging initiative in Korea without first consulting the US. Japan's natural tendency had been to rely on the US for leadership role while keeping a low profile on security issues. See, for example, Kent Calder, 'The Reactive State: Japanese Foreign Policy', *World Politics,* vol. 40, no. 4 (July 1989).
37. 'Japan – US Security Pact Still Vital', *Daily Yomiuri*, 11 May 1991, p.1.
38. In 1993, changes in Japan's domestic politics opened a new possibility of normalization talks with North Korea. After a 38 year reign, Japan's ruling Liberal Democratic Party (LDP) fell from power, and in its place a coalition cabinet supported by seven parties formed a new government. New Prime Minister Hosokawa Morihiro himself was very forthcoming in apologising for Japan's colonial past, and foreign minister Hata Tsutomu said: 'The government will do every effort to make a possible environment for normalization talks with North Korea'. Despite this appeal from Tokyo, Pyongyang did not show any positive response, and focused its diplomatic energy on the US only. Only after the resolution of the nuclear issue

with the US in 1994, did North Korea begin to express its interest in Japan, and talks for normalization resumed in March 1995.

39. *Dong-A Ilbo*, 25 August 1991.
40. *Chosun Ilbo*, 2 September 1991.
41. *Chosun Ilbo*, 20 October 1991.
42. 'Japan – N. Korean talks to be accelerated by US arms proposal', *Agence France Presse*, 31 October 1991.
43. Yonhap cited in *Korea Newsreview*, 29 June 1991, p. 9.
44. This is not to suggest that Washington was keen on the normalization of relations with North Korea. In fact, the US was unable to make progress because of division within the administration, while Seoul's opposition to the New York talk seems to have further complicated the US – North Korean dialogue.
45. *Korea Newsreview*, 19 January 1991, p. 8. See also 'Kaifu sets condition on NK', *Report From Japan (A Yomiuri News Service)*, 10 January 1991.
46. *BBC Summary*, Far East, no. 1366 (24 April 1992).
47. Victor D. Cha, 'Is there still a rational North Korea option for war?' *Security Dialogue*, vol. 29, no. 4 (December 1998), p. 484; and Martin Hart-Landsberg, *Korea: Division, Reunification, and US Foreign Policy* (New York: Monthly Review Press, 1998) p. 231.
48. Kong Dan Oh, 'North Korea in 1989: Touched by Winds of Change?' *Asian Survey*, 30, no. 1, January 1990; Rhee Sang-woo, 'North Korea in 1990: Lonesome Struggle to Keep Juche', *Asian Survey* 31, no. 1, January 1991; and John Phipps, 'North Korea- Will it be the 'Great Leader's "Turn Next?" *Government and Opposition* (Winter 1991), pp. 45-55.
49. In a memorandum to the Soviet Union in September 1990 which strongly opposed Moscow's move towards normalization with Seoul, North Korea argued: 'The essence of *Nordpolitik* is to isolate us [North Korea]'. See *Dong-A Ilbo*, 20 September 1990.
50. Interview with National Security Adviser to President Roh, Kim Chong Whi, 26 August, 2002.
51. US Department of State, *DOS cable*, 'ROK President Roh's Visit: US Policy re N. Korea', 25 October 1988, secret (declassified 1995). Cited in Oberdorfer, *The Two Koreas*, p. 193. The Chairman of the Senate Foreign Relations Subcommittee on East Asian and Pacific Affairs, Senator Alan Cranston, also called Roh's proposals 'a major new initiative. It is the single most positive expression of hope for peace and unification ...'. See 'S.Korean President Tells Unification Plan', *Chicago Tribune*, 7 July 1988. p. C2.
52. Alan D. Romberg, 'Recognize Pyongyang and Break a Dangerous Logjam', *Los Angeles Times (Home Edition)*, 20 November 1990, p. B7.
53. *Chosun Ilbo*, 11 September 1988.
54. *Chosun Ilbo*, 27 October 1988. In March 1989, Takeshita also apologized to Pyongyang for the Japan's colonization of Korea in an attempt to encourage a dialogue between the two countries. See *Chosun Ilbo*, 31 March 1989.
55. Foreign Minister Lee has since stated that Seoul had repeatedly stressed to Washington and Tokyo that an improvement in diplomatic ties with the North would be possible only after the solution of the nuclear problem. Interview with Lee Sang-ok, 12 August 2002.
56. Interview with Kim Chong Whi, National Security Adviser to President Roh, 26 August, 2002. For the public's concern about this point, see *Chosun Ilbo*, 12 October 1990.
57. Melissa Healy, 'Senate Bill Proposes US Troops in South Korea Be Cut By 10 000 Over Next 3 Years', *Los Angeles Times (Home Edition)*, 24 June 1989, p. 10.
58. *Ibid.*
59. Don Oberdorfer, 'Roh Warns Against US Troop Cuts', *Washington Post*, 19 October 1989, p. A16.
60. Under the three-stage troop reduction plan included as part of the East Asia Strategy Initiative (EASI) published by the US Defense Department in April 1990, 7000 out of 43 000 US troops were to be pulled out by early 1993, and in phase II, 6000 to 7000 more US troops were to be withdrawn from South Korea between 1993 and 1995. See Karl Schoenberger, 'Barriers, Real

and Imagined, Still Divided The 2 Koreas', *Los Angeles Times (Home Edition)*, 13 April 1990, p. A30.

61. John M. Broder, 'US To Shed Main Role In S. Korea Military Alliance', *Los Angeles Times (Home Edition)*, 16 February 1990, p. A1.

62. *Ibid.*

63. Although Washington and Seoul agreed to postpone a scheduled withdrawal of US troops in November 1991 because of the North's nuclear status, Seoul did not fail to notice a continuing global retrenchment of the American military in the post-Cold war era. Choe Yong-chol, Minister of Unification during the Roh administration, for example, questioned the credibility of continued US commitment to South Korea, saying 'Until now the US official position on the US forces in the South and peace treaty has been clear. However, nobody knows when and how it will change'. See Choe Yong-chol, *T'ong'il-ro Makhimyŏn Tolasŏ Kacha [Let's go around if the road to unification is blocked]* (Seoul: T'ong'il Ponyong Yonguwon, 1993), p. 283.

64. Of course, North Korea's nuclear programme was not the sole factor leading to the sense of insecurity of the South during this period. Washington's decision to reduce US forces in Korea out of its budgetary consideration increased Seoul's security concerns.

65. For a discussion concerning the influence of the domestic factors on the *Nordpolitik*, see Lee Manwoo, 'Changes in South Korea and Inter-Korean relations', *Pacific Focus* (Spring 1993), pp. 5-25.

66. *Chosun Ilbo*, 26 March 1989.

67. The right-wing newspapers did not hide their displeasure with the radical students or the manner in which the Roh administration was dealing with them. See *Chosun Ilbo*, 17 August 1989.

68. *Chosun Ilbo*, 15 March 1989.

69. *Chosun Ilbo*, 21 March 1989.

70. *Ibid.*

71. Lee, 'Changes in South Korea and Inter-Korean relations', pp. 5-25.

72. *Chosun Ilbo*, 13 and 14 April 1989.

73. *Chosun Ilbo*, 22 January 1990.

74. For motivations and implications of this political merger, see Park Jin, 'Political Change in South Korea: the challenge of the conservative alliance', *Asian Survey*, Vol. 30, no. 12. (December 1990), pp. 1154-1168.

75. Roh's National Security Adviser, Kim Chong Whi, was particularly worried that a large amount of the compensation money that normalization with Japan would bring to the North might make inter-Korean economic cooperation less appealing. Interview with Kim, 26 August, 2002.

76. *Korea Newsreview*, 19 January 1991, p. 8. See also 'Kaifu sets condition on NK', *Report From Japan (A Yomiuri News Service)*, 10 January 1991.

77. *Chosun Ilbo*, 12 September 1991.

78. In an opinion poll conducted in 1990, 36 per cent of the South Koreans believed that Japan's foreign policy was hostile to them, and 55 per cent of those interviewed thought that Japan opposed Korean reunification. *Dong-A Ilbo*, 1 January 1990.

79. The US was well aware of and concerned with North Korea's missile capabilities and its exports to the Middle East. US Undersecretary of State Reginald Bartholomew declared on 25 July 1991 in testimony before the US House Foreign Affairs Subcommittee on Arms Control that 'North Korea has sold Scud missiles to Syria this year' and that 'North Korea is emerging more and more as a major supplier of missiles of this type around the world'. See Federation of American Scientists, *Arms Sales Monitor*, July 1991, p. 2. However, conventional arms control talks between the two Koreas during this time did not deal with weapons of mass destruction (WMD), such as nuclear, biological and chemical weapons, or the missiles to deliver them.

80. Oh Kwan-Chi, 'The Military Balance on the Korean Peninsula', pp. 101-10.

81. Oh Kwan-Chi wrote in 1990: 'There exists today a military imbalance in favour of North Korea'. He also predicted that 'North Korea will be able to maintain military superiority throughout the 1990s'.

82. The quality of weapons notwithstanding, bean-counting methodology also does not take into account such factors as logistical support, training, leadership, and morale. For a critical review of methods of assessment on military capabilities, see Ham Taik-young, *Arming the Two Koreas: State, Capital and Military Power* (London and New York: Routledge, 1999), pp. 38-61.

83. Stephen Goose, 'The Military Situation on the Korean Peninsula', in John Sullivan and Roberta Foss eds, *Two Koreas – One Future?* (Lanham: University Press of America, 1987) p. 68.

84. *Ibid.*, pp. 68-9.

85. Defence Intelligence Agency, *North Korea: The Foundations for Military Strength* (Washington, DC: DIA, October 1995), Chapter. 4 (website version at http://www.fas.org /irp/dia/ product/knfms95/1510~101_chp4.html).

86. Goose, 'The Military Situation on the Korean Peninsula', p. 70.

87. North Korea's main battle tanks were reported to have critical deficiency in areas such as the observation of enemy targets, firepower, mobility and crew environment, while the US-designed South Korean tanks, M-47, M-48 and M-60, do not suffer these problems. See Stuart K. Masaki, 'The Korean Question: Assessing the Military Balance', *Security Studies* 4, no. 2 (Winter 1994/95), p. 379.

88. As far back as 1986, scholars were claiming that North Korea had lost the race to the South. See Edward A. Olsen, 'The Arms Race on the Korean Peninsula', *Asian Survey*, vol. 26, no. 8 (August 1986), p. 861.

89. Despite conceptual and methodological problems associated with differing economic systems, fiscal tools, and price mechanisms between compared states, some scholars believe that the 'military capital stock' derived from defence expenditure is a more valid and reliable indicator than other methods. For a comprehensive analysis of the military balance on the Korean peninsula using the method of military capital stock, see Ham, *Arming the Two Koreas.*

90. Kim Young C., 'The Politics of Arms Control in Korea', *Korean Journal of Defence Analysis,* vol. 1, no. 1 (Summer 1989), pp. 113-26.

91. The ROK Ministry of National Defence, *Defence White Paper 1998*, p. 118.

92. The arms control talks also showed that both North and South Korea had an intention of seeking supremacy over the other side by shifting the military balance in their favour. As in the case of the previous section, it is difficult to separate this intended exploitation from the defensive motive.

93. Richard Nisbett and Lee Ross, *Human Inference: Strategies and Shortcomings of Social Judgment* (Englewood Cliffs, New Jersey: Prentice-Hall, 1980).

94. In short, this psychological tendency means that 'I stood firm because circumstances demanded it, but he was aggressive because of his nature'.

95. Kim, 'The Politics of Arms Control in Korea', p. 118.

96. *Ibid.*

97. Experimental research has established that once an individual has adopted a causal theory or explanation for a particular event, he will be reluctant to change. Attribution researchers refer to this bias as 'belief perseverance'. See Robert Jervis, 'Hypotheses on Misperception', *World Politics,* vol. 20, no. 3 (April 1968).

98. On Shifting resource allocation from defence to social welfare in the midst of democratization, see Moon Chung-in and Paik Won K., 'The Post-Cold War Environment, Democratization, and National Security in South Korea', in Kim Ilpyong J., eds, *Two Koreas In Transition: Implications for US Policy* (Rockville, MD: InDepth Books, 1998), pp. 271-76.

99. *Joong-Ang Ilbo*, 31 August 1988.

100. *Chosun Ilbo*, 26 March 1989.

101. Halperin, *Bureaucratic Politics and Foreign Policy*, pp. 72-3.

102. *Hankyure Shinmun*, 28 June 1988. It was also estimated that there were approximately 1500 subcontractors.

103. *Ibid.* Of the top ten business conglomerates, whose collective annual sales accounted for 40 per cent of the GNP, eight were actively involved in the defence industry.

104. Only two sectors producing aircraft and missiles maintained a 50 per cent capacity utilization rate, while other firms' utilization rate was below 20 per cent. See Moon Chung-in, 'The Political Economy of Defence Industrialization in South Korea: Constraints, Opportunities, and Prospects', *The Journal of East Asian Affairs*, vol. 5, no. 2 (Summer/Fall 1991), pp. 438-65.

105. *Ibid.*, p. 455.

106. Harrison admits that a military-industrial complex has also existed in the North, but he argues that economic troubles there made arms reductions imperative, whereas in the South the pressures for reductions were not strong enough for sincere arms control. See, Harrison, 'US Policy Toward North Korea', p. 75.

107. In 1992, 660 officers including many generals were promoted, and 99 more promotions were announced in 1993. Through these changes, new military elites who would be personally indebted to him began to emerge, such as Oh Kuk-yul, Kim Du-nam, Kim Kang-whan, and Lee Bong-won. But, the generation of military leaders who had fought against the Japanese with Kim Il Sung in the 1940s continued to assume a majority until 1994. See Lee Tonghun, 'Pukhan Kunsa Chŏngch'aek Kyŏlchŏngkujo Mit Kwachŏngkwa Kunbi T'ongjaeŭi Munje [The Structure and Process of Military Policy Making of North Korea and Arms Control Issues]', *Social Science and Policy Studies, Seoul National University*, Vol. 15, No. 2 (June 1993), pp. 143-44.

108. Army unit no. 525, for example, pledged 'their burning loyalty in absolutely crushing the enemy's new war provocation manoeuvres...' See *BBC Summary*, Far East, No. 0999 (18 February 1991), B/1.

109. *Dong-A Ilbo*, 20 February 1991.

110. Oh and Hassig, *North Korea Through the Looking Glass*, pp.119-20.

111. See Jin, 'North Korea-−Japan Relations: political factors of normalization', p. 279.

112. In January 1990, the South Korean government established the 'South−North Economic Cooperation Fund' to help the North's lagging economy, affording $400 million in funds. See *Korea Newsreview*, 20 January 1990, pp. 12-3.

113. Oberdorfer, *The Two Koreas*, p. 195.

114. One of the leading military analysts, Baek Jong-Chun, for example, said: 'Even if Seoul loses the propaganda battle regarding arms control, it would not accept any North Korean peace offensive that might endanger its national security'. According to his estimation, the South's military capabilities at the time of 1990 were at most 60 per cent of the North's, which 'means that South Korea does not maintain sufficient retaliatory force to the North'. See Baek Jong-Chun and Rhee Seonghan, 'Arms Control on the Korean Peninsula: Past, Present, and Future', *The Journal of East Asian Affairs*, vol. 5, no. 2 (Summer/Fall 1991), pp. 382-5.

115. Soviet oil exports to the North in 1992 amounted to only 10 per cent of the 1990 figure, and following Beijing's demand for hard currency in 1993, North Korea was forced to cut its total petroleum consumption by about 30 per cent. Because of this energy shortage, between a third and a half of North Korea's factories were idle in 1992. See Zacek, 'Russia in North Korean Foreign Policy', pp. 82-5; and Reese, *The Prospects for North Korea's Survival*, pp. 27-8.

116. Reese, *The Prospects for North Korea's Survival*, p. 65.

117. With its forward deployed forces and huge firepower and mobility, the North possessed enough capability to make Seoul a 'sea of fire', and this threat of co extinction against the South contributed to military balance on the peninsula despite the North's deteriorating situation. Additionally, given North Korea's logistical disadvantage vis-à-vis US-ROK air superiority, it would be sound reasoning from Pyongyang's perspective to stockpile munitions and other war materials close to the border where initial conflict would occur. See David Kang, 'North Korea's Military and Security Policy', in Samuel Kim, ed., *North Korean Foreign Relations*, pp. 171-2.

118. These findings are perhaps not surprising, given the varying nature of the cases examined. In other words, diplomatic normalization by definition tends to give prominence to external participants, while arms control talks must grant priority to security concerns.

4. From Accommodation to Crisis: 1992–1993

By mid-1992, the nuclear diplomacy instigated by Washington and Seoul had made progress, although there were unresolved issues and weaknesses in the agreements reached. Talks on bilateral nuclear inspections were underway, and moreover, the long-awaited IAEA inspections began in May 1992. Yet this positive trend began to go into reverse later in the year. Bilateral nuclear inspections were substantially delayed, frustrating many South Korean officials, and in October Seoul decided to resume the Team Spirit exercise in 1993. North Korea criticized this decision and complained of insufficient economic and diplomatic benefits from Washington. Circumstances were further aggravated by the IAEA's insistence on 'special inspections.' In the midst of this stalemate, Pyongyang provocatively declared it would withdraw from the NPT in March of 1993. The question central for this period is: why did accommodations in the 1988 to early 1992 period end in confrontation? This chapter's primary objective is the identification of those factors that escalated tension during late 1992 and early 1993. It will also include an examination of their interrelationship and relative importance.

1. Coercion and NPT Withdrawal

Following the signing of the safeguards agreement in January 1992, Pyongyang began to carry out the IAEA mandates required of all states that submit to nuclear safeguards. On 4 May, the North formally submitted an official report of its existing nuclear infrastructure to the agency, followed by a series of 'ad hoc' inspections to verify the submitted information.[1] Shortly thereafter, on 25 May, the first formal regular inspections of the Yongbyon facility began, and they continued throughout the fall of that year.[2] The process went smoothly, and IAEA Director General Hans Blix said in September that their work in the North had 'proceeded well' and was on schedule.[3]

During the spring and summer of 1992, attention shifted from the IAEA inspections, which continued quietly and without any major difficulties, to negotiations on the bilateral inspections between Pyongyang and Seoul via the Joint Nuclear Control Committee (JNCC), established by the nuclear accord of 31 December 1991.[4] Through this nuclear inspection mechanism, Seoul insisted on 'challenge inspections' that would allow both sides to inspect any sites at short notice, including military installations.[5] Inspectors would not be limited to declared nuclear facilities, and would be granted access to any suspicious nuclear sites as long as 24 hours' prior notice was given.[6] As the JNCC meetings proceeded, however, it became clear that North Korea did not intend to accept the South's proposal. Pyongyang insisted that military facilities be excluded from the challenge inspections on the grounds that such intrusive inspections would violate its sovereignty.[7] It also demanded the right to visit US and South Korean military bases, claiming that American tactical nuclear weapons continued to be stored in the South.[8] On 17 September, North Korean Ambassador-at-Large O Chang Rim said: 'If and when South Korea agrees to inspections of US military installations as we demand, a way will be found to resolve the question of mutual inter-Korean nuclear inspections.'[9] Seoul and Washington accepted this demand only partially; intent on protecting sensitive military information, a condition was imposed that US bases would be opened 'under what was called "managed access", which means that North Koreans couldn't go anywhere they wanted to see.'[10] North Korea rejected this offer, demanding that all US bases in the South be opened.[11]

Whatever the North's motives, the stalemate over challenge inspections continued. The initial schedule had stated that inspection guidelines would be determined by 20 May and actual visits would start around 10 June,[12] but both sides failed to narrow the gap and relations began to deteriorate.[13] Pyongyang complained that it had allowed IAEA inspections, but was getting nothing in return, not even verification of American nuclear withdrawal. Seoul began seriously to doubt Pyongyang's interest in resolving the nuclear issue through dialogue, and voices in favour of a tougher approach increased.[14] In June, South Korean Prime Minister Chong Won-sik expressed Seoul's pessimistic mood, saying 'given this attitude by the North Korean side, I cannot help but say that prospects for North–South relations are not optimistic.'[15]

In the midst of such delays in talks, the South made its decision to go ahead with planning Team Spirit 1993. At the annual US–ROK. Security Consultative Meeting (SCM) on 8 October 1992, Seoul successfully persuaded Washington to issue a joint communiqué stipulating 'preparations for Team Spirit '93 in the absence of South-North bilateral nuclear inspections.'[16] North Korea strongly criticized the decision, and talks stalled. Although the JNCC continued to operate until January 1993 despite Pyongyang's threats to terminate the dialogue, meetings were spent entirely on crossfire over the Team Spirit issue.[17] Already by 3 November Pyongyang had suspended all North–South contacts except the JNCC, and a crisis appeared imminent.

It was into this already aggravated situation that another source of tension emerged: the IAEA's demand for 'special inspections' of suspect nuclear sites. In late 1992, inspectors discovered an 'inconsistency' between what the North had declared and the samples taken by the IAEA inspection teams. According to the technical analysis of the samples, the North had reprocessed plutonium not once, as it claimed, but at least three times—in 1989 1990 and 1991.[18] This meant that, theoretically, enough plutonium could have been extracted to produce one or two nuclear weapons. The IAEA's urgent task was to get access to the location where the possible plutonium waste was hidden, and US satellite photographs had identified two suspect nuclear waste sites near Yongbyon.

In late 1992, the IAEA began to discuss the possibility of 'special inspections' of the two sites. The following February, Pyongyang responded harshly, saying 'It is totally unjust of the IAEA to raise the issue of special inspection. The sites mentioned are military bases and have nothing to do with nuclear activities.'[19] The move was further criticized as 'an unpardonable provocation aimed at spying on our military facilities legitimately and stifling our socialist position.'[20] On 25 February, despite Pyongyang's repeated warnings, the IAEA took an unprecedented step in its history by demanding the special inspection of undeclared sites over the objections of the target nation. Many anticipated that if the North did not cede, the IAEA would refer the matter to the UN Security Council.[21] On 8 March, Kim Jong Il declared 'a semi-state of war', ordering the entire Army to assume full combat posture.[22] The next day, the Team Spirit exercise began, involving 70 000 South Korean and 50 000 American troops, and the deployment offshore of the aircraft carrier USS. Independence.[23] On 12 March, North Korea announced that it was withdrawing from the NPT.[24] The Korean peninsula was moving toward a crisis.

2. Explanations

What led the earlier progress to this crisis point and the North's announced withdrawal from the NPT? Two issues seem to have been critical in creating the scenario: one is the dispute over nuclear inspections (inter-Korean challenge inspections and the IAEA's special inspections), and the other is the resumption of the Team Spirit exercise in 1993. Questions arise as to why the US and South Korea insisted on immediate 'challenge inspections', risking everything that had been achieved so far, and as to why the IAEA demanded unprecedented 'special inspections.' On the other hand, one must wonder why Pyongyang demonstrated such resistance to the challenge and special inspections after it had accepted the IAEA regular inspections. Secondly, why were Washington and Seoul unwilling to reward North Korea for the earlier progress on nuclear and other inter-Korean issues, and what led them to go ahead with the potentially counter-productive Team Spirit exercise? This section will examine three perspectives: US domestic politics during the transition of administrations and the IAEA's role, both Koreas' security concerns and possible misperceptions, and the domestic politics of Seoul and Pyongyang.

A. Interregnum politics in Washington and the IAEA's uncompromising stance

The Bush administration's policy towards the North's nuclear issue during the time prior to the period under current consideration can be described as one of 'carrots and sticks'. While Washington tried to maintain its firm security commitment to Seoul by postponing the planned reduction of US forces in Korea, it also offered, as carrots, nuclear withdrawal, the cancellation of the Team Spirit exercise, and a single high-level talk. In return, the North offered the signing of the safeguards agreement and acceptance of the IAEA inspections. Yet, the US soon reverted to a policy of pure 'sticks': while denying any additional incentives for cooperation to Pyongyang, it stepped up its demands for IAEA and inter-Korean inspections. When North Korea repeatedly asked for help in acquiring new light-water reactors and supplying them with nuclear fuel in return for abandoning reprocessing, during the spring and summer of 1992, Washington did not respond.[25] Instead, it urged the IAEA to tighten up its monitoring activities and cooperated with Seoul in pressing Pyongyang to accept intrusive inter-Korean inspections.

Behind Washington's hardened position was a national shift in political mood. With a swift and overwhelming victory in the Gulf War, President Bush had attained a popular approval rating of over 90 per cent. Yet the call within the US to give priority to domestic issues gradually strengthened from the spring of 1991,[26] as a weakened American economy incited a change in public priorities. Harsh criticism of President Bush for ignoring problems at home and spending too much time on foreign affairs sent his approval rating into sharp decline.[27] In early 1992, the administration began to pour all of its energies into the presidential primaries. Although Bush maintained supremacy within the Republican Party, rival Pat Buchanan captured a significant protest vote via an 'America First' slogan.

In response, the Bush camp increasingly emphasized the value of 'prudence' with regard to foreign policy.[28] Washington refused to engage American military power in Yugoslavia, leaving that problem to the Europeans. In Haiti, the Bush administration insisted that no vital interest was threatened and that military intervention was not justified. Despite a strong case for aid to the former Soviet Union, Bush was also very cautious and reluctant in offering economic assistance. Washington's reversal to a pure 'stick' approach towards North Korea also appeared to have been made in the context of this election year policy.[29] Sceptical about the likelihood of success in diplomatic give-and-take, the US refused to be drawn into negotiations with North Korea. The Bush administration may have feared the electoral repercussions of failure, and preferred to keep the volatile issue hidden as much as possible instead of raising the stakes through further diplomatic initiatives, at least during the campaign.

Another source of Washington's toughening position towards North Korea was the failure of US intelligence in uncovering the Iraqi nuclear programme. Bill Clinton's Defence Secretary William J. Perry and his Assistant Secretary, Ashton B. Carter, wrote in their book that beneath the surface of the Gulf War victory was 'a sobering array of close calls and surprises', saying 'Its [Iraq's] nuclear weapons program was much larger and of a totally different technical character than US intelligence had suspected.' [30] Alarmed by Iraq's nuclear potential and increasingly concerned about the non-proliferation issue, the American intelligence community became determined not to repeat the same mistake in Asia. This seems to have contributed to an alarmist estimation of the North's nuclear capabilities. On 25 February 1992, the Director of the Central Intelligence Agency, Robert Gates, told the House Foreign Affairs Committee that North Korea was 'a few months to a couple of years' from acquiring a nuclear bomb.[31] North Koreans, he added: 'had a deception plan for hiding their nuclear capabilities.' Other analysts in the CIA, such as Gordon Oehler, the National Intelligence Officer for Science Technology and Proliferation, also fed fears about North Korean nuclear capabilities in the expert community and the news media.[32] Influenced by these pessimistic official views, nongovernmental experts also expressed their concerns about the North's deception. Gary Milhollin, director of the Wisconsin Project on Nuclear Arms Control, argued that 'US intelligence analysts' believe North Korea now possesses enough plutonium for 'six to eight atomic bombs', but Hans Blix 'is loath to believe it.'[33]

Increasing concern about the prospects of another intelligence failure encouraged such estimates of North Korea's nuclear capabilities, and, despite the Bush administration's desire to maintain a focus on domestic issues, it was hard to keep the matter from the headlines. Determined to avoid appearing as the architect of a disastrous foreign policy failure during the presidential campaign, Washington became more rigid and risk-averse, leaving Seoul to insist on its own intrusive inspections.[34] As has been mentioned, inter-Korean 'challenge inspections' would allow both sides to inspect any sites at short notice. The idea was that IAEA regular inspections, with access only to declared sites, were not rigorous enough, and more rigorous bilateral inspections were needed to make up for this weakness. Furthermore, Washington also generally supported the IAEA's idea of 'special inspections.'[35] In a G-7 summit meeting held in July 1992 in Munich, the US and other nations declared: 'The IAEA must receive the resources necessary to strengthen the existing safeguards regime and to conduct effective special inspections.' [36]

With the presidential election only a few weeks away, the US decided to prepare for a Team Spirit exercise with South Korea–a final, critical move deemed responsible to a large extent for the North's statement of NPT withdrawal. In September 1992, just before the annual US–South Korea Security

Consultative Meeting (SCM), the South Korean Defence Ministry submitted a draft communique to be issued after the meeting, which proposed the resumption of Team Spirit 'unless there is significant progress toward completing the bilateral inspection regime.' Mindful of negative reactions from North Korea, the Korea desk at the US State Department vigorously opposed the resumption idea in an inter-agency review, and Washington managed to soften the communique language into 'preparations' for the exercise.[37] Nonetheless, this was enough to provoke a fierce North Korean response.

Although the two nations officially announced the decision to prepare for the exercise at the SCM on 8 October 1992, Seoul had essentially already made its decision to resume the exercise by that summer. Defence Ministry officials in Seoul began to suggest publicly that the Team Spirit would resume in 1993.[38] Faced with Seoul's strong determination, General RisCassi, the US commander–in–chief in Korea, endorsed the South Korean officers' request for the start of joint planning.[39] RisCassi did not want to pick a fight with allied officers under his command,[40] even though he did not regard the exercise as essential for deterrence or troop readiness. As the issue was basically in the hands of the military, the State Department had limited influence in deciding whether or not the military exercise should take place. Moreover, the voice of caution against resumption 'was [at a] rather low level', according to Charles Kartman, the State Department country director for Korea, and those few people were unable to influence the others.[41]

With the administration's attention turned towards the election, the issue of whether or not Team Spirit would resume did not formally arise in Washington until the fall, despite Seoul's apparent preference. As the presidential campaign unfolded, Bush and his foreign policy team were placed more and more on the defensive. Given the public's disenchantment with the administration's focus on foreign policy, the less said on the subject the better. Furthermore, when Seoul raised the question of resumption, no official at the level of assistant secretary or above was willing to focus on the issue.[42] The administration was not willing to overrule South Korea's preferences, and in particular senior State Department officials were not prepared to intervene in a military matter.[43] By then, President Bush's re-election was in doubt, and policy floated in a political void. 'No decisions were being made on our side. We were getting ready for election. Everything was in neutral', said a State Department official.[44] By November 1992, the conflict between Pyongyang and Seoul/IAEA was coming to a head, but Bill Clinton's victory left the outgoing Bush administration unwilling to contemplate any new diplomatic approach towards North Korea.

In January 1993, William Jefferson Clinton was sworn in as President of the United States, and his foreign policy team was faced with the question of whether Team Spirit should proceed or not. Since plans for the exercise had been set in motion by the previous administration, it was difficult for the Clinton administration to change course. Upon taking office, Secretary of Defense Les Aspin was briefed by the Joint Chiefs of Staff about pending military contingencies, and learned that Korea ranked high on the list.[45] In the briefing, Aspin inquired about the military effect of cancelling the Team Spirit exercise. Gary Luck, an incoming commander-in-chief in Korea, was flexible about its cessation, provided that he was able to make up for the Team Spirit with other joint military exercises. Certain senior officials in the Defense Department also did not regard Team Spirit as militarily essential, and worried about an adverse reaction from Pyongyang. However, General Colin Powell, the Chairman of the Joint Chiefs of Staff during the Bush administration, opposed the idea of unilateral cancellation, insisting that the exercises should not be held hostage to North Korean threats.[46]

In contrast to the indecisive mood in Washington, Seoul was determined to go ahead with the exercise. Only five days after Clinton's inauguration, South Korea's Defence Ministry announced that Team Spirit would take place in mid-March.[47] The new Kim Young Sam administration, which took office in February, also approved the resumption of Team Spirit. Thus, despite the scepticism of senior Clinton administration officials and their concern about North Korean reactions, the fear of adverse South Korean reaction and resulting political fallout in Washington ruled the day.

At the same time, the new Clinton administration was far from equipped to explore new diplomatic initiatives towards North Korea. Foreign affairs was clearly not Clinton's passion or preoccupation.[48] While personally absorbed with domestic issues, vis-à-vis foreign policy decisions, he basically asked his aides to formulate options and then submit them to him to be approved or rejected.[49] He did not attend the meeting where his top foreign policy advisers worked out the administration's policy for the Balkans, its first major foreign policy initiative,[50] nor did he hold a meeting of his National Security Council until the spring of 1993. While some of his aides suggested that he might be somewhat intimidated by foreign policy matters,[51] he was faithfully representing the Democratic Party and the public at that time by focusing on advancing American economic competitiveness and addressing outstanding social problems at home.[52] In the list of the administration's goals for the first 100 days, which had been reviewed by Clinton himself and other top advisers on 6 February, only domestic issues were covered, including economic recovery, health care plans, welfare reform, and public service. There was no mention of a foreign policy objective.[53] The job of his foreign policy aides was to keep these issues away from the president so that he could concentrate on internal matters.[54]

Advances in foreign policy were difficult in a situation where international issues failed to attract a major commitment of time and energy. Top-ranking officials were not keen to take charge of nuclear negotiations with North Korea, despite its repeated requests.[55] Moreover, the incoming Clinton administration was not yet fully organized. Of the 290 top government jobs subject to Senate confirmation, Clinton had submitted just 30 formal nominations by late February 1993,[56] about half the pace of Jimmy Carter and Ronald Reagan in the first month of their presidencies. This delay in nomination and Senate confirmation caused problems. In the Defense Department, for example, when Secretary Aspin was hospitalized with heart problems in February, there was no backup to step in, as Aspin's likely deputy, William Perry, had not yet been nominated for the post.[57] In order to fill the void, the State Department, like some other departments, quietly hired as temporary consultants many of the officials expected to be named to top posts.[58] But such shadow appointees lacked the full authority to take charge of departmental decisions, leaving policy to lower levels, many of which were dominated by holdovers from the Bush administration. Thus, Clinton's lack of confidence in foreign affairs, the imperative of domestic issues at the time, and the delay in appointing senior officials all seem to have contributed to a continuation of the Bush administration's final year of North Korean policy–coercive diplomacy without further 'carrots.'[59] In this sense, nuclear diplomacy towards North Korea during 1992 and early 1993 was a casualty of American interregnum politics.

On the other hand, the same time period saw the IAEA send its own ultimatum to the North, formally endorsing the demand for mandatory 'special inspections' of the two suspect sites at Yongbyon. This demand was spurred by the discovery of inconsistency between the North's initial declaration and technical analysis of the samples taken by the IAEA teams. The realization that reprocessing had occurred on three separate occasions, in contrast to the North's claim that it had separated plutonium just once in 1990, raised suspicion that Pyongyang had already extracted plutonium for making bombs. The IAEA took it as evidence of North Korean deception, and demanded the unprecedented 'special inspections.'

The IAEA's tough stance towards North Korea coincided with its general efforts to strengthen the safeguards regime in 1991 and 1992. The IAEA's reputation as a non-proliferation watchdog had come into question after the Gulf War in 1991. The IAEA removed the analysts in the safeguards division accused of 'dealing with member states as if they were colleagues instead of potential proliferators',[60] and replaced them with a new team led by Demetrios Pericos, famous for his strong determination to uncover Iraq's nuclear programme after the Gulf War. At the same time, IAEA director General Blix adopted new measures designed to prevent another state from trying to follow Iraq's example.[61] The Agency's Board of Governors reaffirmed the IAEA's right to carry out a special inspection, if needed, to confirm that all nuclear material had been reported. The Board also agreed that providing the IAEA with greater access to information and the backing of the Security Council would be essential.[62] North Korea became the target of this newly reinforced system.

B. Security imperatives

In the previous section, US domestic politics at the Cold War's end and the 1992 American presidential election were offered as elements contributing to the shift on the Korean peninsula from initial accommodation to the NPT withdrawal crisis. However, the two primary causes of the crisis–the dispute over challenge inspections and the resumption of the Team Spirit exercise–can also be explained in the context of the security dilemma between Pyongyang and Seoul and their likely respective misperceptions.

Security dilemma

In the case of challenge inspections, South Korea insisted on this intrusive option at a time when IAEA inspections and inter-Korean relations were generally proceeding smoothly. From Seoul's perspective, this attempt to gain transparency of North Korean nuclear capabilities is understandable. If the South failed to ascertain the North's nuclear status and allowed it to make bombs, this would have significant strategic implications. However small and crude they might be, North Korea's nuclear weapons would have the capability of putting enormous psychological pressure on the South, in addition to any potential physical destruction. With its own nuclear inventory, North Korean aircraft or Scud-B missiles could launch nuclear strikes against any major city in South Korea. In this light, William Tow argued that a North Korean nuclear bomb would transform the Korean peninsula's traditional counterforce or military target-oriented battle environment into a largely counter-value or 'city-busting' game of chicken.[63] This would mean, he continued, that 'US–ROK escalation control strategies could be seriously jeopardized.'[64] For example, North Korea could deter a US escalation of hostilities by threatening a port city like Pusan, where major American reinforcements would have to arrive.

Major General Lee Bu-jik, a South Korean delegate to the JNCC, added another worrisome scenario, in which North Korean nuclear bombs would enhance the North's bargaining position enormously at a truce negotiation regardless of the conventional military situation.[65] Although this scenario seems unlikely, given the firm American commitment to the South, it could not be excluded from strategic thinking. Deputy Chief of Staff of the ROK–US Combined Forces Command (CFC), Major General Ahn Kwang-chan, himself involved in the JNCC, even questioned the credibility of the US nuclear umbrella, saying 'if North Koreans have bombs, they could use them at their will. By contrast, it should not be forgotten that the US nuclear umbrella is American bombs. They [Americans], not we [South Koreans], will decide whether to use them or not.'[66] Gong Ro-myung, South Korea's chief delegate to the JNCC, likewise expressed Seoul's determination to verify Pyongyang's nuclear capability, saying, 'We can't give the North a clean bill of health without confirming the truth with our own eyes.'[67]

Despite Seoul's concerns about the North's nuclear capability, the origin of Pyongyang's nuclear programme seems to have stemmed from a fear of conventional and nuclear threats from Seoul and Washington rather than from the offensive motivation to attack South Korea. In addition, one or two primitive nuclear weapons–the estimated number of nuclear weapons that the North might have produced under optimal conditions–would not significantly alter the military balance on the peninsula.[68] If North Korea's nuclear weapons were to be used offensively, they would have to be done so in a way that would exact the maximum amount of political and strategic destruction upon the South. In order to achieve that goal, the minimum targets would have to include major US–ROK military facilities and cities, such as the Chinhae Navy Base, the Kunsan Air Base, the Osan Air Base, the 'Tango' C3I facility, and the Yongsan base.[69] Such attacks would require approximately seven to ten nuclear warheads in the 30–60 kT range.[70] Hence, one or two nuclear warheads would not prove effective as operational military weapons. Despite this realistic assessment of the North's motives and actual battlefield capabilities, however, the worrisome diplomatic scenarios that the North's programmes posed left the South unprepared to compromise on the challenge inspections.[71]

For Pyongyang, the South's demand for challenge inspections was hard to accept for a number of reasons. Assuming that the North did want to use nuclear weapons as a bargaining chip, Pyongyang's hope of extracting maximum benefits from this card was far from being achieved at that point in the JNCC negotiations. To ensure the survival of its regime, a nuclear programme could be bargained away only after ensuring diplomatic and economic concessions from the US and South Korea. After allowing six IAEA regular inspections, Pyongyang had acquired virtually no reward from Washington or Seoul, be it economic aid, investment, or broader diplomatic contacts with the US. Given this situation, the 'challenge inspections' would deprive the North of bargaining power by providing full exposure of its nuclear programme. Even if it had nuclear capability, it would not open its nuclear sites to the world without substantial compensation. Pyongyang appeared well aware that its ambiguous stance in relation to nuclear capabilities was operational as a bargaining chip.[72]

Moreover, the North was denied the opportunity to verify that American nuclear weapons had been completely withdrawn from the South. Strategically speaking, the removal of nuclear weapons did not alleviate Pyongyang's vulnerability to US nuclear threats as long as its umbrella remained over South Korea. Psychologically, however, their removal from Southern soil might have been a partial, if not complete, component in the North's decision as to whether or not it would reveal its nuclear programme. Hence, Pyongyang seems to have demanded the inspection of US bases in the South as a condition for accepting challenge inspections, although it is doubtful that the opening of all American bases would have been incentive enough for its compliance.

Furthermore, the North might have been concerned that its deteriorating conventional military capabilities would be revealed to the outside world, had unconditional and broad access to military facilities been allowed.[73] Given that its external security had been sustained mainly through military threats, any measure that could uncover its weaknesses or remove uncertainties about its actual capabilities would be a substantial blow to the North's survival strategy.[74] In this light, general Lee Bu-jik, South Korean delegate to the JNCC argues: 'If the North's military facilities were opened, the two essences of the North's military strategy–the "blitzkrieg strategy" and the "strategy of ambiguity" about its actual capabilities–would be seriously damaged.'[75]

Finally, it is also possible that Pyongyang was determined to go ahead with its nuclear programme and not offer it as a bargaining chip. According to this view, Pyongyang attempted to cheat on its NPT commitments,[76] falsely believing that it could use its nuclear card for diplomatic leverage while simultaneously making bombs. Under these circumstances, challenge inspections had to be rejected, as such short-notice inspections would betray Pyongyang's intentions.

It was in the midst of such delays and frustrations in North–South nuclear talks that Seoul made the decision to go ahead with planning for the Team Spirit exercise. As North Korea's uncompromising stance on inspections continued, Seoul became increasingly pessimistic about its nuclear motivations and came to believe that Pyongyang was not using its putative nuclear weapons programme merely as a bargaining chip.[77] Most officials felt it necessary to send a strong signal of the South's firm resolve on the issue through advocacy of Team Spirit. Senior officials in the Defence Ministry, including General Director of the Arms Control Bureau Park Yong-ok, General Director of Policy Planning Bureau Cho Sung-tae, and Minister Choi Se-chang, all strongly believed that resuming the exercise was an indispensable part of pressurising the North.[78] They also believed that South Korean and American military preparedness should not be sacrificed when there was no sign of a change in Pyongyang's attitude. Civilian officials agreed as well, and approved resumption. According to Lee Sang-ok, Minister of Foreign Affairs, participants at several NSC meetings held to discuss the Team Spirit issue–the Ministry of Foreign Affairs, the Ministry of Unification, the Ministry of Defence, Office of the President, National Intelligence Agency–all agreed that the renewal of the exercise was inevitable given the North's uncompromising stance on inspections.[79]

Possibility of misperception (psychological insensitivity)
Even though South Korean officials had legitimate concerns about national security, it also seems that they were not sensitive to Pyongyang's security needs. In other words, most South Korean officials did not seem to understand

how the resumption of Team Spirit would be viewed from Pyongyang's perspective at this critical juncture. From January 1993, Pyongyang's reaction to the exercise became extreme and hysterical, as tension was building over the IAEA's call for 'special inspections' and possible UN sanctions. On 8 March, the day before the exercise, Kim Jong Il declared 'a semi-state of war', ordering the entire Army to assume a complete combat posture.[80] Team Spirit, the order contended, was a 'nuclear war test aimed at waging a surprise, pre-emptive strike on the northern half of our Republic.'[81] Senior military officials were ordered to evacuate to underground fortifications and all soldiers were positioned to fight a war, with heads shaved, steel helmets donned and rifle ammunition issued.[82] The civilian population was also mobilized to dig trenches as protection against an air strike.

It could be argued that such a reaction should not be accepted at face value, since it may have been merely propaganda. In this view, Pyongyang's fear of the exercise was not genuine; rather, it was an effort to manipulate North Korean public opinion by stressing an external threat. However, as Peter Hayes has pointed out, the high cost and social disruption caused by the mobilization casts doubt on this 'domestic mobilization' explanation.[83] Pyongyang's mobilization in response to the Team Spirit exercises diverted the North's scarce labour from factories to military tasks by transforming the entire nation into a state of war. Furthermore, such an extreme response had the potential of undermining Kim Il Sung's legitimacy, since the North Korean people would be reminded that their Great Leader could not protect the nation from nuclear threat.[84] In a newly declassified East German record of the 'Kim Il Sung–Erich Honecker conversation' on 30 May 1984, in which Kim had less incentive for propaganda than when speaking in public, Kim did not conceal his sensitivity to the Team Spirit. 'Every time the enemies conduct such military exercises, we have to take measures in response. Every time, we have to mobilize workers into the army. Then, the cost amounts to one and a half month's worth of labour a year', he stated.[85] Although there may have been some element of propaganda in what Pyongyang said publicly, its extreme reaction to the exercise indicates a concern about enemy intentions and possible military conflict.[86]

If North Korea's reaction to Team Spirit was not an excuse but an expression of genuine fear, this episode can be seen to represent the psychological bias of both North and South Korean officials. To South Korean officials, the repeated warnings not to resume the Team Spirit from Pyongyang were no more than propaganda designed 'simply to postpone the inter-Korean dialogue.'[87] Although South Korean officials were aware of some coercive effects the exercise was having on Pyongyang, they did not fully understand the degree of concern that Team Spirit created in North Korea. While their own defensive intentions were obvious to them, they failed to account for Pyongyang's perspective, especially when the atmosphere became increasingly tense over the inspection issue.[88] As 'attribution theories' suggest, many South Korean officials were largely unaware of the 'situational' constraint that evoked Pyongyang's harsh behaviour–for example, North Korea's interpretation of the enemies' massive military exercise at a time of deteriorating internal and external conditions. Instead, Seoul appears to have attributed the North's actions to its 'innate' uncompromising character, dismissing Pyongyang's argument as propaganda. Remarking eight years later that most officials in the Defence Ministry could not have predicted the devastating effects of their Team Spirit decision in the fall of 1993, Han Yong–sup, deputy director of the Arms Control Bureau of the ROK Defence Ministry, acknowledged that key South Korean decision-makers had been insensitive to the political and military implications that resumption would have on the North.[89]

On the other hand, Pyongyang also appeared to have suffered from psychological bias. Although the Team Spirit exercise may have posed legitimate security concerns to Pyongyang, it was never intended as a prelude to waging 'a surprise and pre-emptive strike', as the North alleged.[90] The rationale for the exercise had always been to deter a North Korean attack and defend the South if deterrence failed. In particular, the decision to resume the exercise was designed to pressure Pyongyang into cooperation on challenge inspections. If a rather weak criterion of misperception is used–that is, a judgment will be regarded as biased when it is held with a conviction stronger than warranted by the available evidence–Pyongyang's strong suspicion that the Team Spirit was a prelude to a US nuclear attack against the North was not clearly warranted by the evidence.

In sum, Seoul's assertive decisions (demand of challenge inspections and the resumption of the Team Spirit exercise) and Pyongyang's adverse reactions seem to have stemmed, at least in part, from the security concerns of both sides and their psychological biases.

C. Domestic politics: antagonistic interdependence

As diplomatic negotiations over the nuclear issue came to a halt and signs of regression began to emerge in the second half of 1992, the political climate in both Seoul and Pyongyang worsened. In explaining a number of major incidents that disrupted the cooperation, this section examines the possibility that both Seoul and Pyongyang intentionally generated the crisis for domestic political purposes.

Hawks and electoral politics in Seoul
Many South Korean officials dealing with the North's nuclear issue felt betrayed by the lack of progress in the JNCC talks, and decided on a tougher approach. Although the Team Spirit decision was made because of the delays in bilateral

inspections, it might also have been connected with the politics of the South Korean military. By the fall of 1992, only three months remained in President Roh's term of office, and in the approaching December election a civilian successor would be elected for the first time since the military coup in May 1961. In this changing political climate, the South Korean military, whose privileged status had begun to be undermined by democratization during the Roh administration, might have seen the Team Spirit exercise as a useful political tool in protecting its organizational interests. In other words, the rapidly-moving rapprochement with North Korea and the impending civilian control of the military, if continued or sped up, had the potential to reduce the defence budget and autonomy of the armed forces. Thus, the resumption of Team Spirit may have been taken in order to put the brakes on talks with the North. According to a Defence Ministry official, when the Ministry made its first reports regarding Team Spirit to President Roh in the fall of 1992, the paper dealt only with preparation of the exercise and its prospects without mentioning whether it should be conducted.[91] To Defence Ministry officials, after all, the suspension of Team Spirit in 1992 had only been a one-year decision.

Another move that clearly showed the hard-line mood in Seoul was the government's announcement of the arrest of 95 North Korean espionage agents. On 1 October 1992, the South Korean Agency for National Security Planning (ANSP) announced that it had arrested the largest group of North Korean agents uncovered since 1948, alleging that they had tried to establish political agitation groups with the goal of toppling the South Korean government.[92] The agency even hinted that politicians in the opposition party might be implicated in the case.[93] Not surprisingly, the 'spy ring scandal' cast further doubt on the wisdom of cooperation with North Korea, and the Roh administration was criticized by conservatives for 'underestimating Pyongyang's disguised intentions.'[94]

While there is no evidence to prove or disprove the agency's case, the timing of the announcement and its negative impact on inter-Korean relations made many people suspect a political conspiracy behind the event.[95] There were even rumours that hard-liners in North Korea provided information about the spy ring to the ANSP in an attempt to stall improvement in relations.[96] Given these circumstances, Roh was forced to cancel the scheduled visit of a deputy minister to Pyongyang for discussions about joint economic development with the North.[97] According to Kim Hak Joon, spokesman of President Roh at that time, the ANSP had opposed this proposal for economic cooperation even before the announcement of the spy ring case.[98] The ANSP further hardened Seoul's mood towards Pyongyang by warning that North Korea might attempt a terrorist attack in retaliation for the South's accusations of spying. South Korea's international airports, seaports and other vulnerable areas were put on first-degree alert in preparation for such a contingency.[99]

The spy ring episode and the Team Spirit decision, therefore, appear to have been orchestrated counterattacks aimed at shifting the course of relations from rapprochement to confrontation. One experienced US State Department Korea–watcher notes: 'In late August, the R.O.K. came and told us that President Roh Tae Woo is coming to the end of his term. He's not in a position to make any long-term commitments. We're going to slow the dialogue because he's a lame duck.'[100] On 16 September, South Korean chief representative at the North–South political talks, Lee Dong Bok, refused to table a proposal on reuniting divided families, ignoring the Roh government's instruction.[101] Lee, one of the strongest hawks in the administration, believed the proposal was too accommodating, and his rebellious action effectively shut down the talks with the North without any agreements being reached.

This rebellion, however, did not simply represent a hard-line philosophy or organizational interests, but also seemed to be related to Seoul's electoral politics in the latter half of 1992. With only three months of Roh's term in office remaining, the president's authority and control of his government had been reduced. Instead, Kim Young Sam, who became a presidential candidate in May 1992, began to expand his influence within the administration.[102] In the presidential battle with opposition leader Kim Dae Jung, widely known for his liberal views towards North Korea, Kim Young Sam was apprehensive about any progress in North–South relations. The greater the improvement in inter-Korean relations, the better for Kim Dae Jung, who was regarded as well-equipped in handling rapprochement with North Korea. By contrast, the more inter-Korean relations deteriorated and the South Korean electorate were reminded of North Korean threats, the more dangerous and unreliable Kim Dae Jung would be viewed. In this sense, the ruling party may have determined that confrontation with the North would help it win the coming election, and both the Defence Ministry's preference for resuming the Team Spirit exercises and the ANSP's spy ring announcement were well suited to such a political objective.[103] Hence, when Kim Young Sam was elected President in December 1992, he was not in a position to cancel the exercise. As the first civilian President since 1961, Kim knew that his administration was being closely watched by the military and the conservatives, and he did not want to appear soft on defence. Moreover, since he had ambitious domestic reforms in mind, including the reorganization of the military and the purge of the senior military ranks, he may not have been keen to pick another fight with the armed forces. When Kim came to power in February 1993, Team Spirit was scheduled to begin in less than two weeks, and he had little choice but to let it go ahead as planned.

Succession politics in Pyongyang
The North Korean regime also underwent significant internal political changes during this period, including the gradual rise in power of the armed forces. In trying to consolidate his control over the military, Kim Jong Il promoted many

generals to a higher rank, including O Chin-u, who was given the same title as Kim, that of Marshal.[104] In addition, April 1992 saw North Korea's constitution revised for the first time since 1972 as part of the effort to accommodate Kim Jong Il's legal assumption of the position of Supreme Commander of the North Korean armed forces.[105] Under this revised constitution, the National Defence Commission was given a prominent position within the government, in contrast to the earlier constitution in which the Commission had to work within the Central People's Committee.[106] This change implied that the military's power and influence had substantially increased relative to that of the party.

Even more profound changes were made at the Fourth Session of the Ninth Supreme People's Assembly on 11 December 1992, where reform-minded Premier Yon Hyong-muk was replaced with Kang Song-san.[107] Yon Hyong-muk, who had once been the number three figure in official ranking behind Kim Il Sung and Kim Jong Il, was posted as the governor of a small province called Jakangdo and his ranking was downgraded to twenty–nineth.[108] Another significant downgrading was that of Kim Young Sun, Secretary for international affairs of the Korean Workers' Party (KWP). Kim, a relatively pragmatic figure in Pyongyang, was removed from the Politburo in December 1992, and his post was taken up by Choi Tae-bok in February 1993.[109] In line with these changes, North Korea began to adopt a more conservative stance and started refusing foreign visitors in the winter of 1992.[110]

Until the summer of 1992, although few breakthroughs had been achieved, things appeared to be going smoothly and the military seemed to have supported Yon's conciliatory policy. However, increased pressure from South Korea, the United States, and the IAEA over the nuclear issue and a lack of concrete benefits from its conciliatory policies may have led hard-line groups in Pyongyang, especially the military, to initiate a return to the traditional position of self-reliance. In the face of the South's decision to resume the Team Spirit exercise, the IAEA's increasing pressure on suspect sites at Yongbyon, and Seoul's accusations of spying, the North may well have concluded that the conciliatory measures taken by Yon's administration were futile and should be replaced by a tougher approach, lest the North be betrayed by Seoul and Washington.[111] Given these circumstances in late 1992, Kim Il Sung and Kim Jong Il may have felt they had no choice but to side with this hard-line position.

Pyongyang's uncompromising stance on challenge inspections and the resulting NPT withdrawal can thus be understood in the context of this hardening political climate. As the North had repeatedly argued, opening up military bases virtually without limit would bestow unbearable humiliation on the North Korean regime. It would have been politically unacceptable for Kim Jong Il, still struggling for legitimacy, to give in to pressure from an 'imperial power', the US and its 'puppet' South Korea. The North's NPT gamble might also have been connected with Pyongyang's succession politics. In other words, Kim Jong Il might have attempted to take advantage of the 'NPT crisis' for the purpose of preventing any dissident voices from raising objections to his leadership. It was reported that there were at least three military coup attempts against him in 1992, in which between 10 and 30 high ranking officers were involved at a time. Although it is impossible to confirm such information, the rumours of a coup against Kim Jong Il certainly suggest that his power base was not securely consolidated.[112] The resumption of Team Spirit in 1993, in particular, may have been regarded as a direct challenge by Kim Jong Il and might have compelled him to take firm action, especially as its cancellation the previous year was credited to his personal leadership.[113]

Some observers stress North Korea's Juche (self-reliance) ideology in understanding its continued resistance to special inspections and its announcement to withdraw from the NPT.[114] According to Juche nationalism, the development of a strategic weapons system, including nuclear weapons and long-range missiles, was morally justifiable as self-defence; intrusive 'special inspections' must have been regarded as an unbearable humiliation to North Koreans. Analysts stressing the role of Juche ideology in dictating North Korean behaviour argue that Pyongyang will not negotiate away its nuclear weapons programme for economic or political gains, since national defence, according to this philosophy, is not subject to compromise.[115]

It is difficult to link the North's behaviour during this period directly to Juche ideology, however. Pyongyang's resistance to special inspections and the announcement of NPT withdrawal can be adequately understood in the context of the North's security concerns and domestic politics (e.g. Kim Jung Il's succession) without taking Juche into account. Moreover, Pyongyang proved itself rather calculating during the year and a half of intense negotiations after the announcement of its NPT withdrawal, while later making a deal with the US on the nuclear issue by partially accepting 'special inspections.' In this light, Pyongyang's behaviour does not appear to have been dictated by Juche ideology, often called an unchallengeable principle guiding virtually all fields of North Korean behaviour.[116] Rather, the role of Juche, if any, in determining the North's behaviour during this period seems to have been much less direct than its official status suggests.[117]

3. Conclusion

The deterrence argument, based on the assumption of aggressive North Korean intentions, postulates that concessions from the South encourage the North to redouble its efforts to extract further advantages because it views the initial concession as a sign of weakness. In this view, only a tough stance can restrain the North's aggressiveness and bring about a desirable outcome. Events from mid-1992 to early 1993, however, show the opposite logic operating on the peninsula: the tough measures adopted by Seoul, Washington and the IAEA, such as the South's insistence on challenge inspections, the resumption of the Team Spirit exercise and the IAEA's demand for special inspections, were counter-productive, eliciting a more hostile response from Pyongyang.

Three different perspectives have been proposed for explaining the deterioration from accommodation to crisis. The first explanation stresses Washington's domestic political environment. With increasing pressure to focus on domestic issues in an election year, the Bush administration did not want to be embroiled in quarrels with an ally over Team Spirit, let alone launch its own diplomatic initiatives towards Pyongyang. Preoccupied with internal matters and ill-organized for the first few months in office, the Clinton administration was not capable of dealing with major foreign challenges like the North Korean nuclear problem. This explanation also points to the impact that the intelligence failure in Iraq had on Washington and the IAEA vis-à-vis the inspection issue.

The second perspective, the security dilemma, underscores the security logic behind Seoul's persistence in demanding rigorous inspections and Pyongyang's refusal to accept them: while Seoul felt it essential to obtain complete inspections for the sake of its well-being, Pyongyang saw such intrusive measures as depriving it of negotiating leverage and exposing its conventional military capabilities to the world. There is also a substantial possibility that psychological bias might have played a part in interpreting each other's intentions.

Finally, a focus on domestic politics concentrates on deliberate attempts by the hard-liners in Seoul to slow down rapprochement with the North. The hawks' wish to create self-generated tensions may have been linked to the military's organizational interest and to the ruling party's election strategy. Domestic factors in the North centre around the changes in Pyongyang's political milieu: the rise of the military, the demotion of reform-minded officials, and power transition.

The two key issues in shaping inter-Korean relations during this time were nuclear inspections and the Team Spirit exercise. Hence, a better understanding of the relative importance and relationship of these three explanatory perspectives is gained through a closer look at these two issues. As far as North Korea was concerned, rigorous inspections were hard to accept for security reasons. Allowing the US and the IAEA to inspect suspect sites would deprive the North leverage for nuclear diplomacy, or would, at least, remove a useful bargaining chip without any rewards. The bargaining chip, with its nuclear option, was essential to ensuring the survival of the Pyongyang regime through various rewards from foreign powers, including economic and diplomatic benefits, and–most importantly–security guarantees from the US. Furthermore, Pyongyang might have feared that such an opening would reveal the poor state of North Korea's conventional military capabilities. At the same time, domestic political factors might have played a part in the decision to oppose inspections. The North Korean armed forces, which had been enjoying a privileged status, would be humiliated once their bases were opened.

Nonetheless, this domestic consideration seems less critical than the security reason. Despite potential resistance from the military, the North Korean leadership later accepted 'special inspections' in a nuclear deal with the US Despite its adamant rejection of 'special inspections' throughout negotiations with the US,[118] Pyongyang finally agreed, in October 1994, on an intrusive inspection in return for rewards from the outside world. This suggests that the North Korean leadership had the ability to persuade or disregard the military on inspection issues, as long as it secured enough rewards in return. Rewards promised in the 1994 deal included economic benefits, such as light-water reactors and heavy fuel oil. But the most important incentive for Pyongyang to accept the deal appeared to be American promises to 'provide formal assurance against the threat or use of nuclear weapons' and to 'move toward full diplomatic relations' with North Korea, which were its major motivations in developing a nuclear weapons programme in the first place.[119] Security concerns, then, seem to have been the main factor in North Korea's refusal of special inspections.

With respect to the Team Spirit issue, security and domestic politics seem to have been equally important in their influence on Pyongyang's position. The resumption of the exercise, which came after the pressure for intrusive inspections, could have been a confirmation to the North Koreans that the international community was determined to press them into a corner. Under escalating pressure from the outside, North Korea believed that it had no choice but to take extreme action in line with its survival strategy of utilising nuclear leverage. Pyongyang may have also felt it necessary to stand firm in order to secure a smooth transition of power. In a situation where outside pressure was increasing, a failure to demonstrate strong leadership would greatly undermine Kim Jong Il's authority while simultaneously hindering the succession process. As far as the Team Spirit issue was concerned, then, security logic and domestic politics seem to have held equal weight.

The next question is what prompted the US, South Korea and the IAEA to adopt rigorous inspections and to resume Team Spirit. All three agreed upon the necessity of more rigorous inspections. Behind the hard position of the US and the IAEA was a determination to strengthen the non-proliferation regime after an embarrassing intelligence failure in Iraq. On the part of South Korea, its own security concerns made it tough on inspection issues. The security dilemma lingered due to the difficulty of distinguishing between offensive and defensive behaviours, a difficulty which seems to have compelled Seoul to be tough on challenge inspections.[120] On the other hand, domestic political factors likely had little to do with Seoul's strong preference for rigorous inspections, given its consistent position for 'challenge inspections.' While the signs of hard-liners' deliberate attempts to block inter-Korean rapprochement became clear in late 1992, Seoul had taken its position on inspections ahead of these machinations, leaving little room to argue for a causal relationship between the two. The combination of Seoul's security concerns and the desire of Washington and the IAEA to strengthen the non-proliferation commitment may thus be deemed the main exponents in the hard stance on inspection issues.

The situation surrounding the Team Spirit issue was more intricate. Despite the passive and rather reluctant attitude of the US, South Korea successfully negotiated a resumption of the exercise. Seoul's strong preference for Team Spirit was triggered by both domestic politics and security concerns. On the one hand, the South Korean military probably desired to protect and maintain its special status in the midst of democratization by re-instigating Team Spirit, and civilian authorities had no particular aversion to the military's initiative, as it coincided with their own political purposes in the face of a coming presidential election. On the other hand, genuine and non-political security logic seems to have applied as well. There was little indication of serious bureaucratic debate regarding Team Spirit's reinstatement; all civilian and military officials at senior levels agreed that its resumption was inevitable because of the North's uncompromising stance on inspections.[121] It seems that Seoul's decision over the 1993 Team Spirit exercise was driven by a consensus on the strategic situation among the major governmental actors, a particular bureaucratic interest and the ruling party's election strategy.

In conclusion, both North and South Korean actions vis-à-vis inspection were largely based on security logic. Domestic political factors appear to have been of secondary importance. The Team Spirit issue, on the other hand, demonstrated an equal importance of security and domestic factors in the Koreas, while the external actors' role was limited. All told, security concerns seem to have been more influential than domestic politics, as security logic was applicable to both key issues, while the role of domestic politics was only substantial in the Team Spirit issue. Furthermore, considering their relative potential impact on Pyongyang's nuclear diplomacy, Team Spirit was a relatively minor issue compared with inspections. While the Team Spirit issue exacerbated the situation, the collision over rigorous inspections was mostly to blame for effecting a change of course from accommodation to crisis.

The influence of the external actors was also important, as the US and the IAEA retained significant influence over the inspection issue. It is difficult, however, to weigh the relative importance of external actors and Seoul's security concerns - although the inspections mandate originated in Washington, South Korea and the IAEA did not passively accept the American proposal, but rather adopted their positions based on their own needs.[122]

Notes

1. 'Ad hoc' inspections are undertaken when it is deemed necessary to confirm submitted information or the results of 'regular inspections'. In contrast with 'ad hoc' and 'regular' inspections, which are restricted to declared nuclear facilities, 'special inspections' refer to compulsory inspections of undeclared sites over the objections of the target nation.

2. Mazarr, *North Korea and the Bomb*, p. 85.

3. *FBIS-EAS*, 21 September 1992, pp. 12-3.

4. Mazarr, *North Korea and the Bomb*, pp. 85-6.

5. *BBC Summary*, Far East, No. 1334 (19 March 1992), A3/1; *BBC Summary*, No. 1408 (12 June 1992), A2/5; *BBC Summary*, No. 1491 (19 September 1992), A1/1; *BBC Summary*, No. 1513 (14 October 1992), A1/3; *BBC Summary*, No. 1529 (3 November 1992), A2/2; *BBC Summary*, No. 1575 (29 December 1992), A1/7.

6. *Korea Newsreview*, 6 June 1992, pp. 6-7.

7. *BBC Summary*, Far East, No. 1345 (1 April 1992), A3/3; *BBC Summary*, No. 1491 (19 September 1992), A1/1; *BBC Summary*, No. 1575 (29 December 1992), A1/7.

8. *BBC Summary*, Far East, No. 1378 (10 May 1992), A2/10; *BBC Summary*, No. 1379 (12 May 1992), A2/5; *BBC Summary*, No. 1408 (15 June 1992), A2/5; *BBC Summary*, No. 1420 (26 June 1992), A2/3; *BBC Summary*, No. 1481 (8 September 1992), A1/4.

9. *FBIS-EAS*, 17 September 1992, p. 26.

10. Interview with former State Department official Gary Samore, London, 3 July 2002; and interview with South Korean Foreign Minister Lee Sang-ok, 12 August 2002.

11. *BBC Summary*, Far East, No. 1491 (19 September 1992), A1/1; *BBC Summary*, No. 1575 (29 December 1992), A1/7; *BBC Summary*, No. 1601 (29 January 1993), A1/4.

12. *BBC Summary*, Far East, No. 1330 (14 March 1992).

13. *North Korea News*, 7 September 1992, pp. 2-3.

14. The *Korea Herald*, for instance, advocated 'second thoughts to the earlier decision to forgo the Team Spirit exercises', questioning Pyongyang's sincerity in nuclear inspections. Cited in *Korea Newsreview*, 7 November 1992; and for similar arguments, see *Yonhap* and *Chosun Ilbo* reports cited in *FBIS-EAS*, 10 August 1993, p. 23.

15. *BBC Summary*, Far East, No. 1402 (6 June 1992), A2/2.

16. For the full text of the joint communiqué, see Kwak Tae-Hwan, 'US Military-Security Policy toward the Korean Peninsula in the 1990s', *Korean Journal of Defence Analysis*, vol. 7, no. 2 (Winter 1995), p. 247.

17. See *BBC Summary*, Far East, No. 1519 (20 October 1992), A1/3; *BBC Summary*, No. 1550 (27 November 1992), A1/7; *BBC Summary*, No. 1561 (10 December 1992), A2/2; *BBC Summary*, No. 1596 (25 January 1993), A2/4.

18. David Albright, 'North Korea Drops Out', *The Bulletin of the Atomic Scientists* (May 1993), p. 10.

19. *BBC Summary*, Far East, No. 1613 (13 February 1993), A1/3.

20. *BBC Summary*, Far East, No. 1613 (13 February 1993), A1/3.

21. *BBC Summary*, Far East, No. 1622 (24 February 1993), A1/1.

22. *BBC Summary*, Far East, No. 1632 (8 March 1993), B/3.

23. *Chicago Tribune*, 16 March 1993, p. N3.

24. *BBC Summary*, Far East, No. 1636 (12 March 1993), A1/1.

25. Sigal, *Disarming Strangers*, pp. 39-40.

26. John E. Yang, 'Bush's Year Begins in Australia; President Focusing On Trouble at Home', *Washington Post*, 1 January 1992, A23.

27. Richard Morin, 'Coming November, Will Bush Defy History?', *Washington Post*, 17 August 1992, A11.

28. William G. Hyland, *Clinton's World: Remaking American Foreign Policy* (London: Praeger, 1999), pp. 9-10.

29. *Ibid.*, p. 9.
30. See Carter and Perry, *Preventive Defense: A New Security Strategy for America* (Washington, DC: Brookings Institution Press, 1999), p. 134.
31. Elaine Sciolino, 'C.I.A. Chief Says North Koreans Are Hiding Nuclear Arms Projects', *New York Times*, 26 February 1992, A1. But, according to Toby Gati, director of INR, Gate's estimation was 'the absolute worst-case analysis'. See Elaine Sciolino, 'US Agencies Split over North Korea', *New York Times*, 10 March 1992, A1.
32. Sigal, *Disarming Strangers*, p. 41.
33. Gary Milhollin, 'North Korea's Bomb', *New York Times*, 4 June 1992, A23.
34. Sigal, *Disarming Strangers*, p. 42.
35. Michael R. Gordon, 'North Korea Rebuffs Nuclear Inspectors, Reviving US Nervousness', *New York Times*, 1 February 1993, A9.
36. For the full text of a political declaration of the Group of Seven (G-7) summit leaders, see *The Daily Yomiuri*, 8 July 1992, p, 5.
37. Interview with Han Yong-sup, September 5, 2002. Dr. Han, deputy director of the Arms Control Bureau of the ROK Defence Ministry, was involved in the SCM in 1992.
38. Interview with Han Yong-sup, and see also *Chosun Ilbo*, 2 June 1992.
39. *Dong-A Ilbo*, 6 June 1992.
40. Sigal, *Disarming Strangers*, p. 44.
41. *Ibid.*, p. 46.
42. *Ibid.*, p. 47.
43. Mazarr, *North Korea and the Bomb*, p. 91.
44. Cited in Sigal, *Disarming Strangers*, p. 44.
45. *Ibid.*, p. 48.
46. *Ibid.*, p. 48.
47. *Joong-Ang Ilbo*, 26 January 1993.
48. Although he had been a student of International Relations at Georgetown University in the 1960s and studied abroad for two years at Oxford, Clinton's professional background – attorney general and twice the governor of Arkansas – excluded the traditional foreign policy domains of diplomacy and security. See Clinton's memoirs, *My Life,* (New York: Knopf, 2004).
49. Thomas H. Henriksen, *Clinton's Foreign Policy in Somalia, Bosnia, Haiti, and North Korea,* (Stanford: Hoover Institution on War, Revolution and Peace, 1996), p.8.
50. Thomas L. Friedman, 'Clinton Keeping Foreign Policy on a Back Burner', *New York Times,* 8 February 1993, A9.
51. One adviser said: 'My sense is that he does not like this stuff [foreign policy], because he is not the master of it'. See *ibid.*
52. Tim Hames, 'Foreign Policy', in Paul S. Herrnson and Dilys M. Hill eds, *The Clinton Presidency: The First Term, 1992~96* (London: Macmillan Press, 1999), pp. 126-41.
53. Thomas L. Friedman, 'Clinton Keeping Foreign Policy on a Back Burner', *New York Times,* 8 February 1993, A9.
54. Clinton's selection of the 67 year-old veteran diplomat Warren Christopher as Secretary of State could also be explained in that regard. See Hyland, *Clinton's World: Remaking American Foreign Policy*, p. 18.
55. Sigal, *Disarming Strangers*, p. 48.
56. Douglas Jehl, 'High-Level Grumbling Over Pace of Appointments', *New York Times,* 25 February 1993, A16.
57. *Ibid.*
58. *Ibid.*
59. Clinton promised in his presidential campaign that American policy should pursue more noble goals, such as humanitarian intervention, protection of human rights, and enlargement of democracy, while contending that Bush had laid too much emphasis on maintaining stability rather than promoting values. But Clinton's foreign policy for the first two months turned out to

be rather cautious and timid. On issues such as Bosnia and Haiti, Clinton was criticized for acting 'not much differently from Visionless George'. See Bill Clinton, 'Address to the Los Angeles World Affairs Council', 13 August 1992, in *New York Times*, 14 August 1992; and Richard Cohen, 'Sounds Like Kennedy, Acts Like Bush', *Washington Post*, 24 March 1993, A21.

60. Comments of a State Department official cited in Sigal, *Disarming Strangers*, p. 48.

61. 'Arms Control and Verification: Safeguards in a Changing World', *IAEA BULLETIN*, vol. 39, no. 3 (September 1997), pp. 4–7.

62. The right to carry out special inspections would not be of much practical value unless the IAEA knew where to look. In the case of North Korea, Washington provided the IAEA with the locations of suspected nuclear sites as identified by US satellite photographs.

63. William Tow, 'Reassessing Deterrence on the Korean peninsula', *Korean Journal of Defence Analysis*, vol. 3, no. 1 (Summer 1991), pp. 198–200.

64. Tow, 'Reassessing Deterrence on the Korean peninsula', p. 198.

65. Interview with Lee Bu-jik, 21 August 2002.

66. Interview with Ahn Kwang-chan, 10 September 2002.

67. *Korea Newsreview*, 27 June 1992, p. 8.

68. Kang, 'North Korea's Military and Security Policy', pp. 180~1.

69. Joseph S. Bermudez Jr., 'North Korea's Nuclear Arsenal', *Jane's Intelligence Review* (1 March 1996), p. 21.

70. *Ibid.* In order to complicate allies' reinforcement efforts, further strikes against American bases in Japan and East Asia (such as Guam) would be needed, requiring an additional 3~7 nuclear warheads.

71. General Park Yong-ok, General Director of Arms Control Bureau of the Defence Ministry at that time, expressed the government's determination to insist on 'challenge inspections', saying 'the North's argument for inspection on mutually agreed sites means in effect no nuclear inspections at all'. Interview with Park Yong-ok, 25 August 2002.

72. In this light, Kim Tok, South Korean Director of the Agency for National Security Planning (NSP), analysed that North Korea maintained a 'planned ambiguity' in order not to lose its leverage for political and military gains. See *BBC Summary*, Far East, No. 1641 (17 March 1993), A1/5.

73. This hypothesis was suggested by Ha Yong Son in *Wolgan Chosun*, 26 May 1993. North Korea argued that challenge inspections were Seoul's 'insidious scheme to inspect something that is not the target of nuclear inspection', *BBC Summary*, Far East, No. 1575 (29 December 1992), A1/7.

74. The reasons suggested here for the North's rejection of 'challenge inspections' seem to have been relevant to the case of the 'special inspections' insisted on by the IAEA. In particular, the concern about opening up conventional military capabilities was the North's official reason in rejecting the 'special inspections'. Pyongyang claimed that the IAEA's move was 'aimed at spying on our military facilities...[and] was prompted by the US pressure in a bid to disarm us'. See *FBIS-EAS*, 19 February 1993, p. 8.

75. Interview with Lee Bu-jik, 21 August 2002. Paul Bracken also argues that North Korea links its national security to the development of destructive weapons such as long-range missiles. See Bracken, 'Risks and Promises in the Two Koreas', *Orbis*, vol. 39, no. 1 (Winter 1995), p. 55.

76. Robert A. Manning and Leonard S. Spector, 'North Korea's Nuclear Gambit: Do They Have Dangerous Ambitions, or a More Subtle Strategy?', *Washington Post*, 21 March 1993, p. C3.

77. Even one of the most liberal cabinet members at the time, Unification Minister Choe Yong-chol, acknowledged that Pyongyang's dubious attitude amplified Seoul's suspicion about the North's wish to have bombs. See Choe Yong-chol, *T'ong'il-ro Makhimyŏn Tolasŏ Kacha [Let's go around if the road to unification is blocked]* (Seoul: T'ong'il Ponyong Yonguwon, 1993), p. 65.

78. Interview with Han Yong-sup, deputy director of Arms Control Bureau of the Defence Ministry, 5 September 2002.
79. Interview with Lee Sang-ok, 12 August 2002.
80. *BBC Summary,* Far East, No. 1632 (8 March 1993), B/3.
81. *BBC Summary,* Far East, No. 1632 (8 March 1993), B/3.
82. Oberdorfer, *The Two Koreas,* p. 279.
83. Hayes, *Pacific Powderkeg,* p. 137.
84. Some military analysts have justified US nuclear threats against North Korea during the Korean War with precisely this argument. See *ibid.*, p. 137.
85. *Chosun Ilbo,* 12 November 1995.
86. Pyongyang's harsh reaction to the Team Spirit exercise in 1993 was not particularly different from its past responses. Nonetheless, such reactions can be called extreme in that North Korea had mobilized its population massively despite the tremendous economic damage that would result.
87. *North Korea News,* 28 December 1992, pp. 1-2.
88. The tense mood in Pyongyang at the time was well expressed in the repeated warnings from the North. In March 1993, for example, a Pyongyang broadcast said: 'a war may break out at any moment', cited in *FBIS-EAS,* 8 March 1993, pp. 10~1.
89. Interview with Han Yong-sup, 5 September 2002.
90. Pyongyang argued that Seoul and Washington were 'intending to turn the Team Spirit war game into a real war... by inventing some pretexts after amassing large aggression forces and war supplies under the cloak of an annual military rehearsal'. *Nodong Sinmun* cited in *FBIS-EAS,* 9 March 1993, p. 12.
91. Interview with Han Yong-sup, 5 September 2002.
92. *BBC Summary,* Far East, No. 1506 (6 October 1992), A1/3.
93. *BBC Summary,* Far East, No. 1511 (13 October 1992), A2/3; and *Dong-A Ilbo,* 13 October 1992.
94. *Chosun Ilbo,* 8 October 1992.
95. Lee Jong-suk, *Pundansidaeŭi T'ong'ilhak [The Study of Reunification in the Divided Era]* (Seoul: Hanul, 1999), p. 48.
96. *Mazarr, North Korea and the Bomb,* p. 89.
97. *BBC Summary,* Far East, No. 1507 (8 October 1992), A1/3; *Korea Newsreview,* 17 October 1992, p. 9. Major South Korean newspapers pressed the government to secure an apology from Pyongyang first, even if it slowed down dialogue. See *Joong-Ang Ilbo,* 8 October 1992.
98. Oberdorfer, *The Two Koreas,* p. 274.
99. *Korea Newsreview,* 24 October 1992, p. 10.
100. Cited in Sigal, *Disarming Strangers,* p. 45.
101. Hwang Yi Bong, Nambuk Taehwapoda Namnamtaehwa Tŏ Ŏryŏpda [South – South dialogue is more difficult than North – South talks], Shin Dong-A [monthly magazine], January 1994, pp. 211-5.
102. Beginning in early 1992, power was shared by President Roh and candidate Kim Young Sam, but from the summer of 1992, Kim was believed to exercise virtually full control over the ruling party. See *Dong-A Ilbo,* 15 August 1992.
103. Lee Jong-suk points out that the 'North Korea issue' has contributed to the victory of the ruling party in almost every election in the South since 1987. See Lee, *Pundansidaeŭi T'ong'ilhak [The Study of Reunification in the Divided Era],* p.48.
104. Suh, 'North Korea: The Present and the Future', p. 68.
105. *BBC Summary,* Far East, No. 1358 (9 April 1992), C3/1.
106. Suh, 'North Korea: The Present and the Future', p. 68.
107. *BBC Summary,* Far East, No. 1562 (11 December 1992).
108. Choe Yong-chol, *T'ong'il-ro Makhimyŏn Tolasŏ Kacha [Let's go around if the road to unification is blocked]* (Seoul: T'ong'il Ponyong Yonguwon, 1993), p. 283.
109. *Dong-A Ilbo,* 6 February 1993.

110. *North Korea News,* 21 December 1992, pp. 1-3.
111. Until October 1992, Kim Young Sun, Secretary for International Affairs of the Korean Workers' Party (KWP), still expressed an optimistic view about Pyongyang – Washington relations, saying 'relations will improve in the near future'. But, when Kim and other party officials tried to attend a meeting organized by the US Congress to find out the Korean policy of the new administration, the American government refused to issue visas to them on the grounds that their entry would send a wrong signal to Pyongyang about Washington's stance on the nuclear issue. See *Dong-A Ilbo,* 13 October 1992 and 1 February 1993; and Suh, 'North Korea: The Present and the Future', pp. 62-3.
112. Choe, *T'ong'il-ro Makhimyŏn Tolasŏ Kacha [Let's go around if the road to unification is blocked],* pp. 190~5.
113. As Seoul and Washington decided to go ahead with Team Spirit in 1993, they argued that Pyongyang was well aware that its suspension in 1992 had been a one-year decision. However, Han Yong-sup has intimated that Pyongyang was perhaps led to believe that the exercise would be permanently ended at the final North – South negotiation in December 1991. Interview with Han Yong-sup, 5 September 2002.
114. Lee Jung-Yong, *North Korea's Arms Control Policy and the Challenge of South Korea's Sunshine Policy,* Doctoral Thesis (University of Aberdeen, 2002), pp. 223-4.
115. Park Han S., *North Korea: The Politics of Unconventional Wisdom* (Boulder, CO.: Lynne Reiner, 2002), p. 91.
116. Kongdan Oh and Ralph C. Hassig, *North Korea Through the Looking Glass* (Washington, DC: Brookings Institution Press, 2000), pp. 11-5.
117. Similarly, Juche did not constrain the North from holding talks with the US and Japan in an attempt to relieve military and economic difficulties. On the interpretation of Juche as a comprehensive and flexible concept that can be stretched to fit diverse situations, see Oh and Hassig, *North Korea Through the Looking Glass;* and David C. Kang, 'Preventive War and North Korea', *Security Studies,* vol. 4, no. 2 (Winter 1994/5), pp. 330~63.
118. North Korea's Ambassador to the UN in Geneva Ri Chul said on 16 February 1993: 'If we accept the request to inspect ordinary military sites, at the end, we will have to reveal all of our military facilities', thus representing the military's interests or concerns. Cited in Mazarr, *North Korea and the Bomb,* p. 96.
119. Quoted in the 1994 nuclear pact between the US and North Korea, 'Agreed Framework of the United States of America and the Democratic People's Republic of Korea'. The nuclear deal will be examined in detail in a following chapter.
120. However, because of the mutual deterrence on the Korean peninsula, North Korea's primitive nuclear capabilities did not pose an imminent 'life or death' scenario worthy of risking all-out war. This might explain why Seoul did not undertake military action. This was discussed in chapter one as 'an ameliorated security dilemma'.
121. Interview with Lee Sang-ok, 12 August 2002.
122. According to Leon Sigal's interview with a State Department official, the Bush administration urged the IAEA to tighten up monitoring procedures and pressed Seoul to insist on intrusive inspections. As seen earlier, however, both the IAEA and Seoul had compelling reasons for their preference of special inspections. In particular, questioning the IAEA's ability to inspect effectively, Seoul vehemently pursued the right to institute rigorous inspections of its own. 'Only the South Korean government can read what the North is up to. For this reason, the South Korean government placed a great weight on mutual (challenge) inspections', said Unification Minister Choe Yong-chol at that time in his book, *T'ong'il-ro Makhimyŏn Tolasŏ Kacha [Let's go around if the road to unification is blocked],* p. 58.

5. Dramatic Reversal at the Brink of a Collision 1993–1994

This chapter explores nuclear diplomacy from North Korea's NPT withdrawal to the resolution of the subsequent crisis. There were three distinct phases. During the first phase, from the North's NPT withdrawal in March 1993 to the second round of high-level talks in July 1993, diplomatic solutions seemed to work and there existed cautiously optimistic prospects for a peaceful resolution. In particular, Washington made a strategic decision in November 1993 to accept Pyongyang's offer of a 'package solution' that entailed a sequence of give-and-take elements between North Korea and the US. However, entering into the second phase in the fall of 1993, negotiations came to a stalemate over the inspection issue, and tensions began mounting towards a possible military conflict. The final phase began in June 1994 with the former US President Jimmy Carter contributing an unexpected role as a mediator. Carter spearheaded a dramatic reversal back to the diplomatic course, and the nuclear dispute was settled four months later.

This chapter examines why the initial progress was not sustained and the resolution was so delayed. The final nuclear settlement, known as the Agreed Framework, was signed in October 1994, almost one year after the US's initial acceptance of the North Korean offer for a package deal. Considering that the Agreed Framework basically contained the same conditions as the initial package deal had suggested in November 1993, it is necessary to explain the reasons for such an extended stalemate that could have resulted in military conflict. This chapter explores various possible factors for this stalemate, including the international environment (the US, China, Russia, Japan and the IAEA), South Korea's security concerns, and Seoul's domestic politics. This chapter also intends to provide an understanding of the extent to which each factor was responsible for the diplomatic delays, and how they are interrelated.

1. A Long Delayed 'Package Solution'

A. Diplomatic progress

Pyongyang's announcement of withdrawal from the NPT posed a serious challenge to both the non-proliferation regime and the stability of eastern Asia. If

North Korea had nuclear weapons, not only would the security of the Korean peninsula be threatened, but South Korea, Japan and other Asian countries would be given an excuse for going nuclear, 'setting in motion a domino proliferation effect in East Asia.'[1] Given its rapidly increasing missile capability, moreover, it was feared that Pyongyang was not far from an ICBM with nuclear warheads capable of targeting the North American continent. In addition, North Korea's nuclear weapons might be made available to nations in the Middle East, including Iran and Iraq, thus posing a nuclear threat to Israel.[2]

Despite the gravity of the situation, the initial response of both Washington and Seoul was moderate, and focused on diplomacy. While urging North Korea to return to the NPT, each avoided the sort of inflammatory criticism that might have exacerbated the situation. On 15 March 1993, Foreign Minister Han Sung Joo expressed Seoul's desire for a diplomatic solution.[3] Fearful of further escalation, the Clinton administration showed similar restraint, calling on the North to fulfil its responsibilities without making threats or criticisms.[4] China also stressed dialogue, opposing the use of sanctions against the North. On 23 March, Chinese Foreign Minister Qian Qichen said: 'If the matter goes before the Security Council, that will only complicate things.'[5] In this dangerous but controlled atmosphere, North Korea and the US held a high-level meeting in New York, and, on 12 June, US Assistant Secretary of State Robert Gallucci and North Korean chief negotiator First Vice Foreign Minister Kang Sok Ju agreed that North Korea would suspend its NPT withdrawal 'as long as it considers necessary.'[6] In return, the US agreed to a principle of 'assurances against the threat and use of force, including nuclear weapons.'[7] Initial talks, then, ended with a temporary suspension of North Korea's NPT withdrawal and a symbolic American promise of future rewards.[8] On 14 July, a second round of high-level talks began in Geneva, and further agreements were reached, including an expression of North Korean interest in resuming dialogue with the IAEA and South Korea.[9] Although the US failed to persuade North Korea to accept special inspections, Gallucci evaluated the result of the talks as 'a small but significant step.'[10] Although there was no imminent breakthrough, the crisis appeared on its way to resolution.[11]

B. Stalemate and preparation of sanctions

As the autumn of 1993 progressed, however, the optimism of early July evaporated. Stark differences between the IAEA and North Korea as to the scope of inspections quickly emerged. The IAEA demanded a full range of ad hoc and regular inspections, while North Korea was only willing to allow IAEA technicians to replace the film and batteries in monitoring equipment, a measure that could only inhibit North Korea from removing and reprocessing more spent fuel. Confrontation continued for three months, and on 1 November, IAEA

Director Hans Blix provided a report to the UN General Assembly that Pyongyang had refused to cooperate and that continuity of some safeguard–relevant data was on the verge of being broken.[12] As the prospects for a diplomatic solution of the North Korean nuclear issue became grim, hard-line voices demanding tougher approaches gained strength in the American and South Korean media.[13] Most Clinton administration officials, excepting a small group of moderates such as Under Secretary of State Peter Tarnoff and Assistant Secretary Robert Gallucci, also believed that a more hard-line approach would be necessary.[14]

North Korea responded with a new proposal for a 'package deal', rekindling the possibility of diplomatic solution. In October 1993, when US State Department desk officer for North Korea C. Kenneth Quinones travelled to Pyongyang, the North Korean Foreign Ministry presented him with a comprehensive proposal that contained a series of trade-off measures between the US and North Korea. This proposal for trade-offs, later termed 'a package solution', already contained all the elements of what would become the final agreement of October 1994: North Korea would remain in the NPT in return for economic and diplomatic benefits from the US.[15] On 11 November, the chief North Korean negotiator in US–DPRK talks, Kang Sok Ju, again called for American agreement to a package solution, while rejecting the IAEA's requests for regular and special inspections.[16]

Bureaucratic debate ensued in Washington as to whether to accept North Korea's 'package deal.' The Joint Chiefs of Staff wanted to hold Pyongyang to special inspections as well as ad hoc and regular inspections.[17] Civilians in the Office of the Secretary of Defense argued for an alternative to the package deal.[18] Betraying deep scepticism about diplomatic channels, this offer–replete with the flavour of an ultimatum–was to approach Kim Il Sung directly and present a list of inducements and a list of demands. National Security Adviser Anthony Lake was also sceptical about Pyongyang's proposal. Nonetheless, debate ended with a victory for the State Department and support for the package deal.[19] Chief negotiator Gallucci particularly advocated the comprehensive approach, persuading Lake that the US should place a higher priority on stopping more plutonium production than clearing up the North's pre-existing nuclear programme through special inspections.[20]

On 15 November 1993, the Principals Committee finally decided to endorse the basic elements of the package deal. The decision to accept was made based on the recognition that the existing mid-level meetings were not working, and the incremental approach was garnering increased frustration from Washington.[21] After the package approach was adopted, negotiations stepped up in New York, as US Deputy Assistant Secretary of State Thomas Hubbard and North Korea's United Nations delegate Ho Jong tried to secure the best outcome for their respective sides as to the substance of the deal.[22]

American attempts to broaden diplomacy with North Korea through the 'package approach' encountered strong resistance from Seoul, however. South Korean officials attempted to downplay its importance and even rejected the idea. Foreign Minister Han, for example, said on 13 November: 'We haven't reached the stage where we can talk about such a deal, much less what should be included in such a deal.'[23] The growing disagreements between Washington and Seoul over the 'package approach' were even more obvious when President Kim vehemently opposed a package deal in an Oval Office meeting with Bill Clinton on 23 November 1993.[24] Surprised by Kim's strong objection, Clinton and his aides agreed that the US would not make a simultaneous compromise with North Korea.[25] On the final day of Kim's visit to Washington, Foreign Minister Han said bluntly: 'There is no package deal.'[26] With the US thus failing to provide a specific response to the North's package offer, there was no sign of an immediate breakthrough in negotiations between Washington and Pyongyang in sight.[27]

Nonetheless, on 29 December 1993, after a long exchange of working-level contacts, the two nations reached an agreement that North Korea would accept inspections of all seven nuclear sites. As the number and scope of inspections required was left for the IAEA to determine, however, the 'December agreement' quickly led to a dispute between the IAEA and Pyongyang.[28] While the IAEA demanded full access to and the right to sample from the seven nuclear sites, North Korea insisted that it would accept only a single inspection aimed at maintaining the continuity of the safeguards. The IAEA refused to send inspectors under such conditions, and negotiations between the two broke down.[29] In addition, as Washington consulted with Seoul on every detail regarding the US–North Korean talks in New York, the US diplomatic efforts became further complicated.[30] Under such circumstances, a third round of US–DPRK high-level talks could not take place for almost a year after the second round of high-level talks in July 1993.

Amidst this stalemate, North Korea began to refuel the main Yongbyon reactor without IAEA supervision[31] and on 2 June IAEA, Director General Hans Blix finally declared that the agency's ability to assess the history of North Korea's reactor core had 'been lost' and was 'irreversible.'[32] After receiving the IAEA's assessment, the US produced a draft of UN sanctions, and began to consult with the members of the UN Security Council.[33] International sanctions appeared imminent, and the situation was moving in an increasingly dangerous direction.

Military preparations accompanied the growing possibility of sanctions. On 18 May, in a Pentagon conference room, Secretary of Defense Perry and every active four-star general in the American military discussed the war plan for the Korean peninsula. The Defense Department 'significantly increased intelligence assets' in Korea and studied a four-step military plan that the US and its allied forces would carry out at a time of war on the peninsula.[34] On 16 June, Clinton,

Vice-President Al Gore, Christopher Perry and Commander in Chief of US forces in Korea Gary Luck attended a meeting at the White House where three military options were drawn up.[35] Throughout the spring and summer of 1994, heavy tanks, Bradley armoured vehicles and new ammunition-loading equipment arrived, and a total of six batteries with 48 launchers and over 300 Patriot missiles were deployed to South Korea. For its part, the South Korean government also displayed firm resolve and military preparedness. On 8 June, a massive combined air–ground–sea war exercise was conducted.[36] A week later, a civil defence exercise was performed across the country, stressing war preparedness, and 6.6 million South Korean reserves were called up for a massive mobilization drill.[37] The Korean peninsula had become more militarized than ever before.

C. Dramatic reversal and final hurdle

On 15 June 1994, former US President Jimmy Carter travelled to Pyongyang. Although not an official emissary, he met Kim Il Sung and received 'a package deal' offer from him.[38] Believing that this was an important breakthrough, Carter publicly declared in a live CNN broadcast that the crisis was over, adding that 'the pursuit of sanctions is counterproductive in this particular and unique society.'[39] The CNN interview embarrassed Washington, as Carter appeared to be taking over diplomacy from a sitting president.[40] More importantly, Carter's public repudiation of the sanctions strategy led its international support to evaporate.[41]

On the other hand, Carter's visit provided the Clinton administration with another, and perhaps final, chance to resolve the nuclear crisis diplomatically. On 21 June, the Clinton administration announced that a long-awaited third-round of US–DPRK talks would take place on 8 July in Geneva.[42] Reinforcement plans, including the dispatch of forces, were also postponed.[43] A major crisis had suddenly been averted, and the prospect of a diplomatic solution looked promising. On 12 August, talks yielded an 'Agreed Statement' laying out mutual commitments and spelling out the long-awaited package deal as 'part of a final resolution of the nuclear issue.'[44] The US vowed to make arrangements for the supply of light-water reactors, and North Korea would freeze construction of its two new reactors and forgo reprocessing in return. The two sides also agreed to establish liaison offices in each other's capitals and 'reduce barriers to trade and investment, as a move toward full normalization of political and economic relations.'[45]

Although the prospect of a peaceful solution looked ever more promising, there was another difficult and embarrassing hurdle for US negotiators to overcome—South Korea's opposition to a package deal, particularly the deferment of special inspections. In a phone call to Clinton on 17 August,

President Kim stated that North Korea should fully disclose its past nuclear activities and accept special inspections.[46] He also pointed out that the Agreed Statement in August made no mention of North–South dialogue. Foreign Minister Han Sung Joo likewise tried to slow US–North Korean talks, insisting that any deal would be predicated on the supply of a Korean model reactor and an account of the North's nuclear past. Moreover, as the agreement neared completion, President Kim Young Sam criticized it in a series of interviews with American, Japanese and South Korean newspapers in early October 1994 for its concessions on key issues.[47]

North Korea's response to the South's demand for complete transparency of its nuclear history was harsh. On 19 August, the Foreign Ministry blamed Seoul for getting in the way of the Geneva talks between the US and North Korea.[48] Then, Kang insisted that the South Korean reactor was unacceptable, calling it a Trojan horse.[49] From the North Korean perspective, the timing of special inspections should be delayed until it had received a substantial portion of the reactor, lest the South cancel the reactor project for political or other reasons.[50] Due to the rigidity of both Koreas, intensive negotiations between Washington and Pyongyang continued in Geneva for two months after the August Agreed Statement, while consultation and confrontation between the US and South Korea also continued.

Despite Seoul's resistance, however, the US finally acknowledged that achieving immediate special inspections was impossible and agreed to delay them until the delivery of 'sensitive components' of the first light-water reactor (LWR). Washington had also concluded that Seoul was no longer playing a constructive role.[51] South Korea's attempts to establish a link between North–South talks and the Geneva negotiations had proven ineffective to many US officials. National Security Adviser Lake, expressing his unhappiness about President Kim's newspaper interviews in which he attacked Clinton and his negotiator, bluntly told his South Korean counterpart, Chung Jong Wook, that if Seoul insisted on waiting for unconditional concessions from the North, it risked being blamed for any failure in the negotiations.[52] Faced with the spectre of a major confrontation with its closest ally, Seoul gave in. The 'Agreed Framework' was reached on 16 October 1994, based on a package solution which proposed a number of reciprocal measures for every issue involved.[53]

2. Explanations

Despite the grave challenge posed by North Korea's announcement of its NPT withdrawal, the first response from the US and South Korea emphasized a diplomatic approach. However, initial progress stalled, and the stand off took a dangerous turn. Although the dispute was resolved peacefully, the outcome was not a major accomplishment in terms of its initial objectives. The final Agreed Framework, though constructed of the same basic elements as the initial 'package deal' proposed by Pyongyang in November 1993, ceded a delay in special inspections. Moreover, this modest success involved almost one year of confrontation and serious military tensions.

Two questions need to be answered. First, what accounted for the delay in acceptance of the package solution? Why did the early diplomatic mood turn into confrontation? Second, how should we understand the military tensions during this period? The three perspectives outlined in Chapter 1 will again be utilized for these questions.

A. International factors

Although the US and North Korea were the main actors in diplomatic negotiations, other international players, such as the IAEA, China, Japan, and Russia were also involved. This section will focus on the roles of these participants in shaping the diplomacy. In explaining the military tensions, deliberate and conscious American contributions will be stressed.

Difficulties of multiple bargaining
As has been noted, tensions on the peninsula mounted contributing to the waning of the initial diplomatic overtures towards North Korea. Although the US did not completely abandon diplomacy, more hard-line approaches, including economic sanctions and military preparations, gained strength over time. A number of factors contributed to this shift. First, the IAEA's uncompromising and legalistic stance on inspections became a source of increasing tension with the diplomatically-minded State Department. When the tentative agreement of December 1993 between Washington and Pyongyang was disrupted by an IAEA–North Korea dispute, one State Department official complained: 'We became a prisoner of the IAEA.'[54] The *New York Times* also criticized the Clinton administration for 'letting the IAEA decide how to carry out a deal Washington reached with Pyongyang.' It contended: 'By changing the terms of that deal, the IAEA could embroil the US in a dangerous confrontation on the Korean peninsula.'[55] From the State Department's perspective, the IAEA was a narrow-minded institution preoccupied with its own technical accomplishments and oblivious to the wider implications of its behaviour.[56]

As far as the IAEA was concerned, however, nothing less than full compliance was acceptable. After its disastrous performance in Iraq, wherein inspectors had found no evidence of the vast nuclear weapons complex uncovered during the Gulf War, the IAEA was determined not to lose its credibility again.[57] Although the agency tried to stay in step with American diplomacy, it leaned in favour of its own prerogatives.[58] After the suspension of

Pyongyang's NPT withdrawal in June 1993, the IAEA argued that North Korea, like any other member state, had a legal obligation to accept full IAEA inspections. Pyongyang insisted that its 'special' and 'unique' status allowed it to determine which demands to accept.[59] This disagreement put Washington in a difficult position.

A second factor contributing to the hard-line shift was a change of power dynamics in the Clinton foreign policy team. Initially, with the President's attention focused on domestic and economic issues, much of the foreign policy responsibility fell on the State Department; Secretary Warren Christopher was a low-key style diplomat whose preference was clearly not for a hard-line approach.[60] Given the less prominent role assigned to the Defense Department, Secretary Les Aspin, the highly intelligent but volatile former chairman of the House Armed Services Committee, played a relatively less important role.[61] Furthermore, Clinton appointees to Asia–among them Under Secretary of State for Political Affairs Peter Tarnoff and Assistant Secretary of State Winston Lord–tended to be more liberal-minded than the previous Bush administration, wherein hard-liners such as Ambassador to Korea James Lilley and Under Secretary of Defense for Policy Paul Wolfowitz had been influential voices on Korean issues. As far as the North Korean nuclear issue was concerned, Tarnoff, Assistant Secretary Robert Gallucci, and other working level officials at the State Department, were playing leading roles and advocating a diplomatic approach.[62] As a result of Clinton's decision to turn over his foreign policies to subordinates, the role of these mid-level officials increased.

Additionally, failures in Bosnia, Somalia and Haiti during the administration's first few months contributed to a risk-averse foreign policy.[63] American credibility was particularly tarnished in Somalia, as the bodies of deceased American soldiers were dragged around the streets of Mogadishu. Confronted by negative public opinion and angry congressional questions about the administration's handling of operations, Clinton seemed to decide that he would live within the limits of US power. That included negotiated outcomes to outstanding conflicts on the best terms he could achieve. For Somalia, this entailed a quiet retreat.[64] In North Korea, it meant accepting a give-and-take deal with a potential proliferator.

The State Department's preference for a diplomatic approach to the North Korean nuclear issue was increasingly undermined, however. The IAEA's strict legal stance repeatedly disrupted its efforts. Moreover, Clinton began to question the State Department's ability after an unpleasant meeting with President Kim Young Sam, wherein he and his foreign policy aides were surprised by Seoul's unexpected opposition to a package deal.[65] Clinton was particularly embarrassed, as he himself had explained the deal to Chinese President Jiang Zemin as a new US diplomatic approach on 19 November at the APEC meeting in Seattle.[66] He consequently shifted his attention from State Department officials to his White

House staff and other departments. In order to maintain close contact with the South Korean presidential office, Anthony Lake began regular conversations with National Security Adviser Chung Jong Wook, and instructed Daniel Poneman, Senior Director for Non-proliferation at the NSC, to keep an open channel with his South Korean counterpart.[67] Moderates in the State Department were bypassed, and hard-liners in the Defense Department, CIA and NSC staff gained strength. Anthony Lake and Daniel Poneman gained especial influence in North Korean policy making.[68]

Finally, the vacillations of other powers regarding UN sanctions provided room for Washington to shift its policy direction. Beijing's initial opposition to UN sanctions against North Korea left Washington unable to consider seriously such a strategy.[69] From the beginning, China had defined itself as an advocate of a moderate diplomatic campaign. On 8 April, Chinese Foreign Ministry spokesman Wu Jianmin stated: 'Dialogue is more effective than pressure. To bring pressure to bear is not appropriate now.'[70] Although China also hoped to keep North Korea non-nuclear, it disagreed with the US as to how this could be achieved. Fearing any destabilizing effect that stringent sanctions would have on its neighbour, China chose to exercise indirect influence in discouraging confrontation between North Korea and the US, and called on Washington to engage in direct talks with Pyongyang.[71] Washington 'bowed to Chinese entreaties', and, in June 1993, a first round of high-level talks began between two nations.[72]

However, Beijing slowly changed its attitude and began to pressure Pyongyang more directly. Frustrated with North Korea's continuous provocations, increasingly worried about rising tension on the peninsula, and wanting to make a positive gesture towards President Clinton after his renewal of China's MFN status on 29 May, China became more actively involved. The North Korean ambassador in Beijing was warned that Pyongyang should not expect indefinite Chinese support for its confrontational position towards the US The same message was sent to the North Korean ambassador to the UN and the South Korean government.[73] Although Chinese support was not guaranteed, Washington estimated that a UN Security Council resolution would be passed with a Chinese abstention.[74] The sanctions strategy also gained support from Moscow, as the South Korean President secured Yeltsin's promise for cooperation during his visit to Russia in May.[75] Yeltsin announced that Russia would support international sanctions against North Korea if Pyongyang continued to refuse cooperation on nuclear inspections. During the summit meeting in Moscow, South Korean President Kim Young Sam agreed to postpone Russia's debt repayment schedule if Moscow would pressure North Korea to cooperate on the nuclear issue.[76] Despite opposition by the Japanese Social Democratic Party, Japan also agreed to include the cessation of remittance payments in a resolution drafted by the United States.[77]

These factors–the IAEA's tough stance on inspections, the rise of hard-liners in the Clinton foreign policy team and gathering international support for UN sanctions–along with Pyongyang's determination to exploit a nuclear card to its limit, seem to have contributed to tensions and the danger of military conflict.

Counter-proliferation

In the midst of the nuclear dispute, the US undertook a series of military reinforcements which contributed to military tensions. Regarding a possible military conflict, it is useful to understand the new concept of 'counterproliferation.' The term was introduced in a December 1993 speech by Secretary of Defense Les Aspin.[78] In the past, Aspin contended, the US had attempted to stop proliferation. Its increasing recognition 'that proliferation may still occur', however, meant that it should be prepared for regional conflicts of a nuclear or biological nature.[79] This new emphasis had two distinct elements. One was defence–to provide the American military with the ability to protect itself against weapons of mass destruction. This meant, in practical terms, regional missile defences. The other element was prevention–to take preventive action to destroy the WMD programmes of threatening states.[80]

Confirming this new policy, Secretary of Defense William Perry and his Assistant Secretary Ashton Carter later acknowledged: 'We readied a detailed plan to attack the Yongbyon facility with precision-guided bombs.'[81] 'We were highly confident that it could be destroyed without causing a meltdown that would release radioactivity into the air', they added. However, this option was not recommended to President Clinton due to its unacceptably high costs.[82] General Luck estimated that troop casualties could reach the hundreds of thousands, including 100 000 American soldiers, and the cost of a war could top one trillion US dollars, far higher than the $60 billion spent in the Gulf War.[83] 'People believed there was a very high likelihood that an attack on the North Korean nuclear facilities would spark a broad war', said Gary Samore, former Director of the Office of Regional Non-Proliferation Affairs of the State Department, who was one of the US negotiators of the 1994 Agreed Framework as a Deputy to Robert Gallucci.[84] 'People looked at military options, but ruled them out as being unattractive', he added.

Despite this downplaying of the 'surgical strike option', it seems clear that a preventive military strike was a serious option to the Clinton administration. Certainly, the Defense Department had thoroughly studied it. Perry and Carter were fully aware of its inherent dangers, understanding 'a strike on Yongbyon, while surgical in and of itself, would hardly be surgical in its overall effect.' Nonetheless, they believed 'the nuclear program on which North Korea embarked was even more dangerous', and they 'were prepared to risk a war to stop it.'[85] At the 14 June principals' meeting, the plan of an attack on Yongbyon, called the 'Osirak option' after a 1981 Israeli strike against Iraq's nuclear reactor, took centre stage.[86] Support for initiating military action also existed outside the administration–Brent Scowcroft and Arnold Kanter advocated a military strike, and the Senate called for all actions necessary to 'deter and, if necessary, repel an attack from North Korea.'[87]

Even if rationalized as counter-proliferation, it could be argued that conscious and deliberate measures of the US military were responsible for contributing to the prospect of war. Conventional thought propounded that war would break out on the Korean peninsula if the North's aggression were not deterred. However, this section has demonstrated that war could have been initiated by the US, since the threat of North Korea extended beyond conventional warfare in its own region. South Korea now faced the dual danger of a war under the new WMD spectre–not only the failure of deterrence against North Korea but also US preventive action.

B. Security fear and risk of preventive and pre-emptive war

Seoul's opposition to a package deal contributed to the delay in a diplomatic solution of the North Korean nuclear issue. This next section will investigate how South Korean security fears led to this unusual divergence from Washington. Unlike the threat of an American military initiative, as described in the previous section, this discussion will explore a different possibility of military clash–a pre-emptive attack by Pyongyang in the face of growing military pressure from the US.

Security driven resistance

Different explanations could be offered to explain Seoul's relentless objection to a package deal. But most of all, a 'fear of abandonment' seems to have pushed South Korea into an uncompromising stance on the issue. As implied by the term, a 'package deal' would substantially and comprehensively alter the strategic landscape on the peninsula. From Seoul's view, normalized diplomatic relations between the United States and North Korea, and the North's almost certain renegotiation of the American presence in the South, would ultimately raise the issue of US force withdrawal. As North Korea and the US neared the exchange of consular-level liaison offices, national security adviser Chung made it clear to Lake that President Kim was concerned about the rapid pace of US–North Korean efforts to establish diplomatic relations.[88] 'The idea of resolving the nuclear issue with simultaneous US–North Korean normalization may appear sensible at first, but it was not that simple at all', President Kim wrote in his memoirs.[89] '[North Korea] would insist on new conditions, such as the withdrawal of US forces, a new peace treaty with the US, and respect for North Korea, and it would continue to threaten the peace of the peninsula with missiles and biochemical weapons even if the nuclear issue were resolved.'[90]

A former Chun administration cabinet member also expressed concern over a package deal. 'There is a growing consensus among...analysts in South Korea that North Korea is pursuing a Vietnamese-style unification strategy', and he added that: 'After the US signed a peace treaty and withdrew its soldiers from Vietnam in 1973, it took only two years and three months until Vietnam was taken over by the communists.'[91] Choe Yong-chol, Minister of Unification during the Roh administration, was also critical of the package approach. 'There was fear in [South] Korea concerning a direct deal between the US and North Korea, excluding the South, for the critical issues that are directly linked to the security of the peninsula, such as the US forces' withdrawal and a new peace treaty, will continue to emerge.'[92]

The postponement of special inspections was another concern for South Korea in the fall of 1994. As has been shown, the deal was struck with mutual compromise on the matter of special inspections: while Pyongyang finally accepted them for its two suspect sites, Washington agreed to delay their actual occurrence until the delivery of key nuclear components of the LWRs. Washington's initial objective of uncovering the past operations of the North's nuclear programme had changed to the more moderate aim of freezing nuclear facilities while any pre-existing nuclear capabilities would remain in a black box.[93] Although defending a failure to address special inspections might prove politically difficult, stopping future nuclear developments was deemed a more urgent and pressing problem by most American officials than clarifying the history of the programme.[94]

From Seoul's perspective, however, ensuring the certainty of the North's current nuclear potential with its past record was as urgent as inhibiting its future. If the North had succeeded in making bombs from past operations, however small and crude they might be, it would have serious security ramifications for the peninsula. National security adviser Chung Jong Wook acknowledged that there was a disagreement between the American and South Korean governments, saying 'whereas the South Korean government wanted a complete transparency of the North's nuclear capability, the US wished an early solution of this troubled North Korean nuclear issue with the "NPT Review and Extension Conference" ahead', which was scheduled for 1995 to reaffirm the treaty.[95] President Kim was determined to prevent the North from having 'even half a nuclear bomb', and argued: 'Why is North Korea developing nuclear weapons? It is evident that it targets South Korea.'[96] South Korean scholar Ahn Byung-joon further elaborated Seoul's sense of vulnerability: 'Kim Jong Il with a nuclear arsenal is the South's strategic nightmare ... [and] getting a full accounting of Pyongyang's past record through timely IAEA and mutual North–South inspections' was essential, given doubts about the US commitment to defend the South 'in the teeth of a North Korean nuclear threat.'[97] This concern made Seoul uncompromising on special inspections and resistant to the

Agreed Framework.

Mirror image and risk of pre-emptive war

At the time, security experts in both Seoul and Washington generally agreed on two different possibilities in which the dispute could lead to war.[98] The first possibility, as shown earlier, was that US attempts to destroy the North Korean nuclear facilities, including surgical strikes, could escalate. In order to save the global non-proliferation regime, it was suspected that the US might be willing to take military action. The second possibility was that North Korea, driven into a corner, could attack the South out of desperation. Seoul and Washington were particularly concerned about the negative signals that American military reinforcements might send to the North. A large scale military build-up in South Korea, however defensive the Pentagon's motivation, could have been misread by Pyongyang as a signal of an imminent attack. The North might have then felt compelled to strike first. If the US military build-up had been completed, the North's small chance for military success would have been even more unlikely.

Some senior American officers in South Korea were well aware of the danger of a pre-emptive North Korean strike. 'I always got this feeling that the North Koreans studied the desert [Operation Desert Storm in the Gulf War] more than we did almost', said a general in the US Command in Seoul at the time of a major reinforcement.[99] 'And they learned one thing: you don't let the United States build up its forces and then let them go to war against you... They would see their window of opportunity closing.' That May, Pyongyang made exactly the same point at Panmunjom. 'We are not going to let you do a build-up', said a North Korean colonel to a US officer.[100] State Department official Robert Carlin, a member of an interagency group, made the same point regarding the effects that the deployment of Patriot missiles might have on Pyongyang. 'The North Koreans are thinking, "When were the Patriot missiles used? Desert Storm. And what were those missiles used for? To support an invasion of Iraq"', he concluded.[101]

Pyongyang's sense of urgency was well expressed in its almost daily accusations against Washington. On 9 June, for example, Pyongyang criticized American military moves, saying that they were 'not a mere threat but a war blast signalling the green light to the actual provocation of a second Korean war.'[102] Although it is impossible to know exactly how close Pyongyang was to a 'pre-emptive war', it was probably serious about the possibility. Vis-à-vis North Korea's military moves, South Korean Defence Minister Yi Pyong Tae said: 'North Korea has conducted inspections assessing the combat-readiness of the entire armed forces.'[103] According to Kim Tok, director of the South Korean intelligence agency, North Korea initiated a wartime system, suspending the issuance of travel permits to its residents, examining its emergency communications network, and increasing construction of defence facilities such as barriers.[104] It was also reported that fears of war drove North Korean elites–including party, government and military officials–to convert their local currency into US dollars, gold, jewellery and other valuables.[105]

Given the unclear and conflicting signals that Washington and Seoul had sent to the North, Pyongyang's fear of war should not be taken as total paranoia or simple propaganda. While Washington pursued a diplomatic approach, hawks outside the administration often argued publicly for military strikes against North Korea.[106] Even Secretary of Defense Perry, who was managing to strike a balance between diplomacy and military preparedness, hinted that a pre-emptive attack against North Korea could not be ruled out.[107] According to Perry, American forces were 'position[ed] to strike Yongbyon' in order to 'make our [US] willingness to use military forces crystal clear to the North Koreans.'[108]

South Korean President Kim Young Sam also tried to send a strong signal to Pyongyang that the South was willing to do anything to prevent a nuclear-armed North Korea. 'North Korea's nuclear programme is a matter of life and death ... We will not tolerate North Korean possession of even half a nuclear weapon. I will stop the North from developing nuclear weapons by all means', a determined Kim said in June 1994.[109] Furthermore, in late March 1994, amid mounting public fears about a war and after North Korea had threatened to turn Seoul into a 'sea of fire', South Korean Defence Minister Lee Pyong Tae publicly briefed the National Assembly on the newly devised 'ROK–US Combined Operations Plan (OPLAN) 5027', which put emphasis on offensive strikes well north of the military demarcation line.[110] He also said: 'If North Korea perpetrates a provocation in the five northwestern islands or specific areas, the ROK–US Combined Forces or the ROK Armed Forces alone will offer powerful punitive retaliation and link this to an opportunity to wage a war to achieve reunification.'[111] This was the first official declaration that South Korea had a plan not only of defending itself, but also of pursuing unification via the armed forces before an all-out provocation by the North.[112] Although the disclosure of this highly furtive and incendiary military plan was taken 'as a threat to the North Koreans ... as a deterrent measure', according to a senior US officer in Seoul, it was unlikely that Pyongyang simply dismissed the US–ROK war plan as a deterrent gesture by the South.[113]

Therefore, a dilemma arose for the US and South Korea, because war preparation on their part stemmed from defensive motivations. On the one hand, reinforcement and war planning were pursued as a kind of pressure strategy and were related to the concept of counter proliferation. On the other, military reinforcement was an inevitable and precautionary measure designed to deal with Pyongyang's unpredictable reaction to possible UN sanctions. North Korea repeated its position clearly, warning that 'sanctions mean war, and there is no mercy in war.'[114] When the Principals Committee recommended to President Clinton that he approve the deployment of a Patriot on 8 February, it took heed of Secretary Perry's concerns about the dangers of pursuing a sanctions strategy in the Security Council without Patriots on the ground in South Korea.[115] Calling the situation 'a dilemma', State Department official Gary Samore said: 'If the negotiation had collapsed, I am convinced President Clinton would have ordered increasing US forces for defensive purposes, even if the North might have seen that as a preparation for attack.'[116] The difficulty was that additional military deployments would have to be carefully calibrated so as to deter and deal with, rather than provoke, a North Korean attack.

There was no direct evidence that North Korea perceived the US–South Korean reinforcement as preparation for an imminent strike. However, Pyongyang's escalating rhetoric of war and its unusual military moves, including longer winter training and the display of new ballistic missiles, set off alarm bells inside the American intelligence community. Faced with troubling indicators of the North Korean military forces' status, the national intelligence officer (NIO) for warning, Charlie Allen, came close to issuing a 'warning of war' in early 1994.[117] The situation was so tense that even South Korean President Kim Young Sam believed that US military action was imminent.[118] Furthermore, no one can know for sure how Pyongyang would have perceived and reacted to the deployment of 50 000 more American combat troops to South Korea–the preferred military option of the president, and one he would have authorized on 16 June, had Carter not gone to North Korea.[119] With the impending dispatch of US forces, there were signs of panic in South Korea. The stock market plummeted and people began hoarding food and provisions in anticipation of war.[120] 'There is no question', recalls Charles Kartman, the deputy chief of mission in the South, 'that in the summer of 1994 we were headed toward a substantially increased possibility of a war.'[121]

The series of events in early 1994, thus, demonstrate that the Korean peninsula was facing the danger of spiral interactions rather than deterrence failure. The most serious threat does not seem to have stemmed from Pyongyang's aggressive or irrational motivations, but from its entrapment in situations wherein it felt compelled to act in order to ensure its survival.[122]

C. Domestic politics

Domestic politics also seem to have played a role in the South's strong opposition to the US–DPRK package deal. One aspect was President Kim's determination not to be sidelined in a nuclear deal between the US and North Korea amidst popular demand for proper involvement. Another domestic factor was pressure from hard-liners and the subsequent confusion as to the direction of South Korea's strategy.

President Kim's determination not to be sidelined

As Washington exercised flexibility and accepted the North's package deal offer in November 1993, President Kim Young Sam feared that Seoul stood on the sidelines while the US was taking control of diplomacy on the peninsula.[123] A 'package deal' implied that all the important Korean issues were being comprehensively dealt with by the Americans without the input of Seoul. Kim was a politician with little experience or interest in diplomacy, and was well known for his obsession with polls in running the government. He was adamant that South Korea should play an important role in resolving the peninsula's nuclear issue.

Prior to Kim's summit with Clinton, the South Korean media criticized Pyongyang's effort to strike a direct deal with Washington and pressed the administration to make sure that the primary participants in Korean matters would be Koreans.[124] In the face of such publicity, Presidential Chief of Staff Park Kwan Yong strongly advised Kim that he should block the package approach. In an interview with South Korean monthly magazine *Shin Dong-A* in November 1997, Park said: 'I told the President that the public would not tolerate such an approach and that public emotion should be taken into account in dealing with the North Korean issue.' Park also revealed that he had had a dispute with Foreign Minister Han over the matter, as Han had agreed with Washington's approach.[125]

In addition to apprehension about the repercussions of being sidelined, President's Kim's personal rivalry with a defacto opposition leader, Kim Dae Jung, also seems to have affected his aversion to the package approach. Kim Dae Jung had publicly advocated an idea similar in name and concept to that proposed by the North since the spring of 1993.[126] Despite a mutual concern about being left out of Washington–Pyongyang negotiations, the opposition party then supported the package approach.[127] While faithfully following their boss's support of the package deal, opposition members were also ready to attack the Kim Young Sam administration for any failure to involve Seoul fully in it.[128] Under such circumstances, yielding to Kim Dae Jung's initiative and accepting a Washington–Pyongyang direct deal was anathema to Kim Young Sam both politically and personally. Clinton and Kim thus devised a new name for the policy–a 'broad and thorough' approach–though it had little substantial difference from the 'package' approach.

In sum, as Halperin has pointed out regarding most presidents' domestic calculations, President Kim needed to deny a potential opponent a key issue that might have undermined his own prestige as the pre-eminent decision-maker.[129] At the same time, in the face of possible criticism, he also needed to demonstrate to his domestic audience that he was in command and seeking solutions to problems, even if their consequences were not yet known or might prove counterproductive.[130]

Pressure from the hawks in a right-wing political atmosphere
Following Carter's visit to Pyongyang came a brief period of hope that an historic summit meeting between North and South Korea would be achieved. However, Seoul's resistance to the US–North Korean deal continued even after the resumption of high-level talks in July 1994. Moreover, disputes inside the South's bureaucracy were often made public, creating confusion among South Korean observers as well as US officials about the South's strategy.[131] This section will attempt to elucidate these battles by examining the South Korean political landscape during the summer of 1994.

First, anti-North Korean sentiments were fuelled when condolences were offered to Pyongyang after the sudden death of Kim Il Sung. On 11 July 1994, four opposition legislators, including Lee Boo Young and Lim Chae Jung, suggested that the government dispatch sympathies, touching off an impassioned debate.[132] On some college campuses, dissident students took part in memorial ceremonies and handed out pamphlets eulogising Kim. This stood in stark contrast to the views of most South Koreans, to whom Kim Il Sung was an instigator of the Korean War and a perpetrator of national division. On 16 July, several thousand people gathered to criticize the expression of condolences, accusing the opposition legislators of 'reckless' and 'irresponsible behaviour.'[133] The four legislators were forced to apologize, and the opposition party disowned their remarks.[134]

Conservatives took advantage of this sudden rise in anti-Northern sentiment. Park Hong, President of Sogang University, argued that North Korea had already organized terrorist and other pro-North Korean groups on campuses in the South.[135] He also said that dissident students were operating under direct instruction from Pyongyang.[136] Although Park argued that he had evidence for his claims, he was never able to provide it. Others questioned the ideology of Kim administration officials. In a public letter to the President, Hunjung-whei [The Parliamentarians, Society of the Republic of Korea], a group of retired legislators, argued that some of his aides were ideologically suspect, and demanded that they be removed.[137] Although the request had no practical legal or political power, this influential group's direct attack against the Presidential office had wide repercussions.

In such a climate, the administration had no choice but to side with the conservatives. A week later, the government announced that it would crack down on any domestic attempts to eulogize Kim Il Sung. On 18 July, South Korean Prime Minister Lee Yung-duk denounced the proposal for offering condolences as a 'regrettable, thoughtless attitude that ignores grim historical facts.' The government prohibited crossing the border, and dozens of people travelling to the funeral were arrested.[138] A nationwide search was conducted for 140 or so college students charged with praising North Korea and eulogising Kim Il Sung.[139] The government not only responded to the conservative mood of the nation, it took deliberate advantage of it. For the upcoming by-election on 2 August, the ruling party successfully utilized the condolences issue in an appeal to conservative voters.[140] Although the opposition tried to shift the focus to matters like government financial scandals and a failed trade negotiation in the Uruguay Round, it lost all three constituencies.[141]

Given this political atmosphere, it would have been terrible timing for Kim's administration to allow a nuclear deal between Washington and Pyongyang, and in effect, hard-liners attempted to put a brake on the dialogue. On 27 July, a North Korean defector named Kang Myong Do said at a news conference arranged by the Agency for National Security Planning (ANSP), the South Korean intelligence organization, that North Korea already possessed five nuclear warheads and was in the process of making five more.[142] Identifying himself as the son-in-law of North Korea's Prime Minister, Kang said that he was an executive for a government-run trading company and that his information came from a North Korean intelligence official.[143] He also said that North Korea's new leader, Kim Jong Il, saw the development of nuclear weapons not as a bargaining chip, but as the muscle he needed to stand up to the US. While there was no way to confirm Kang's claims, which would exceed even the gloomiest estimates of the CIA, most western intelligence officials expressed deep scepticism. US State Department spokesman Mike McCurry said that Kang's claims were not consistent with US intelligence estimates, adding 'the reliability of the information is something, that, frankly, we're not certain we can assess at this point.'[144] The IAEA released an official statement that said: 'The statement made by the defector is not judged to be plausible.'[145] In any case, concern was raised over the South Korean intelligence service's motives in choosing this sensitive moment, two months after Kang's reported defection, to release this information.[146] Some saw them as an attempt to poison the high-level talks set to resume between the US and North Korea the following week, and national security adviser Lake interrogated Chung Jong Wook as to why the press conference was held.[147] There was speculation that the ANSP might have been trying to pre-empt a diplomatic deal by painting the North Korean nuclear programme in the starkest possible terms.[148]

This incident may be presented as an example of the bureaucratic politics model. As it would suggest, there was no single 'South Korean' position at the time. The hard-line position of ANSP Director Kim Deok, Defence Minister Kwon Young-hye, and National Security Adviser Chung Jong Wook stood against the more moderate stance of Foreign Affairs Minister Han Sung Joo and Vice-Premier and Unification Minister Lee Hong-koo.[149] Whatever its motives, the ANSP clearly appeared to be pursuing its own goals, and officials at the Foreign Ministry and the National Unification Board were furious.[150] The next day, after a meeting between Vice-Premier and Unification Minister Lee Hong-koo and other key Cabinet members to coordinate views, the South Korean government formally dismissed the defector's claim.[151] According to one official involved in the meeting, it was agreed that 'North Korea has an intention to develop nuclear weapons but there is no evidence that it already has them.'[152] Another official stated: 'What he said was based on what he heard from a third party in North Korea, with nothing else to back up the information.'[153]

More confusion emerged a month later. On 21 August, South Korean Foreign Minister Han expressed openness to nuclear inspections, if they could help clear up the suspicions about Pyongyang's nuclear programme.[154] Although Minister Han seems to have been searching for a practical way to clarify Pyongyang's past nuclear activities without hurting its honour, his remarks caused some consternation. The presidential secretaries were especially irritated, as Han's remarks could have been considered a retreat from Seoul's long-standing policy of demanding 'special inspections', which President Kim had himself repeatedly confirmed.[155] National Security Adviser Chung Jong Wook attacked the remarks, saying that there was no change in the government's stance on the issue.[156] Another official called Han's comments 'inappropriate' at a time when the government position remained firm.[157] This time the administration was even slower in addressing the confusion than in the Kang case. In an attempt to work out differences, Vice-Premier and Unification Minister Lee Hong-koo called a Unification and Security Policy Coordination Committee (USSPCC) meeting on 24 August, but it was postponed without appropriate reasons provided.[158] Lawmakers in both the ruling and opposition parties called for a reshuffle of the foreign policy team. Some speculated about a personal rivalry between Chung and Han from their days in academia.[159] These inconsistent and even conflicting messages led some experts to conclude that 'the government had no policy toward North Korea.'[160]

The confusion between key foreign policy-makers was in part the result of a lack of central control. As Stephen Krasner has noted, the ability of bureaucracies independently to establish policies is a function of Presidential attention.[161] The President has a major role in determining who participates in the decision-making process and to what extent. During the Kim administration, where presidential power was relatively strong, policy inconsistency or confusion would develop not because of the independent power of government organizations, but because of failures by the President to assert control. During both the Kang controversy and the Han/Chung dispute, Kim's role was negligible. Perhaps he had lost his personal interest in inter-Korean relations after a summit meeting was cancelled because of Kim Il Sung's death. Moreover, as the South's public mood towards Pyongyang hardened in the wake of the condolences' controversy, it seemed that he indirectly allowed hard-liners to take actions aimed at undermining Han's moderate policy.[162] Han later recalled: 'Kim Young Sam was not a hard-liner at first. But opposition from inside the administration, media, and the Parliament made the diplomacy difficult.'[163] The coupling of Seoul's hard-line bureaucracies with President Kim's own political calculations, then, seems to have complicated the moderates' efforts to strike a package deal with Pyongyang.

3. Conclusion

This chapter has examined three different aspects of Korean nuclear diplomacy between March 1993 and October 1994 in order to address two main issues. The first was why initial diplomatic progress gave way to a long-lasting stalemate that could have resulted in military conflict. Considering that the US and North Korea had already reached a consensus on a package deal by the fall of 1993, we need to explain why there was a lapse of one year until the final agreement, which was not essentially different from the original terms, was reached. The second issue pertained to the origin and character of the military confrontation during the stalemate. Who was to blame for creating these circumstances, and how and why did the crisis escalate to such a point? Answering these questions should offer a better understanding of the danger of war on the Korean peninsula in the post-Cold War period.

Regarding the stalemate, a look at the role played by international actors has suggested that the IAEA's uncompromising demand of thorough inspections stalled negotiations and hence undermined the US State Department's diplomatic efforts. At the same time, China's more flexible attitude vis-à-vis UN sanctions against North Korea allowed Washington to pursue a more coercive strategy. The security dilemma theory has argued that the South Korean government opposed a US led deal because it feared the security implications. Domestic politics also inhibited diplomacy. Hard-liners deliberately undermined diplomatic progress by using a conservative political environment for their own advantage. President Kim's personal determination to be seen as in charge also complicated diplomacy.

All things taken into account, the IAEA's legalistic and stubborn stance and Seoul's continuous resistance were the two most powerful factors in delaying the final diplomatic solution. Negotiations had been conducted by the US and North Korea; whereas Pyongyang consistently pushed for a deal on its terms, the US shifted from dialogue to a sanctions strategy and then back towards a package solution. American diplomatic fluctuations were the function of internal and external factors, representing bureaucratic politics in Washington and the roles of international participants, including South Korea and the IAEA. While Beijing's more flexible attitude towards UN sanctions against North Korea may be seen to have afforded the Clinton administration with more leverage for an aggressive approach towards North Korea, the opposing positions of the IAEA and Seoul directly undermined the State Department's diplomatic efforts.[164] While the

IAEA disrupted an incremental diplomatic approach during the second half of 1993, Seoul contributed to delaying a package deal from the winter of 1993 until the end of October 1994. Given Clinton's preference for his domestic agenda and the embarrassing foreign policy failures in Somalia and Haiti, the administration was more inclined towards diplomacy than sanctions, and would certainly have continued in this direction, had Seoul and the IAEA not interfered. It is hard to tell, however, which factor–Seoul or the IAEA–was more responsible for delaying a diplomatic solution, as each seems to have been powerful enough to block an early diplomatic breakthrough independently.

If Seoul's objection to a US-led package deal was one of the two main factors in hampering American diplomacy, what was the source of its opposition? The security dilemma and domestic politics explanations stress different perspectives. In domestic politics accounts, the hawks' deliberate attempt to undermine the North Korean regime seems to have limited explanatory power. The hawks' dislike of the package approach had not been evident before the summer of 1994 and it affected only four to five months of the final phase of nuclear diplomacy, while the stalemate and confrontation had already begun in the fall of 1993. In contrast, the Kim administration's resolve not to be sidelined was obvious during the whole period. Thus, this strong desire to get fully involved in a nuclear deal was a more comprehensive factor in contributing to the stalemate.

In order to understand Seoul's attitude, then, it is necessary to compare the two factors, 'the security dilemma' and President Kim's 'determination not to be sidelined'. They differ primarily in their origin: the 'security dilemma' points at 'fear' and the 'determination not to be sidelined' explanation stresses the public's demand for Seoul's proper involvement in inter-Korean matters. While both seem to point to relevant sources, the security dilemma's 'fear'-based explanation might be more helpful in understanding the deeper roots of Seoul's behaviour. A direct Washington–Pyongyang deal might have failed to take the South's position into account and South Koreans 'fear[ed] a diplomatic triangular relationship with Pyongyang starting to rival Seoul as an American partner.'[165] In other words, the Kim administration's concern that the South Korean government not be viewed as an outsider seems to have stemmed from the same 'fear of abandonment' held by the South Korean public.[166]

On the other hand, the 'domestic politics' explanation seems to be better at showing the complex dynamics of decision-making in the South Korean government. The security dilemma explanation might give the impression that Seoul was monolithic and rational, and that its fear was alone responsible for the situation. The reality was more complex. Key policy-makers had different degrees of fear, and they had different ideas of the proper way to deal with Pyongyang. Although 'fear' was a major factor in Seoul's behaviour, it was filtered through complex bureaucratic dynamics.

In sum, the IAEA's uncompromising stance on inspections and South Korea's resistance to a package approach (stemming from security concerns and President Kim's determination not to be sidelined) complicated and prolonged negotiations for more than a year. Although the US was ultimately successful in striking a deal with North Korea, it was not able simply to disregard its ally and the IAEA during negotiations. As a result, the Clinton administration was split regarding its course of action, and it seems inconceivable that the nuclear problem could have been resolved any earlier than the fall of 1994.[167]

Concerning the military crisis, two perspectives have been provided. The first points to the US war plan and reinforcement as a main cause for the escalating tension. In this view, a preventive strategy based on counter-proliferation was responsible for aggravating the already sensitive situation. The second stresses spiral reactions from North Korea in response to defensive military measures by the US and South Korea. Even if their primary concern was to prepare for unpredictable North Korean actions, the reinforcement may have been seen as war preparation by Pyongyang. If it concluded that war was inevitable and imminent, the North may have been prompted to consider pre-emptive military action rather than wait to be attacked. Misperception on the part of the North operates behind this logic.

In contrast with the traditional view that war breaks out only in the case of deterrence failure, these two examples suggest that different catalysts for military engagement are active. The difference between them is that, while the US counter-proliferation account assumes conscious action on the part of the US to initiate a military strike, the security dilemma explanation points out that pre-emptive logic may provoke a war even if neither party involved is actively initiating military actions. The two views are not necessarily inconsistent or contradictory. If the US were to reinforce its military with the intention of striking North Korea, then Pyongyang might attempt to pre-empt it by initiating military actions under the, in this case, correct perception that war is inevitable and imminent. In this scenario, a double pre-emptive logic operates: the US would act pre-emptively to save the NPT regime and North Korea would react pre-emptively before the American military is activated. In either case, both perspectives offer an alternative to the conventional wisdom that peace may be maintained as long as North Korea's aggressions are successfully deterred. As circumstances broadened to include threats beyond mere North Korean aggression, so did the question of war and peace on the peninsula become more complex.

Notes

1. Ashton B. Carter and William J. Perry, 'Back to the Brink', *Washington Post*, 20 October 2002, p. B01.
2. Clyde Haberman, 'Israel Seeks to Keep North Korea From Aiding Iran', *New York Times*, 20 June 1993, p. 6; and David E. Sanger, 'Missile Is Tested by North Korea', *New York Times*, 13 June 1993, p.7.
3. Minister Han said: 'the present situation is not as extreme a crisis as the outbreak of war or military provocation. Therefore, we are continuing diplomatic efforts in a calm, prudent and efficient manner', KBS report cited in *FBIS-EAS*, 15 March 1993, p. 31.
4. Yonhap report cited in *FBIS-EAS*, 15 March 1993, p. 34.
5. Nicholas D. Kristof, 'China Opposes UN Over North Korea', *New York Times*, 24 March 1993, p. 6. On Chinese role, see also Samuel S. Kim, 'The Making of China's Korea Policy in the Era of Reform', in David M. Lampton, ed., *The Making of Chinese Foreign and Security Policy in the Era of Reform, 1978 – 2000* (Stanford: Stanford University Press, 2001), pp. 371-472.
6. The Joint Statement of the DPRK and the USA, New York, 11 June 1993.
7. *Ibid.*
8. There was hard bargaining over the special inspection of two suspect sites, but strong North Korean resistance led the US finally to agree that regular inspections of declared sites would begin first, leaving special inspections for future negotiations. See Chung, *Bukhaek 588il [588 days of North Korean nuclear bombs]*, pp. 45-8.
9. Richard W. Stevenson, 'US-North Korea Meeting Yields Some Gains on Arms', *New York Times*, 20 July 1993, p. A2.
10. *Ibid.*
11. 'North Korea chose the right direction... the government notes the result of the North Korea~US contacts as important progress', said South Korean Foreign Ministry spokesman. Cited in *BBC Summary, Far East*, No. 1746, (20 July 1993), C1/1.
12. Stanley Meisler, 'UN Agency Says Pyongyang Has Refused To Permit Inspections', *Los Angeles Times (Home Edition)*, 2 November 1993, p. A4.
13. For example, former Bush administration defence official Zalmay Khalilzad advocated imposing a deadline and economic sanctions. See Zalmay M. Khalilzad, 'A Deadline on Diplomacy', *New York Times*, 8 November 1993, p. 19. Similar arguments can be found in Charles Krauthammer, 'North Korea's Coming Bomb: It's Clinton's crisis, and he's not ready to lead', *Washington Post*, 5 November 1993, p. A27 and *Chosun Ilbo*, 22 October 1993.
14. Michael Breen, 'US searches for deal to diffuse nuclear controversy in N. Korea', *Washington Times*, 29 September 1993, p. 11.
15. For the full text of the proposal, see Kenneth Quinones, *Hanbando Unmyŏng: Pukpokyınya Hyŏpsangyinya [North Korea's nuclear threat 'off the record' memories]* (Seoul: Jongang M&B, 2000), pp. 242-3.
16. *BBC Summary, Far East*, No. 1845, (11 November 1993), D/3.
17. R. Jeffrey Smith, 'US Weighs N. Korean Incentives: New Approach Taken On Nuclear Inspection', *Washington Post*, 15 November 1993, A15
18. Sigal, *Disarming Strangers*, p. 82.
19. R. Jeffrey Smith, 'North Korea Deal Urged By State Dept.: Cancelling Exercise Linked to Inspection', *Washington Post*, 17 November 1993, A31.
20. Joel S. Wit, Daniel B. Poneman, and Robert L. Gallucci, *Going Critical: The First North Korean Nuclear Crisis*, (Washington, DC: Brookings Institution Press, 2004), pp. 139-42.
21. R. Jeffrey Smith, 'US Weighs N. Korean Incentives: New Approach Taken On Nuclear Inspection', *Washington Post*, 15 November 1993, A15.

22. Interview with Gary Samore, London, 3 July 2002; and Wit, Poneman and Gallucci, *Going Critical*, pp. 98-106.
23. Ruth Marcus and R. Jeffrey Smith, 'US, South Korea Shift Strategy on North', *Washington Post*, 24 November 1993, p. 12.
24. 'Seoul Gets the Shake', *New York Times*, 27 November 1993, p. 18.
25. US National Security adviser Anthony Lake, Senior Director for Non-proliferation at the NSC Daniel Poneman, and South Korean National Security Adviser Chung Jong Wook discussed a new arrangement and agreed that Team Spirit would only be cancelled after a serious inter-Korean dialogue. See Wit, Poneman and Gallucci, *Going Critical*, p. 112.
26. Cited in *FBIS-EAS*, 24 November 1993, 28.
27. After the summit meeting, North Korea's UN delegate Ho Jong complained to US Deputy Assistant Secretary of State Hubbard that he had given Seoul control over the pace of US~North Korean talks. Hubbard told Lake that talks in New York were destined to fail. See Wit, Poneman and Gallucci, *Going Critical*, pp.112-5.
28. Sigal, *Disarming Strangers*, p. 98.
29. In March, another dispute between the IAEA and North Korea over sampling issues led to the withdrawal of inspectors from the North. On March 15, the IAEA declared that it was unable to verify the North's nuclear programme. See Laura King, 'North Korea continues to reject nuke inspections', *Washington Times*, 22 January 1994, p. A9.
30. One of the key US participants in the New York talks, Kenneth Quinones believed that delaying and complicating US-North Korean talks was the first priority of South Korean president Kim Young Sam. See Quinones, *Hanbando Unmyŏng [North Korea's nuclear threat 'off the record' memories]*, pp. 267-8.
31. On 19 April 1994, North Korea informed the IAEA that the reactor needed to be refuelled quickly, and expressed its willingness to have inspectors monitor the refuelling process. But the agency wanted not only to monitor refuelling, but also to extract samples to obtain a clear reading of the reactor's past operations and information on how much plutonium North Korea had acquired thus far. North Korea refused to let the inspectors take samples, and began removing the fuel rods from the reactor.
32. Ann Devroy, 'Nuclear Inspectors Cite "Lost" Chance To Monitor Reactor', *Washington Post*, 3 June 1994, p. A1. However, not all observers agreed with Blix's pessimistic assessment. For example, some US officials privately conceded that Blix's assessment was 'something of an exaggeration'. See Mazarr, *North Korea and the Bomb*, p. 159.
33. Paul Lewis, 'US Offers a Plan For UN Sanctions On North Korea', *New York Times*, 16 June 1994, p. A1.
34. Douglas Jehl, 'US Is Pressing Sanctions for North Korea', *New York Times*, 11 June 1994, p. 7.
35. The first option was the immediate dispatch to Korea of additional counter-battery radars, a reconnaissance system, and around 2000 troops composed mainly of logistic, administrative and supply personnel in preparation for a rapid deployment of larger forces later. Another option included the dispatch of 30~40 fighter planes and other aircraft, including F-117 Stealth fighter-bombers and long-range bombers, the deployment of several battalions of ground forces, and the stationing of a second US aircraft-carrier battle group in the area. This would involve deployment of more than 10 000 American troops. The third, most robust option was to send tens of thousands more Army and Marine combat troops and even more combat air power. For the US war plan, see Oberdorfer, *The Two Koreas*, pp. 323-5; and Leon V. Sigal, 'US~DPRK Relations and Military Issues on the Korean Peninsula', *KNDU (Korean National Defence University) Review*, vol. 6, no. 2 (December 2001) p. 84.
36. *FBIS-EAS*, 14 June 1994, p. 16.
37. *BBC Summary, Far East*, No. 2023, (15 June 1994), D/1.
38. *BBC Summary, Far East*, No. 2023 (15 June 1994), D/5.

39. T.R. Reid, 'Leaders of 2 Koreas Seek First Summit', *Washington Post*, 19 June 1994, p. 28.
40. A White House official later recalled: 'It looked like as if we were contracting out our foreign policy, like we were bystanders'. See R. Jeffrey Smith and Ann Devroy, 'Carter's Call From N. Korea Offered Option' *Washington Post*, 26 June 1994, p. 1.
41. The day after Carter's public announcement, the Chinese Foreign Ministry spokesman hardened China's opposition to sanctions. The Russian Foreign Minister Andrei Kozyrev also opposed the American proposal on grounds that Moscow had not been consulted in advance. See Lena H. Sun, 'North Korea Presents China with Dilemma', *Washington Post*, 17 June 1994, p. A20; 'N. Korea and US narrow differences', *Independent (London)*, 17 June 1994, p. 12.
42. R. Jeffrey Smith and Ann Devroy, 'Carter's Call From N. Korea Offered Option' *Washington Post*, 26 June 1994, p. 1.
43. R. Jeffrey Smith and Ann Devroy, 'One Small Concession Looms Large', *Washington Post*, 26 June 1994, p. A1.
44. For the text of an agreed statement, see *BBC Summary*, Far East, No. 2074, (13 August 1994), D/1.
45. Alan Riding, 'US and N. Korea Agree on a Move to Diplomatic Ties', *New York Times*, 13 August 1994, p. A1.
46. Sigal, *Disarming Strangers*, p. 181.
47. In a draft compromise delivered to South Korea by the US, North Korea was allowed to delay 'special inspections' until the completion of approximately 75 per cent of the LWR. *BBC Summary*, Far East, No. 2123, (19 October 1994), D/7. Yonhap cited in *FBIS-EAS*, 11 October 1994, p. 58.
48. 'North Korea Reaffirms It Will Never Allow Special Nuclear Inspections', *North Korea News*, no. 750, 29 August 1994.
49. Wit, Poneman and Gallucci, *Going Critical*, p.284.
50. For this reason, North Korea searched for a non-South Korean reactor, investigating models from Germany, Russia and the United States, while opposing 'special inspections'. See *ibid.*, pp.283-316.
51. Mazarr, *North Korea and the bomb*, pp. 169-71.
52. Wit, Poneman and Gallucci, *Going Critical*, p.315.
53. More specifically, the Agreed Framework was composed of several phases. In the first phase, the North would freeze all existing reactors and facilities, and permit regular IAEA inspections. In return, the US would provide two light-water reactors (LWRs), and supply 500 000 tons of heavy fuel oil annually. In addition, the US would provide formal assurance against the threat or use of nuclear weapons, and would reduce political and economic barriers. In the second phase, after North Korea accepted the IAEA 'special inspections', the US would deliver 'sensitive components' of the LWR and would enter full diplomatic relations with Pyongyang. In the final phase, the North's existing nuclear reactors would be completely dismantled parallel to American completion of the second LWR. For details and an assessment of the agreement, see Mazarr, *North Korea and the Bomb*, pp. 173-80.
54. Sigal, *Disarming Strangers*, p. 100.
55. 'Who Is Running Our Korea Policy?', *New York Times*, 11 February 1994, p. A34.
56. Chung, *Bukhaek 588il [588 days of North Korean nuclear bombs]*, p. 154.
57. Sigal, *Disarming Strangers*, p. 97.
58. 'Safeguard hawks' in the IAEA were determined to monitor against cheating and protect the agency's reputation. The director of the agency's safeguards division, Dimitri Perricos, was known to be the model for the post-Iraq IAEA bureaucrat because of his aggressive style. On the other hand, others, including director Hans Blix who had extensive experience as Swedish foreign minister, were more politically adept. See Wit, Poneman and Gallucci, *Going Critical*, pp.79-80, and p. 120.

59. *BBC Summary,* Far East, No. 1768, (14 August 1993), A1/1; *BBC Summary,* Far East, No. 1809, (1 October 1993), D/3.

60. The selection of Christopher as Secretary of State was criticized even by Clinton's supporters, on the grounds that he was fearful of the use of force and obsessed with negotiations. See William G. Hyland, *Clinton's World: Remaking American Foreign Policy* (London: Praeger, 1999), p. 20.

61. Hyland, *Clinton's World,* pp. 20~1.

62. Chung, Bukhaek 588il [588 days of North Korean nuclear bombs], p. 154.

63. Hyland, *Clinton's World,* pp. 25-34.

64. By the time American forces left on 25 March 1994, approximately 100 000 US troops had served in Somalia. The operation had cost 13 American lives and left 175 wounded. See Thomas H. Henriksen, *Clinton's Foreign Policy in Somalia, Bosnia, Haiti, and North Korea.* (Stanford: Hoover Institution on War, Revolution and Peace, 1996), p.12.

65. Chung, *Bukhaek 588il [588 days of North Korean nuclear bombs],* p. 90.

66. Nam Chan-soon, 'Cross summit meetings of the US, China, Japan, and Korea', *Dong-A Ilbo,* 21 November 1993.

67. Wit, Poneman and Gallucci, *Going Critical,* p. 114.

68. Chung, *Bukhaek 588il [588 days of North Korean nuclear bombs],* p. 91.

69. In establishing UN sanctions, it was essential to avoid a Chinese veto in the Security Council.

70. 'China Insists on Dialogue, Not Pressure, on North Korea', UPI wire report, 8 April 1993.

71. Lena H. Sun and Jackson Diehl, 'N. Korea Reportedly Snubs China; Beijing Sought Talks Over Nuclear Arms', *Washington Post,* 28 April 1993, p. A13.

72. 'US may join nuclear talks with N. Korea', *Chicago Tribune,* 23 April 1993, p. 3.

73. Jim Mann, 'China Assisted US Efforts on N. Korea, Officials Say', *Lost Angeles Times (Home Edition),* 29 June 1994, p. A1.

74. Robin Wright, 'Christopher Predicts UN Approval of N. Korean Sanctions', *Los Angeles Times (Home Edition),* 10 June, 1994, p. A8.

75. See Wit, Poneman and Gallucci, *Going Critical,* p. 197; and R. Jeffrey Smith and William Drozdiak, 'US Aides Say Other Powers Are Leaning toward Tougher North Korean Sanctions', *Washington Post,* 11 June 1994, p. A17.

76. Eugene Bazhanov, 'Soviet Policy toward South Korea under Gorbachev', in Il Yung Chung ed., *Korea and Russia: Toward the 21ˢᵗ Century,* (Seoul: Sejong Institute, 1992), pp. 75-77.

77. 'Japan agrees to halt remittances', *Daily Yomiuri,* 15 June 1994, p. 1.

78. Stephen J. Cimbala, *Clinton and post-Cold War defense* (Westport, CO: Praeger, 1996), p. 61.

79. *Ibid.*

80. Preventive action occurs when a country is driven to war through a fear of greater military and economic disadvantage vis-à-vis its adversary over time. Pre-emption occurs when it is perceived that an attack by the opponent is imminent, and action to forestall the impending attack is deemed imperative. In both cases, military action is not driven by expansionist aims or domestic political agendas, but is defensive in nature. The difference is how imminent the threat is; a preventive situation is more diffuse. See Victor D. Cha, 'Is There Still a Rational North Korean Option for War?', *Security Dialogue,* vol. 29, no. 4 (December 1998).

81. Ashton B. Carter and William J. Perry, 'Back to the Brink', *Washington Post,* 20 October 2002, B1.

82. Wit, Poneman and Gallucci, *Going Critical,* p. 244.

83. Susan Rosegrant in collaboration with Michael D. Watkins, *Carrots, Sticks, and Question Marks: Negotiating the North Korean Nuclear Crisis,* (Harvard University, John F. Kennedy School of Government, 1995), p. 39.

84. Interview with Gary Samore, London, 3 July 2002.

85. Ashton B. Carter and William J. Perry, 'Back to the Brink', *Washington Post*, 20 October 2002, B1.

86. Wit, Poneman and Gallucci, *Going Critical*, p. 210.

87. Rosegrant and Watkins, *Carrots, Sticks, and Question Marks*, p. 38.

88. Seoul also insisted that the liaison offices should have only limited functions, such as the construction of LWRs and searching for the remains of US soldiers, and that they should not serve as a step towards establishing formal diplomatic relations. See *BBC Summary*, Far East, No. 2103, (16 September 1994), D/3; and *BBC Summary*, No. 2105, (18 September 1994), D/1.

89. Kim Young Sam, *Kim Young Sam Taet'ongnyŏng Hoegorok: Minjujuurul Wihan Naŭi T'ujaeng [President Kim Young Sam Memoir: My Struggle for Democracy]* (Seoul: Chosun Ilbo Press, 2001), p. 193.

90. *Ibid.*, p. 214.

91. T.R. Reid, 'US – North Korea Ties Worry Seoul', *Washington Post*, 6 September 1994, A12.

92. Choe, *T'ong'il-ro Makhimyŏn Tolasŏ Kacha [Let's go around if the road to unification is blocked]*, p. 222.

93. Officially, on 16 March, the Principals Committee agreed that the US would be prepared to compromise on the timing of the special inspections. See Wit, Poneman and Gallucci, *Going Critical*, pp. 140~3.

94. In that sense, Gallucci declared in September 1994 that 'the actual implementation of special inspections need not be undertaken immediately for a settlement to be successful'. Cited in *Washington Post*, 'US Won't Condition North Korea Nuclear Agreement on Special Inspections', 10 September 1994.

95. Interview with Chung Jong Wook, 17 September 2002. Right before the 'Agreed Framework' was reached, Vice-Premier and Unification Minister Lee Hong-koo also said that there was disagreement between Seoul and Washington as to the order of priority. 'The US was dealing with the North Korean nuclear issue in a universal outlook, that is, to retain the NPT regime, while South Korea, as a direct party to the Korean question, emphasized the transparency of the North Korean nuclear activities of the past, present and future', he said. See *BBC Summary*, Far East, No. 2126, (12 October 1994), D/5.

96. Cited in *Korea Newsreview*, 11 June 1994, p. 4.

97. Ahn Byung-joon, 'The Man Who Would Be Kim', *Foreign Affairs*, vol. 73, no. 6 (November /December 1994), p. 105.

98. *Korea Newsreview*, 18 June 1994, pp. 4-5.

99. Oberdorfer, *The Two Koreas*, p. 325.

100. *Ibid.*, pp. 325-6.

101. Rosegrant, *Carrots, Sticks, and Question Marks*, p. 32.

102. Pyongyang KCNA cited in *FBIS-EAS*, 9 June 1994, p. 18. Pyongyang radio also said: 'The US military action to crush us has now entered an adventurous stage for carrying out a real warfare'. See *ibid.*

103. KBS Radio report cited in *FBIS-EAS*, 15 June 1994, p. 38.

104. *BBC Summary*, Far East, No. 1956, (25 March 1994), D/2.

105. *BBC Summary*, Far East, No. 1982, (26 April 1994), D/2.

106. Brent Scowcroft and Arnold Kanter, 'Korea: Time For Action', *Washington Post*, 15 June 1994, p. A25; and Karen Elliott House, 'Korea: Raise Another Desert Shield', *Wall Street Journal*, 15 June 1994, p. A18.

107. This occurred at a time when the crisis was at its peak after the North's unsupervised refuelling. See Sharon LaFraniere, 'Perry Says Washington May Act If UN Balks', *Washington Post*, 6 June 1994, P. A13.

108. Ashton B. Carter and William J. Perry, 'Back to the Brink', *Washington Post*, 20 October 2002, p. B01.

109. *Korea Newsreview*, 11 June 1994, p. 4.
110. '"Counter-attack Plan" To Deter DPRK Reported', *Korea Herald*, cited in *FBIS-EAS*, 25 March 1994, pp. 20~21.
111. *BBC Summary*, Far East, No. 1956, (24 March, 1994), D/1.
112. 'US – Seoul "Strategic Concept" on DPRK Noted', *Joong-Ang Ilbo*, 24 March 1994 cited in *FBIS-EAS*, 24 March 1994, p. 26.
113. Oberdorfer, *The Two Koreas*, p. 312.
114. *BBC Summary*, Far East, No. 2016, (5 June 1994), D/4.
115. Wit, Poneman and Gallucci, *Going Critical*, p. 125.
116. Interview with Gary Samore, London, 3 July 2002.
117. Wit, Poneman and Gallucci, *Going Critical*, pp.127-9.
118. After being informed that the US embassy was planning to conduct non-combatant evacuation operations, or NEOs, President Kim strongly urged American Ambassador Laney to cancel the plan. Kim perceived the evacuation of American civilians as a common measure taken by the US before initiating military action. See Kim, *Kim Young Sam Taet'ongnyŏng Hoegorok [President Kim Young Sam Memoir]*, pp. 315-7.
119. Wit, Poneman and Gallucci, *Going Critical*, p. 243.
120. Mazarr, *North Korea and the bomb*, p. 160.
121. Sigal, *Disarming Strangers*, p. 122.
122. It should be noted that a pre-emptive strike, by definition, is motivated more by fear than by aggression. See Cha, 'Is There Still a Rational North Korean Option for War?' pp. 478-9.
123. President Kim's National Security Advisor Chung Jong Wook later acknowledged that the apprehension of being left out of the nuclear deal and its political repercussions at home were important factors in Seoul's get-tough approach. Interview with Chung Jong Wook, 17 September 2002.
124. See, for example, *Dong-A Ilbo*, 17~8 November 1993; and *Joong-Ang Ilbo*, 18 November 1993.
125. In a response to the criticism that his interference created inconsistency in government policy, Park said that any policy towards Pyongyang should inevitably be flexible in light of changing domestic opinion, or it would not be sustainable.
126. *Dong-A Ilbo*, 12 November 1993.
127. *Chosun Ilbo*, 30 October 1993.
128. This inconsistency or conflict in the opposition party's arguments is evident in their criticism of President Kim's summit in Washington. On the one hand, they criticized Kim for disrupting diplomacy by opposing a package deal. On the other hand, some argued that Kim had failed to acquire Clinton's confirmation that Seoul would be properly involved in the talks despite the government's claim. See *Dong-A Ilbo*, 27 November 1993.
129. Morton H. Halperin, *Bureaucratic Politics and Foreign Policy* (Washington, DC: The Brookings Institution, 1974), pp. 68-70.
130. Halperin argues that, in general, presidential popularity goes up at least in the short run, when the President is seen acting vigorously on almost any issue. Presidential initiatives in foreign policy, in this regard, are frequently seen as desirable. See *ibid.*, pp. 67-8.
131. For critical views about the South Korean government's inconsistent policy on North Korea, see Mazarr, *North Korea and the Bomb*, pp. 169-71.
132. *Chosun Ilbo*, 13 July 1994.
133. 'Sympathy in South Korea for Kim Angers Critics', *Reuters*, 12 July 1994.
134. 'DP Lawmakers Retract Remarks about Kim Il Sung', *Yonhap*, 13 July 1994.
135. *Chosun Ilbo*, 19 July 1994.
136. 'Seoul to crack down on leftist youths', *United Press International*, 18 July 1994.
137. Education and Culture Adviser Kim Jung Nam, who had a 'dissident student' background, was the central target. See *Dong-A Ilbo*, 27 July 1994.

138. 'Seoul Renews No-Condolence Policy, Summit Prospects Seen Dimming', *United Press International*, 18 July 1994.

139. 'Seoul to Deal Sternly with Pro-North Students', *Yonhap*, 18 July 1994.

140. *Joong-Ang Ilbo*, 23 July 1994.

141. *Joong-Ang Ilbo*, 3 August 1994.

142. *Chosun Ilbo*, 28 July 1994.

143. Some South Korean analysts raised questions about Kang's identity. If the son-in-law of North Korea's prime minister had fled the country two months ago, the prime minister would presumably have been in serious trouble in such a regime. Broadcasts had repeatedly shown Kang Song San in positions of high honour and had cited him as the third-ranking official in the Pyongyang hierarchy. After Kang's press conference, Pyongyang denied his relation to the Prime Minister, and said that he was a fugitive. See Lee Keumhyun, 'N. Korea Has 5 Nuclear Warheads, No Delivery System, Defector Says', *Washington Post*, 28 July 1994, p. A25.

144. 'N. Korea defector's bomb claim played down', *United Press International*, 29 July 1994.

145. 'IAEA refutes N. Korea defector's bomb claim', *United Press International*, 29 July 1994.

146. James Sterngold, 'Defector Says North Korea Has 5 A-Bombs and May Make More', *New York Times*, 28 July 1994, p. A7.

147. Wit, Poneman and Gallucci, *Going Critical*, p. 262.

148. *New York Times* editorial argued that South Korean hard-liners were sowing doubts about how much bomb-making plutonium the North may have already produced. It argued: 'Their shrill opposition to accommodation could complicate Washington's efforts to make a deal with Pyongyang'. See 'Seoul's Show-Stoppers', *New York Times*, 23 September 1994, p. A34.

149. This classification is based on Foreign Minister Han's interview with *Shin Dong-A*, January 2002. The fact that their different positions were consistent with the core missions of their respective agencies does not necessarily mean that the agencies were pursuing their own parochial interests. Nonetheless, in a situation where information about Pyongyang's nuclear motives and capabilities was ambiguous and national interests in dealing with North Korea were debatable, the interpretation of the situation and the definition of proper goals might have been coloured by the roles that the individuals played.

150. Kim Chae Il, 'Disharmony in Government's DPRK Policy Studies', Seoul, *SISA Journal*, cited in *FBIS-EAS*, 9 August 1994, p. 40.

151. US State Department spokesman Mike McCurry said that Washington expressed displeasure at Seoul for arranging such a news conference at a sensitive time. The Clinton administration had known about Kang's defection for weeks, but it was not aware of his assertions about the size of North Korea's nuclear arsenal until the news conference. Thus, pressure from Washington might also have affected Seoul's playing down Kang's claim. See 'N. Korea defector's bomb claim played down', *United Press International*, 29 July 1994.

152. 'N. Korea defector's bomb claim played down', *United Press International*, 29 July 1994.

153. *Ibid.*

154. *Chosun Ilbo*, 23 August 1994.

155. Han's remarks actually seemed to be a response to Pyongyang's latest statement that it would not accept special inspections. *BBC Summary*, Far East, No. 2080 (21 August 1994), D/3.

156. *Chosun Ilbo*, 24 August 1994.

157. *Ibid.*

158. *BBC Summary*, Far East, No. 2083 (24 August 1994), D/1.

159. *Dong-A Ilbo*, 31 August 1994.

160. Kim Chae Il, 'Disharmony in Government's DPRK Policy Studies', Seoul *SISA Journal*, cited in *FBIS-EAS*, 9 August 1994, p. 40.

161. Stephen D. Krasner, 'Are Bureaucracies Important? A Re-examination of Accounts of the Cuban Missile Crisis', in Charles W. Kegley, Jr., and Eugene R. Wittkopf eds, *The Domestic*

Sources of American Foreign Policy: Insights and Evidence (New York: St. Martin's, 1988), pp. 159-79.

162. In this regard, *New York Times* editorial said that 'some of Seoul's top leaders seem sympathetic to the hard-liners' complaints' about Washington's diplomatic efforts. See 'Seoul's Show-Stoppers', *New York Times*, 23 September 1994, p. A34.

163. Cited in Foreign Minister Han's interview with *Shin Dong-A*, January 2002.

164. The opposing position of Seoul and the IAEA not only disrupted US diplomacy, but also affected the power dimension in Clinton's foreign policy team. As Clinton shifted his attention to the tougher approach advocated by hard-liners, including the CIA, the Department of Defence, and the White House staffs, the position of moderates in the State Department was undermined.

165. T. R. Reid, 'US-North Korea Ties Worry Seoul', *Washington Post*, 6 September 1994, p. A12.

166. Ahn Byung-joon, a South Korean scholar, said: 'Seoul fears that Washington may even strike a separate peace with Pyongyang, de-linking its relationship with the North from its alliance with the South'. See Ahn, 'The Man Who Would Be Kim', p. 104.

167. The Clinton administration decided to negotiate with North Korea through a package deal in the autumn of 1993, as had been advocated by the State Department. This initiative wavered, however, under the persistent objection of Seoul and the IAEA, undermining the State Department while bolstering the position of the hawkish NSC and the Department of Defense.

6. Recurrent Hostilities: 1994–1997

The Agreed Framework of 1994, though it represented something of a compromise, marked significant progress in the security of the Korean Peninsula. The deal carried with it hopes for more normalized economic and diplomatic dealings between the US and North Korea, and heightened the expectation for more positive changes in inter-Korean relations. However, virtually none took place between 1994 and 1997. There was no substantive removal of trade barriers, nor was the establishment of inter-Korean liaison offices ever executed, and North Korea remained on the US's list of countries supporting international terrorism. Turbulent inter-Korean relations continued to raise fears of military action. Tension and conflict were perpetuated after the accord by Seoul's response to the North's food shortages in the mid 1990s, North Korean provocations in the DMZ, and the infiltration of a North Korean submarine into South Korean waters. Though each event carried with it mounting tensions, compromise was reached in all three cases and the crises receded. This chapter will examine the three main explanatory factors in order to help us understand these outcomes. This chapter's structure differs from the others in that it examines cooperation, breakdown and a renewed compromise while the others tend to outline positive developments and then their breakdown. The security dilemma and the domestic politics of both North and South Korea will help us explain the breakdown, while the role of international actors, the United States in particular, will be explored as a key factor on the road to compromise.

1. The North Korean Food Crisis and its Attendant Military Confrontation

A. The Food Crisis

Pyongyang suffered increasingly poor economic conditions in the mid-1990s. It experienced negative GNP growth after 1990, and by 1995 the economy had contracted by over a fifth.[1] Although the economic depression was rooted in the structural problems of the Communist command economy and an excessive resource allocation to heavy industry, it was also instigated by the loss of protected trading relationships with the former Soviet Union and China. Conditions worsened as a series of droughts and floods over the next three years critically destroyed the economic system and precipitated a food crisis. Grain output in 1995 met only 42 per cent of the total demand, down from 4.1 million tons the previous year to some 2.6 million.[2] Though difficult to estimate, famine deaths from August 1995 to March 1998 were reported to have reached as high as three million.[3] This crisis resulted in a mass exodus of starving refugees to neighbouring countries, most of all, China. The US Committee for Refugees estimated the number of North Korean refugees living in China in 1999 at about 50 000.[4]

The economic deterioration and food shortages posed a great threat to the political viability of Kim Jong Il's regime. As has been asserted by defector Hwang Jang Yop, secretary of the Workers Party for international affairs and a great authority on 'Juche' philosophy in North Korea, the regime's inability to feed its own people created a high-level of discontent among North Koreans, undermining Kim Jong Il's political authority.[5] According to one survey conducted by a South Korean NGO, upwards of 60 per cent of the refugees blamed the regime for the prevalent famine, citing an absence of economic reform, bureaucratic misrule, and excessive military spending as contributing factors.[6] The famine may have also damaged the regime's control over the military, as a large proportion of troops certainly witnessed the deaths of relatives.[7] A corps-level military coup was apparently uncovered in the autumn of 1995 at Hamhung, the second-most populated and the worst-hit city by the famine in the country.[8]

In the midst of this crisis and growing rumours of its possible collapse, Pyongyang undertook 'unusual military moves' in late 1995.[9] Military exercises increased in frequency 1.3 to 1.6 times, culminating in the large scale demonstration on 21–22 October of 350 fighter jets at three air bases within 40 kilometres of the military demarcation line.[10] The North also conducted infiltration trainings of 100 000 special operation troops into the rear area of the military border, and positioned artillery closer to the front line.[11] About 20 more fighter jets were deployed to bases within five minutes of Seoul. South Korean officials repeatedly warned that the North might attempt armed provocations or infiltration to defuse unrest.[12] Both Seoul and Washington were concerned that Pyongyang might try to exploit foreign affairs to divert attention from its desperate economic and social circumstances.[13]

The South Korean government adopted a policy that reinforced this mentality. On 29 March 1996, the DPRK ambassador in Geneva requested food aid from the UN, saying North Korea was in 'urgent need'.[14] Seoul initially expressed a willingness to help.[15] On 21 June 1995, after five days of secret talks in Beijing, the South Korean government agreed to grant 150 000 tons of rice to the North.[16] In the latter half of the year, however, it became reluctant to provide aid. In his New Year policy speech on 9 January 1996, President Kim made it clear that Seoul would not help Pyongyang unless it 'scale[d] down its military and change[d] its hostile attitude toward South Korea'.[17]

This hard-line position was in contrast to other countries. The US provided more than 500000 tons of rice and $6.2 million in food aid in June 1996, on top of its February commitment of $2 million.[18] Japan also agreed to provide North Korea with two shipments of rice aid, 300000 tons in June 1995 and another 200000 tons in October.[19] China also provided a substantial amount of food to North Korea, including two million tons of food grain in 1996. Although the terms and exact amount of China's aid to North Korea remain unclear, the annual food assistance since 1995 has been estimated at more than 500000 tons.[20] In contrast, Seoul had provided only 150000 tons of rice and $3 million in food aid by the end of 1996.[21] Despite criticism from the US and other western countries for its reluctance to help,[22] the South Korean government even attempted to prevent the US and Japan from providing assistance. In a meeting with the two nations in late January 1996, Seoul contended that the North's food crises were not as serious as had been thought, and insisted that American and Japanese aid should not precede the resumption of a North–South dialogue.[23]

B. Military Confrontation in the DMZ

In the spring of 1996, military confrontation near the demilitarized zone exacerbated the already mounting tensions. On 4 April, North Korea announced that it would give up its DMZ maintenance duties, and held a series of armed provocations in the Joint Security Area (JSA) a few days later. For three successive days, up to 230 North Korean soldiers held offensive positions with heavy artillery, including two 60mm mortars, an 82mm recoilless gun, and rocket propelled grenades.[24] Such actions stood in direct violation of the 1953 Armistice Agreement, which mandates that both sides suspend all hostile actions, particularly as pertains to the DMZ.

South Korea's response was immediate and decisive. The Defence Ministry issued a statement that the North's move 'was meant to launch a major military provocation ... We will retaliate promptly and firmly under the joint ROK–US defence system'.[25] The Ministry upgraded its intelligence alert level to 'WatchCon 2', which dictated that all forces intensify their surveillance activities.[26] WatchCon 2 had not been declared since 1981–throughout the period of nuclear confrontation, including the North's 'sea of fire' threat, the NPT withdrawal announcement of 1993, and Kim Il Sung's death in July 1994, Watchcon 3 had been maintained. Both Pyongyang's provocations and Seoul's response contributed to the military tension along the DMZ.

C. The North Korean Submarine Incident

In response to North Korea's hostile behaviour in the DMZ, the US proposed a new diplomatic initiative with South Korea. On 16 April, Presidents Kim and Clinton announced a joint proposal for four-party talks, wherein the two Koreas, the US and China would 'initiate a process aimed at achieving a permanent peace agreement' on the Korean peninsula.[27] Pyongyang did not immediately accept or reject the proposal, but rather asked for a detailed explanation of the objectives; a joint briefing was scheduled for September.

On 18 September 1996, however, just prior to the scheduled briefing, a North Korean submarine of the 325-ton Shark-class infiltrated South Korea's eastern coast, and crew members fled into the coastal mountains. The South Korean Defence Ministry took immediate action, mobilising 60 000 troops to hunt down the intruders. The massive operation lasted for more than six weeks. Of the 25 North Koreans on the submarine, 11 were killed, 13 wounded, and one was captured. Thirteen South Korean soldiers and policemen were killed, as were four civilians, and more than a dozen soldiers were wounded during the intensive manhunt.

The South Korean government described the infiltration as 'a grave provocation'. President Kim Young Sam declared that this was proof of North Korea's desire to communize the South by force. 'What we have to realize is that North Koreans are impatient and feel they have to implement a plan to communize the South with arms,' he said.[28] He added that there was a 'real possibility of war ... In the worst case, we will have to resolve upon going to war'.[29] Demanding an apology from Pyongyang, Kim suspended all economic cooperation with the North, including participation in the Korean Peninsula Energy Development Organization (KEDO), which had been established under the 1994 Agreed Framework to provide North Korea with the light-water reactors. In his interview with *The Washington Post,* Kim also said that his government would not proceed with the four-party proposal until Pyongyang apologized.[30]

North Korea claimed that the submarine, which had been on a routine training mission, drifted into South Korean waters after encountering engine trouble, and demanded the return of the submarine and the remains of the dead. Angered by Seoul's criticism, the North threatened to make 'a hundred or a thousand fold retaliation'.[31] It also threatened to abandon the Agreed Framework and resume its nuclear programme if the South interfered with progress on the light reactor project.[32] The rising tensions led the UN Security Council to issue a statement that called on 'both sides of the Korean peninsula to settle their outstanding issues by peaceful means through dialogue'.[33] The issue was resolved when the North expressed 'deep regret' for the submarine incident on 29 December 1996. Although the announcement was 'short and had indirect expressions'–using 'regret' rather than 'apology'–Seoul accepted the vaguely worded confession.[34] Inter-Korean relations got back on track in 1997, but time had run out for President Kim to achieve any further diplomatic progress while in office.

2. Explanations

North Korea's actions in the midst of economic hardship, especially military demonstrations in the DMZ and the submarine incursion into South Korean waters, jeopardized its desperate appeal for food assistance and economic reform. Except for its offer of four-party talks in April, Seoul's unusually tough responses to these provocations exacerbated instability and tension. In particular, its suspension of all inter-Korean cooperation and refusal to continue participation in the KEDO could have incited Pyongyang to abandon the Agreed Framework, returning the peninsula to a nuclear crisis. Ultimately, the standoff was resolved with compromise. Seoul agreed with Washington's idea of four-party talks to solve the armistice issue diplomatically and accepted Pyongyang's apology regarding the submarine incident. This section will attempt to shed light on Pyongyang's motivations and perplexing timing, as well as the primary causes of Seoul's reactions. It will also examine the extent of Washington's influence and why the US acted as mediator.

A. The Security Dilemma

(1) Food aid policies: the controversy of food diversion to the military and the danger of preventive war

The main motivation behind the South's reluctance to help the North during its food shortage was a concern that the aid provided would not reach the North's hungry, but instead be stored for the military. In December 1995, the Mainichi Shimbun, a Japanese newspaper, reported that rice had been diverted to feed the North Korean military, quoting sources in Seoul.[35] Foreign Minister Gong Ro-myung claimed that a substantial amount of food was being set aside, and that the North's food shortage was being exaggerated.[36] President Kim also expressed concern over food assistance to the North, announcing that most of the 150 000 tons of rice that South Korea had offered had been used to feed the military.[37] It was the first official confirmation that the military was the major beneficiary of Seoul's food aid to the North. After the North Korean submarine incident in September 1996, the South Korean embassy in Washington organized a campaign in the US to counteract NGO lobbying for Washington to give generous food aid to North Korea, believing that any famine assistance would only be diverted to military rations.[38] Pyongyang's military incursion and the ensuing clash may have intensified South Koreans' security sensitivity. Officials in the US Defense Department and the NSC also expressed concern, and members of Congress claimed that the food aid being sent to North Korea was provisioning the country's military.[39]

In keeping with governmental apprehensions, many South Korean civilian agencies produced reports stating that the North was storing a substantial amount of rice for the military at a time of millions of famine deaths.[40] North Korean Ko Jun, who defected to the South in July 1996, was reported to have said: 'I witnessed three 10 meter-deep military warehouses filled with piles of rice bags from South Korea in my county of Yangdok, while residents still suffered from food shortage.'[41] Another defector, An Yong Kil, who had worked at the Rear Area Food Control Bureau of the Ministry of the People's Armed Forces, said that the North Korean Army was saving enough rice to sustain war for 170 days.[42]

Given these reports and official remarks, it seems clear that concerns about how food aid would be appropriated played a role in hardening the South Korean government's policy. It is not clear, however, whether its intentions were purely defensive. There may have been a motivation to exploit the situation, opportunistically weakening the North's war-fighting capacity or even precipitating regime collapse.[43] President Kim had long been ambivalent about North Korea. On one hand, he had tried to help Pyongyang, repeatedly rejecting the idea of absorption strategy.[44] On the other hand, he often justified hard-line policies on the grounds that Kim Jong Il's regime was collapsing and time was on South Korea's side.[45] The offensive desire to exploit an adversary and the defensive motivation to enhance security are not necessarily contradictory. In the zero-sum situation on the Korean peninsula, the existence of one was viewed as a threat to the other. Therefore, no action could be purely defensive or offensive, and any South Korean attempt to weaken Pyongyang's war-fighting capacity would have been intertwined with its fear of the North.[46]

It is not clear to what extent security concerns alone accounted for the South's food aid policy, but its stance was undoubtedly dangerous and counterproductive. The 'preventive war' theory propounds that a country suffering worsening inferiority in military and economic capabilities vis-á-vis the adversary over time may decide to initiate a war if it concludes that war now is better than war later.[47] In such a situation, maintaining the status quo means future defeat.[48] This logic seems to have been relevant on the peninsula, given Pyongyang's growing fear of extinction-through-absorption.[49] During the food crisis, the Kim Jong Il regime likely felt especially insecure, faced as it was by both internal instability and external threat. In his speech to party cadres in December 1996 at Kim Il Sung University, Kim Jong Il expressed a certain unease about the loyalty of the military. He said the 'food problem is creating a state of anarchy', possibly alluding to a failed coup at Hamheung the previous year.[50] He also argued that the military was suffering from such serious food supply problems that the US might be encouraged to take advantage of the situation and launch an attack.[51]

Korea watchers in Washington and Seoul energetically deliberated how and when the Pyongyang regime would fall. One US official said to reporters in December 1995, speaking on condition of anonymity, 'We continue to see anecdotal evidence of some civil discontent.'[52] Harvard University professor Ezra Vogel, who had worked at the CIA as an Asia specialist during the Clinton administration, also remarked that Pyongyang could collapse in the next two or three years.[53] Concern grew that Pyongyang, threatened by domestic instability, might be compelled to advance south.[54] Gary E. Luck, US Commander-in-chief in Korea, told a congressional hearing in March 1996 that 'the question is not will this country disintegrate, but how will it disintegrate: by implosion or explosion'.[55] Watching the North's unusual 'total mobilization' exercises in spring 1997, Luck's successor General Tilelli was also deeply concerned that circumstances in the North might compel the regime to seek a military solution.[56]

Pyongyang was probably aware of the dire prospects of military action against US–ROK alliance forces.[57] Nonetheless, with no other choice but to wait for collapse, it was certainly a possibility that Pyongyang might instigate a war out of preventive motivations. Choi Ju-hwal, a former North Korean army colonel and the highest-ranking military officer to defect to the South, said that while Pyongyang was not convinced that it could win a war against South Korea, it would attempt one if faced with a grave enough political and economic crisis.[58] Seoul was aware of such possible preventive measures of on the part of North Korea. 'Our concern is that because of their desperation and frustration, they may start on a course of adventurous military provocation,' said President Kim.[59] Yet some of South Korea's policies encouraged Pyongyang's preventive thinking. It could thus be said that Seoul's security-based actions ironically worsened its security status by facilitating the possibility of military confrontation.

(2) The Armistice issue: Pyongyang's new peace treaty offensive

Pyongyang's DMZ provocation in April 1996 was part of a more extended effort to undermine the armistice mechanism.[60] North Korea had essentially nullified the Military Armistice Commission (MAC) by withdrawing its delegates on 28 April 1994, and had also successfully persuaded China to recall its delegates on 15 December.[61] Initially, Beijing did not accede to Pyongyang's request to withdraw Chinese delegates, as it was concerned about the destabilizing effects that undermining the armistice mechanism would have on the Korean peninsula.[62] Faced with continued appeals from Pyongyang, however, China finally agreed to recall its representatives. The dispatch of Vice-Minister Song Ho-gyong, on 1 September, as the special envoy to meet Tang Jiaxuan, China's Vice-Minister of Foreign Affairs, and Qian Qichen, the Minister of Foreign Affairs, was one example of Pyongyang's concerted efforts to persuade Beijing.[63] On 28 February 1995, Pyongyang paralysed the Neutral Nations Supervisory Commission (NNSC), another key feature of the armistice mechanism, by forcing the Polish delegates to leave North Korea.[64] Such unilateral actions effectively impaired these two bodies, and were part of a plan to replace the current armistice agreement with a bilateral peace treaty between North Korea and the United States.[65]

Why did Pyongyang attempt to undermine the armistice system and replace it with a new treaty? Taking account of the critical role the US played on the peninsula, the North probably believed that the establishment of a new peace mechanism through direct dealings with Washington was essential to regime survival. The United States, North Korea's most threatening opponent, was also the only country capable of providing the means for survival. The American control of South Korean forces during wartime may have further convinced Pyongyang that Washington was the only partner worth negotiating with.[66]

More importantly, North Korea may have reasoned that the process of transforming the armistice into a new peace pact and the attendant dismantlement of the United Nations Command (UNC) would assist in raising the issue of US forces in Korea. Unlike Pyongyang's official position, however, it is not clear whether the North was pursuing a total withdrawal of US forces from South Korea. Off the record, key North Korean officials often admitted that a total pull out of US troops was not expected.[67] General Ri Chan Bok, the North Korean representative at Panmunjom, also explicitly stated that Pyongyang would not bring up the issue if the armistice and the UN Command were dismantled:[68]

> It's clear from the Asian strategy of the United States that the US Army will not pull out tomorrow. It will take a long time. Accordingly, we will set up a new peace mechanism on the basis of a mutual understanding that US forces will continue to be stationed in Korea indefinitely.[69]

In his summit meeting with South Korean president Kim Dae Jung in June 2000, Kim Jong Il made it clear that US troops in Korea would be necessary to maintain regional balance even after the reunification of the peninsula, provided that their objective is to maintain the peace. When Kim Dae Jung asked why North Korea continued to demand the total withdrawal of the US troops, Kim Jong Il responded that this was propaganda for domestic politics.[70]

What form of American presence in Korea would the North accept, then? According to one South Korean analyst, a possible solution would be the dissolution of the UN Command, the conversion of some US ground forces into neutral peace-keeping forces, and the maintenance of some American garrison forces. This included combined planning level command forces, staff to receive and deploy reinforcements in an emergency situation, and one fighter wing from the 7th air force.[71] This view argues that the North's demands included a reduction in the number of troops, and a shift in the US's role from hostile force to more neutral and balanced participant.[72]

While North Korea's genuine intentions may not be clear in these remarks, it is certain that it wished to move relations with Washington into a more neutral or friendly realm. Given that the North had virtually lost its traditional allies of Russia and China, the existence of the UN Command, which continues to brand North Korea 'an aggressor' in its 1951 resolution, may no longer have been acceptable.[73] Once in motion, negotiations for replacing the Armistice with a peace treaty with the US would raise many critical issues, including a lifting of economic sanctions, diplomatic normalization, and American troop withdrawal. The military provocation in the DMZ during April 1996 may thus be seen as Pyongyang's projected effort to force the US into negotiations to replace the armistice with a peace treaty. The day after the DMZ provocation, the Clinton administration acknowledged that the moves seemed to be motivated by political, rather than military, considerations.[74]

But if the North's actions were so obviously political in origin, why did Seoul react so vehemently? First of all, replacing the armistice agreement would have had a negative impact on the deployment of US or UN reinforcements during an emergency. As its replacement would entail an inevitable dissolution of the UN Command, restrictions might be imposed on the use of US bases in Japan. American forces are allowed the free utilization of six main bases in Japan– located at Yokota, Jama, Sasebo, Futenma, and White Beach–in accordance with the 'Acheson-Yoshida exchanged document', which agrees to provide Japanese facilities and services to all nations participating in UN operations on the Korean peninsula. Since the Japanese obligation to provide bases would terminate 90 days before the withdrawal of UN forces, dissolution of the UNC might affect American military operations. In addition, its dismantlement would have negative diplomatic implications for Korean defence. In the case of an emergency on the peninsula, those UN nations which participated in the Korean War can become immediately involved without a renewed UN resolution. If the UNC were dismantled, however, another dispatch of multinational forces would require a new Security Council resolution in accordance with UN Chapter 7; this would obviously prolong the process.[75]

Some South Koreans held a simpler interpretation of the North's demand. They felt that this was a malicious scheme to communize the South by dissolving the current military structure.[76] The Arms Control Bureau of the South Korean Defence Ministry, which was in charge of the Armistice issue, wrote in its internal document: 'North Korea's intention behind the 'US–North Korea peace treaty' is to dismantle the UNC, withdraw US forces, and ultimately communize the Korean peninsula.'[77] The majority of South Koreans viewed the North's ultimate goal to be the withdrawal of US troops and the estrangement of relations between Seoul and Washington.[78]

The South Korean Defence Ministry noted that North Korea first proposed a peace treaty with the US in 1974, the year after the Paris Peace Agreement between the US and North Vietnam. This agreement, which eventually led to the communization of Vietnam, stipulated the total withdrawal of foreign troops.[79] The Ministry argued that, should the American presence be redefined as a 'peace-keeping' force, the US–ROK alliance would be weakened.[80] In this light, Seoul may have found it necessary to respond as strongly as possible, upgrading the Watch-con status to demonstrate its firm resolve. Pyongyang's attempts to guarantee its own survival by undermining the Armistice had only invited heightened tensions. If South Korea had not been affected by security fears, it might have responded more diplomatically, such as sending a verbal warning while coordinating its stance with Washington.

(3) Submarine incursion: intelligence gap and war-reconnaissance

In response to the submarine incursion, the South suspended all inter-Korean cooperation projects, including the KEDO established by the nuclear deal in October 1994. Such an extreme measure reflected a genuine fear that Pyongyang was still contemplating a military solution to Korean reunification. Kwon Yong Hae, the head of the South Korean intelligence agency, said that the submarine was on a 'major mission', as its on-board officers were all second lieutenants or higher, and included the head of the People's Armed Forces Reconnaissance Bureau's maritime section.[81] General Park Yong-ok, the Assistant Defence Minister, suggested that the plan may have been to set up an armed hideout in the mountains, where future terrorist attacks could be prepared.[82] 'It was not purely an intelligence mission,' he said. The only surviving captive, a 31-year-old captain named Li Kwang Su, upheld Seoul's claim when he confessed that the mission was to 'destroy military installations and create disturbances as part of preparation for war'.[83]

The submarine equipment and the light weaponry of the crew suggested a more moderate interpretation of the mission, however. No heavy weapons or hand grenades appropriate to the alleged sabotage were found. The submarine contained only a few rolls of films and camera equipment.[84] One analyst at the Korea Defence Intelligence Agency (KDIA) later said that the mission was to gather intelligence on the Kangnung air base and radar facilities.[85]

Nevertheless, the mission was replete with negative strategic implications for Seoul.[86] It was possible to interpret such a special military reconnaissance operation as an indication of a war preparation effort, even if it was impossible to tell how imminent that war was.[87] In this light, Ministry of Defence spokesman Yoon Chang-ro said: 'North Korea aimed to map out plans for possible large–scale armed provocations and to test infiltration methods using submarines.'[88] Given the detailed military maps of South Korea and the rolls of film found in the submarine, the Joint Chiefs of Staff agreed that the mission appeared to be associated with revising a war plan.[89] Unable to rule out such an ominous possibility, South Korea had to take a firm stance, regardless of its impact on inter-Korean relations. Furthermore, this event revealed South Korea's vulnerability to infiltration, and seriously impaired the self-confidence of its military.[90] The navy had failed to detect the submarine and the Army had struggled to capture the commandos, taking more than six weeks and the lives of seventeen South Korean soldiers and civilians. North Korea was believed to have nearly 100 000 special operation forces (SOF), whose assigned mission was to infiltrate the rear area of the South at the beginning of a war. South Korea's Defence Ministry, which had focused on front-line warfare, was compelled to revise its military doctrine to emphasize the early detection of infiltrators.[91]

Although it is difficult to discern Pyongyang's intention, it is important to note the substantial intelligence capability gap between North and South Korea. South Korea has enjoyed access to sophisticated intelligence capabilities: American reconnaissance satellites and U-2 aircraft, as well as many other advanced intelligence aircraft and ground equipment, have gathered information on any significant North Korean military movements. This data is then sent to the Korean Combat Operations Intelligence Centre (KCOIC) and the Combined Analysis Control Centre (CACC), where real-time analysis on the movements is conducted.[92] North Korea, apparently lacking such technical capability, had no choice but to rely on human intelligence.[93] The desire to obtain military information on one's adversary could be either offensive or defensive in orientation. Even without the intent to initiate war, a country might seek to collect intelligence on its enemy through whatever means available, as is the case for North Korea.

There is a possibility that the motivation behind the submarine incident was not offensive, and such an interpretation could have yielded a less hard-line response from Seoul. Nevertheless, Pyongyang's attempt to reduce the intelligence gap, whether offensive or defensive, appeared threatening to the South. As has been illustrated, Seoul could not rule out the possibility that the submarine was sent for 'war-reconnaissance aimed at an all-out attack against South Korea'.[94] Had Seoul not been led through its security fears to a worst-case scenario, its reaction would have been more moderate, and circumstances would not have developed as they did. This episode, then–the submarine infiltration, Seoul's negative interpretation, and the interactions that followed–was another reminder that the 'security dilemma', once provoked, could still aggravate relations on the peninsula.

B. Domestic Politics

(1) Seoul's reactions: political pressure and manipulation of the North Korean threat

As might be suspected, Seoul's resistance to food aid, its harsh reactions to the DMZ provocation, and its response to the submarine incident were all fuelled to some degree by domestic political interests. In June 1995, President Kim declared that his government was willing to provide 150 000 tons of rice, with more aid to come. 'If our reserves are not enough, we will buy rice from foreign countries ... We have the money to do that,' he said.[95] But this enthusiasm quickly disappeared after a series of hostile North Korean actions. As a South Korean ship transporting rice entered a port in the North, local DPRK officials forced it to hoist the North Korean flag. Although Pyongyang later apologized, the incident infuriated the South Korean public and resulted in a three day suspension of the second rice shipment.[96] Later, another South Korean rice transporting ship was detained on charges of 'reconnaissance'.[97] As a result, Seoul's position on food aid hardened.[98]

Furthermore, a crushing defeat of Kim Young Sam's ruling party in local elections on 27 June 1995 seems to have stimulated a reconsideration of the administration's aid to Pyongyang. Many political analysts attributed the defeat to the government's policy–its excessive generosity and Pyongyang's impudent ingratitude enraged the South Korean public, costing the ruling party 'millions of votes'.[99] Three days after the election, the ruling party analysed the defeat and concluded that its major causes included the food aid policy towards North Korea, insufficient reform and the party's internal conflict.[100] Emergency measures were recommended to the president, and the ruling party raised its voice for strong opposition to unconditional food aid during policy consultations with the cabinet. Pressured by public discontent and the party's demand, Kim decided to adjust his policy.

Electoral politics also seem to have affected Seoul's response to the DMZ provocation. The North's violation of the Armistice agreement came just one week before the South Korean parliamentary election on 11 April 1996, and the ruling party successfully exploited it. Financial scandals involving presidential aides had left the ruling New Korea Party (NKP) trailing the opposing National Council for New Politics (NCNP) in opinion polls. However, the DMZ incident underscored the reality of the Northern threat and strengthened voter turnout for Kim's party.[101] Election analysts concluded that the provocation had boosted the electorate's support of the ruling party by more than 15 per cent, substantially contributing to their victory.[102]

Did the government deliberately manipulate the North's military moves to gain ground in the incipient election? Many of the South Korean Defence Ministry's actions suggest that Seoul's response was not purely security-based. The upgrade of Watchcon status from 3 to 2 appears disproportionate and an over-reaction. Watchcon 2 was designed for a situation when 'the enemy's threat and attack symptoms are substantial'. American and South Korean forces had maintained Watchcon 3 for the last 15 years, and even when tensions had peaked–during the North's announcement of its NPT withdrawal, the subsequent nuclear confrontation, or Kim Il Sung's death–Watchcon 2 had never been declared.

The USFK (US Forces in Korea) position suggested that the upgrade of Watchcon status was not fully supported by the US Jim Colls, spokesman of the US Forces in Korea, hinted that there was apparent disagreement between the two nations over the issue:

> South Korean media said that Watchcon was upgraded from 3 into 2, but it was announced by the South Korean government. We never announced such a measure, using [a] concrete number, although we can say that level of WatchCon was raised ... We didn't have to take any extra measures because of the North's action in the DMZ ...[103]

The US never increased US reconnaissance airplanes or dispatched intelligence teams to South Korea, measures necessary to the Watchcon 2 status.

When Kim Dae Jung took office, an official investigation on whether Kim Young Sam's administration had exaggerated the DMZ incident for political purposes was conducted. It found that most of the suspicions were true, providing ample illustration of how the situation had been exploited by the president and ruling party.[104] According to the October 1999 report, as leaked to the monthly magazine *Shin Dong-A,* the presidential office of Kim Young Sam and the Defence Ministry distorted the incident and systematically exaggerated it for political advantage.[105] It claimed: 'The Presidential Office, the Defence Ministry, and the Joint Chiefs of Staff created a sense of fear and tension among the public who did not know the very nature of the incident and situation, as if North Korea were about to wage a war, and they used it for the 15th parliamentary election.' According to the report, manipulation began on 6 April when National Security Adviser You Jong Ha made a phone call to Kim Dong Shin, Chief Directorate of Operations, ordering a media briefing. Then General Kim and several auxiliary officers, all wearing military combat gear, held a press conference that provided the headline in most newspapers the following morning.

The report also claimed that Chairman of the Joint Chiefs of Staff Kim Dong Jin unduly pressured his subordinate officers to make their evaluation more severe. The Joint Chiefs of Staff's initial judgment was that 'North Korea's intention is to nullify the Armistice agreement and achieve a direct military channel with the US,' adding that its military action 'was a recurrence of past demonstrative action. Despite a slim chance of military provocation, close attention is desirable'.[106] The Chairman disputed this judgment, and replaced an officer after their meeting. The position then dramatically reversed, saying that 'North Korean troops in the DMZ are very hostile and bellicose, having a history of killing American soldiers with axes in 1976. The possibility of military provocation is seriously high, thereby requiring a tight level of military preparedness.'[107]

Domestic politics were also at play in Seoul's response to the submarine incident. Regardless of its mission, the large number of casualties inflicted on South Korean forces and civilians created a great deal of popular antagonism. Faced with this hardened view, the South Korean government may have been compelled to act so staunchly that inter-Korean relations were damaged.[108] Moreover, President Kim, becoming an increasingly lame duck, used the incident to build a consensus between the ruling and opposition parties and raise public support for him and his administration.[109] 'Politically, it's a way for Kim Young Sam to maintain tension and authority to prevent himself from becoming a lame duck,' argued Michael Breen, a Seoul resident and North Korean expert and consultant.[110] Specifically, Kim courted political leaders from both parties and managed to garner 'supra-partisan support to help the administration overcome the current crisis'.[111] The opposition party had planned to use parliamentary inspections to attack the Kim administration on issues like economic mismanagement,[112] but the submarine incursion left the plan substantively nullified.[113] At the same time, presidential candidates had to restrain their political moves in the wake of the call for nationwide unity, and calls for the nomination of a presidential candidate in the ruling party were considerably subdued.[114] President Kim's control over his party strengthened.[115] In all possibility, the domestic political rationale of President Kim and his ruling party served as an impetus for the South Korean government's North Korea policy.

(2) The timing of North Korea's provocations

One of the puzzles surrounding these events was the seemingly inconsistent and incompatible behaviour of the North. During the second half of 1995, Pyongyang initiated its unusual military actions, including large-scale exercises and the deployment of aircraft and other heavy weaponry along the frontline, jeopardising emergency food aid from the South and other countries. Furthermore, its public rejection of the Armistice Agreement and subsequent armed incursion into the DMZ in April 1996 came only a week after a request to the UN for 'urgent' food aid.

The timing of such behaviour has perplexed many analysts. The Pyongyang regime surely knew that any military tension on the peninsula would operate in favour of the conservative party in South Korea.[116] It seems rather paradoxical that North Korea would coordinate such risky military actions with the South's election.[117] Coupling such dubious timing with the South's deliberate exaggeration has led some analysts to describe inter-Korean relations as 'antagonistic interdependence.'[118] In other words, despite the public condemnation, leaders in both nations sometimes need confrontation and tension to succeed politically. In this instance, the gain in Seoul was an electoral victory by the ruling party. In Pyongyang, Kim Jong Il might have needed a certain level of tension to consolidate his power base.

The submarine incident occurred on 18 September 1996, just prior to the scheduled joint briefing session on the four-party talks, and substantially damaged inter-Korean relations and Pyongyang's efforts to get out of economic trouble and diplomatic isolation. In particular, it also coincided with 'the Forum for the Promotion of Foreign Investment' held from 13th to 15th of September to foster foreign interest in the Rajin-Sonbong Free Economic and Trade Zone (FETZ).[119] The forum was critical in boosting the interests of foreign investment, and the North Korean team had exerted great efforts for its success, advertising the event abroad for the previous two years. Pyongyang's hopes to attract large-scale foreign investment, however, ended unsatisfactorily–its initial goal was $3 US billion in new contracts with foreign entrepreneurs, but only $840 million was obtained.[120] The biggest setback to South Korean investors was the poor state of North–South Korean relations,[121] while the North's military provocations made potential foreign investors, already cautious of the North's poor Social Overhead Capital (SOC) facilities, more reluctant to invest in this politically and militarily unstable region.[122] Why, then, would Pyongyang send the submarine on 14 September, in the middle of the Rajin–Sonbong forum?

One possible explanation is that there might have been internal strife between hard-liners and pragmatists as to the right direction for North Korea. Despite opposition from ideologues, pragmatists were advocating reform and an open door policy to assist with solving the structural problems of the socialist economy. Chairman of the Committee on External Relations Kim Jong U, who was in charge of the Rajin–Sonbong project, was a leading figure in this group. Kim had superseded the limited role technical specialists held in North Korean politics by using personal ties to Kim Jong Il and his family.[123] In fact, Kim Il Sung had begun to pave the way for such reform before his death. In his 1994 New Year address, he indicated that there would be a shift in policy emphasis from heavy industry to agriculture, light industry and trade. The Rajin–Sonbong project was initiated during his rule, and received his personal support. The pragmatism of Kim Jong Il's regime seems to be part of Kim Il Sung's legacy in North Korean politics.

At the same time, however, the clout of the military was growing. Since Kim Il Sung's death, high-ranking military officers had been elevated in the official hierarchy of North Korea. Top generals were listed ahead of some full Politburo members, and, while prior to Kim Il Sung's death vice-marshal level leaders were ranked below 77th in the standing, upon his death they were rapidly promoted to assume ranks between 19th and 26th.[124] This ascent placed the vice-marshal level above the deputy prime minister of the Administration.[125] Most of Kim Jong Il's public appearances were visits to military units, another indicator that he was soliciting the loyalty of the armed forces.[126] The anniversary of the founding of the Workers Party was feted with a large scale military parade, and defence minister Choe Kwang made the keynote address at an event that had previously been non-military in character.[127] The Cabinet and Supreme People's Assembly lost their roles, and it was speculated that the National Defence Commission (NDC) was operating as a kind of interim government, making virtually all the important decisions.[128] Under Kim Il Sung, the military had enjoyed an honoured but subordinate position in North Korean politics,[129] but under his son it appeared that the traditional balance between the armed forces, the party and the government had shifted towards the military.

The rise of the military and its concomitant rivalry with pragmatists might have been the background for the untimely military provocations. Choe Kwang, Minister of the People's Armed forces, Kim Young-chun, Chief of the General Staff, Cho Myong-nok, director of the General Political Bureau, and air force commander O Kum-chol, all of whom received their position during the personnel reshuffle of Kim Jong Il in the summer of 1995, were hard-liners known to be in charge of the abnormal military moves in December 1995.[130] For the three years following Kim Il Sung's death, the debate over opening the country for foreign investment seemingly intensified. It was even carried out in the Party's official publications and theoretical journals. On 10 May 1996, the Party newspaper *Nodong Shinmun* attacked the pragmatists, warning 'the revisionists in the leadership positions are actually hurting the supreme leader by derailing the socialist road towards the abandonment of the revolution as if they were pretending to support the supreme leader'. A week later, on 17 May, the same paper stressed: 'we have nothing to open or to be opened.'

Such distinct political polarities led some analysts to become increasingly suspicious of the traditional view that North Korea was pursuing a single national interest under the control of an absolute ruler.[131] Rather, various elites from the military, politburo and administration might be competing and bargaining over important national issues. The South Korean presidential office also raised the possibility of ongoing internal conflict, as Kim Jong Il did not appear to have full control of his regime.[132]

On the other hand, the classic example of implementation failure can be taken as another explanation of the North's inconsistent behaviour during this period. Unlike the previous illustrations of bureaucratic strife, this explanation does not have to assume an insufficiency of central control; even if a leader is in absolute control, his officials could still produce conflicting policies at the implementation stage. One reason is an uncertainty about orders.[133] Presidential decisions often lack specificity, conveying only general directions without specifying when they should be executed or how they should be performed. As Morton Halperin has argued, based on his observation of American presidents, the leader seldom makes a single comprehensive decision covering a wide range of interrelated issues.[134] Rather, he responds to a series of issues discretely, each on its own merits, yielding a series of diffuse and even contradictory instructions to the bureaucracy about what should be done.

In the case of North Korea, according to the testimony of defector Ko Young-hwan, who worked for the North Korean Ministry of Foreign Affairs, the North determined diplomatic action through written instructions from Kim Jong Il.[135] Every Saturday morning, diplomats received Kim's instructions and returned to their bureau, where they discussed how to implement them. It was often difficult to enact these orders, as many were quite unspecific. In addition, Kim Jong Il's personal character and governing style might have impeded the coordination of economic, diplomatic, and military objectives. North Korean defectors and South Koreans who have spoken with him and observed his behaviour consistently point out that Kim Jong Il feels uncomfortable in public and prefers to deal with a small circle of associates.[136] He does not deliver a New Year's message, and likes to keep people guessing. Unlike his father, Kim Jong Il dislikes the sort of large, official meetings wherein more coherent policies can be made. He relies instead on a small cabinet composed of friends and family.[137] Even in these meetings, he receives separate reports and makes separate decisions regarding the various functional groups of North Korean government.[138] In this light, it is possible to speculate that the Rajin–Sonbong foreign investment forum and the submarine incursion were both approved by Kim Jong Il, then implemented by different bureaucratic groups according to their own judgement. If this was the case, Pyongyang's poorly coordinated behaviour during this period might have stemmed from intrinsic implementation problems, and have been further aggravated by Kim's peculiar governing style.

C. US influence

Discussion will now turn to the role played by the US in resolving tensions, including an overview of the Clinton administration's North Korean and Asian policy and its domestic political circumstances. Although China also contributed to easing tensions to some extent, this section will focus on the role of the US In terms of shaping developments, Beijing's role seems limited to its influence on Pyongyang, while Washington affected both North and South Korean behaviour through active engagement.[139]

(1) Washington's role in restraining Seoul
During this period, the United States adopted quite a different position on North Korea from Seoul, one rooted in a divergence from its ally on how to evaluate stability on the peninsula and what should be done to reduce potential dangers. Washington found North Korea to be an increasingly vulnerable and isolated regime that needed incentives for accommodation. On the other hand, Seoul continued to possess a no-tolerance mentality vis-à-vis Pyongyang, and its North Korean policy was often more rigid than Washington's.[140] This difference strained US–ROK relations, and created a great deal of distrust between the

two.[141] In terms of mitigating potentially dangerous interactions between the Koreas, however, Washington's mollification of Seoul's hard-line position certainly prevented further aggravation.

Regarding food aid to North Korea, Washington was more willing to assist Pyongyang than Seoul. On 13 January 1996, the South Korean government requested National Security Adviser Anthony Lake that the US be prudent about food aid to North Korea.[142] When senior diplomats from the US, Japan and South Korea met in Honolulu on 24 January to coordinate their assistance to Pyongyang, they failed to concur on how and when aid would be given.[143] Assistant Secretary of State for East Asian and Pacific Affairs Winston Lord, the American representative at the meeting, implied a substantial gap between his government and that of South Korea. 'The basic theme was the need for coordination,' he said at a post-meeting press conference. 'But does that mean the three sovereign countries, with their own national interest[s], don't have a certain degree of tactical differences at times? Of course not.'[144] Despite Seoul's objection, Washington decided in February to donate $2 million to a U.N. food assistance program, while simultaneously attempting to soothe South Korean concerns by portraying the decision as a largely 'symbolic and humanitarian gesture'.[145]

Despite its donations, human rights NGOs criticized the US government for not responding to the North Korean famine seriously enough. It does, in fact, seem true that not until the summer of 1997 did the US make any aid commitments commensurate to the severity of the crisis.[146] Several factors contributed to this initial constraint. The first was the bureaucratic inertia of four decades of hostility between the US and North Korea. The Defense Department was particularly reluctant to feed a hostile country, and repeatedly expressed concerns that the food would be diverted for military purposes.[147] The Central Intelligence Agency (CIA) and the Defense Intelligence Agency (DIA) were also reluctant to help, and often dismissed the State Department's reports of the crisis as an attempt by Pyongyang to obtain aid.[148] Assistance was further hindered by the decision to use food aid as a diplomatic carrot for inducing North Korea's participation in the four-party talks.

Nevertheless, the US recognized the risk posed by a sudden collapse of the North Korean government. Assistant Secretary Lord said in this regard: 'North Korea's food shortage threatens [an] 18-month long peace process on the peninsula obtained from the nuclear freeze.'[149] The US certainly endeavoured to stabilize the Pyongyang regime through food assistance despite adamant objection from Seoul, although the amount supplied was insufficient.

US policy also seems to have been vital in the midst of the DMZ incident. The US proposal for four-party talks was the first point at which Seoul showed a willingness to actively deal with Pyongyang's peace initiative in an international setting. Seoul had long held that constructing a new peace was a strictly Korean matter, but Washington's influence apparently played a role in the South's more flexible attitude. Although Clinton and Kim made the four-party talks proposal together in their joint communique, Kim was 'very reluctant to support the idea' behind the scenes.[150] Clinton's decision to postpone any visits to South Korea until Kim agreed to four-party talks, however, left him no choice but to cede.[151]

If precedent held true, diplomacy with the American president would boost the Korean leaders' support at home. Clinton had visited Seoul in 1993 and had hosted Kim in Washington twice, in 1993 and 1995.[152] In April 1996, however, with no agreement from Seoul on the four-party issue, Clinton scheduled a trip to Japan without allocating time to stop in Korea.[153] Given that American presidents typically visited while travelling to neighbouring countries, Clinton's bypass of Seoul could have been interpreted as a sign of Washington's ill-regard for President Kim. Such a revelation could make the Kim administration vulnerable to domestic criticism of a rift in US–South Korean relations. Furthermore, Clinton's scheduled visit to Japan on 17 April was just five days after South Korea's nationwide parliamentary election, and opposition leader Kim Dae Jung raised the issue of the snub, criticising President Kim for his mismanagement of relations with Washington. He argued: 'Due to strained US–South Korean relations, President Clinton is not scheduled to drop by South Korea while he is visiting Japan and Russia.'[154] The Kim administration thus agreed on a four-party formula, and Kim arranged a meeting with Clinton on 16 April, five days after his party's victory in the National Assembly election.[155]

The submarine incident revealed greater dissension between Washington and Seoul, and their respective position vis-à-vis North Korea. On the day of the incursion, the Clinton administration refused to define it as a military provocation. The State Department instead asked open-ended questions as to the submarine's mission and the cause of the crew members' death. Secretary of State Christopher urged 'all parties' to avoid further provocations. This statement infuriated South Korean officials.[156]

Despite Seoul's resentment of the US's even-handed stance, the resolution of tensions surrounding the event owed a great deal to Washington's diplomatic efforts. In the face of Seoul's strong demand for a North Korean apology and Pyongyang's outright rejection, American officials were actively involved with both parties to facilitate compromise. Following his visit to Seoul on 10-12 October, Assistant Secretary of State for East Asian and Pacific affairs Winston Lord held a secret meeting in Beijing with Yi Hyong-chol, director-general of the American Affairs Bureau at the North Korean Foreign Ministry, where they discussed the light-water reactor project and the submarine incident apology.[157] On October 24, Yi Hyong-chol was in New York for another meeting with State Department officials, including Mark Minton, head of the Korean desk.[158] Three days later, Deputy Assistant Secretary of State Charles Kartman flew to Seoul for talks with South Korean officials on the New York meeting.[159] The next month, representative Bill Richardson reportedly held high-level dialogues with influential North Koreans, including Vice Foreign Minister Kang Sok-chu, to discuss the issue of four-party talks and other US-North Korean matters.[160]

In December, after three months of active American involvement, Seoul began to relax its position, and finally accepted 'deep regret' rather than direct 'apology'.[161] The wording was carefully negotiated between North Korea and the United States, and was designed to meet Seoul's minimum requirements for resuming cooperation with the North. The South Korean government had found it increasingly difficult to maintain its position in the face of Washington's determination to engage Pyongyang.[162] President Clinton welcomed the apology, calling it a 'significant development, which I hope will contribute to the reduction of tensions on the Korean peninsula'.[163] The *New York Times* praised the Clinton administration for 'an impressive diplomatic triumph'.[164] In sum, US engagement policy was a vital component in reducing tensions vis-à-vis the North Korean food crisis, the DMZ provocation and the submarine incursion.

(2) US engagement strategy and domestic politics of the Clinton administration

What were the US's motives in pursuing its engagement policy to the extent it did, creating tensions in its alliance with South Korea? First, Washington acknowledged it had important interests in both Koreas. In the post-Cold War era, and especially after the nuclear deal with Pyongyang in 1994, Washington wanted to maintain its new relationship with the North in order to manage nuclear proliferation and eventually to seek new security arrangements on the peninsula.[165] The Clinton administration had other interests in maintaining a good working relationship with Pyongyang as well, including the North's long-range missiles and the return of American soldiers missing in action from the Korean War.[166] Furthermore, Washington feared that the Agreed Framework was vulnerable to political pressure and regional tensions if a broader framework addressing the fundamental sources of tension on the peninsula was not outlined.[167] In this light, the American government pressed the Kim administration to accept the four-party talks, and called for restraint from both Seoul and Pyongyang.[168]

Washington's North Korean strategy was termed 'the soft-landing policy'. As North Korea declined into a position of greater unrest, refugees, and even military provocation, the Clinton administration came to believe that the regime should not be pushed further into a corner.[169] It felt that aggravating North Korea would threaten the stability of the peninsula and Northeast Asia, and hurt American interests in the region. Leading advocates of this policy included Winston Lord and James Laney, the US ambassador to South Korea, who cogently expressed the strategy in his address 'Beyond Deterrence'.[170]

The soft-landing approach should be understood in the context of Clinton's regional strategy. During much of his first term, the president had been widely faulted for the absence of sustained high-level attention to and clarity in Asian policy.[171] With a lack of coherent foreign policy, escalating tensions over Taiwan, trade, and human rights often stymied advances in US–Sino relations.[172] Faced with growing trade deficits with Japan and the aftermath of the trade dispute, the Clinton administration had also strained relations with Tokyo.[173] However, the Clinton administration soon learned that US-Sino relations were not simply about trade, technology, or the promotion of human rights.[174] Recognizing their strategic importance, the administration sought a comprehensive partnership with Beijing and renewed its efforts.[175] With the trade imbalance narrowing and growing concerns in Washington and Tokyo about political and security relations between the US and Japan, the Clinton administration also sought to shore up the American–Japanese alliance.[176] The president visited Japan and signed a joint security declaration with Prime Minister Hashimoto, reaffirming the commitment of both countries to the maintenance of their robust alliance.

The administration's engagement policy was well expressed in the February 1996 National Security Strategy Report to Congress.[177] Noting that a new era was presenting the US with a complex set of new international challenges, the report stressed: 'US engagement is indispensable to the forging of stable political relations and open trade to advance our interests.' It also pointed to East Asia as 'a region of growing importance for US security and prosperity; nowhere are the strands of our three-pronged strategy more intertwined, nor is the need for continued US engagement more evident'. The Agreed Framework of October 1994 and the subsequent diplomatic efforts to implement it were, in a sense, an early product of this engagement policy.[178] In this light, the report refers to the Agreed Framework as 'a key element of our strategic commitment to the [Asian] region'.

The administration also had a political incentive to engage North Korea. The Agreed Framework was one of its few diplomatic achievements. Although it was not a major public issue, Clinton himself regarded his handling of the nuclear ambitions of North Korea as 'one of his major foreign policy successes'.[179] On the other hand, his opponent Bob Dole, the Republican presidential candidate, was attempting to use the nuclear deal with North Korea as an election issue, calling it a 'failed negotiation'.[180] A disruption of the deal and the reopening of nuclear danger on the Korean peninsula would have burdened Clinton's campaign. Likewise, any emergency situation in North Korea involving large numbers of refugees would embarrass the president in the midst of his campaigning.[181] Even in the face of Seoul's complaints, then, the Clinton administration pursued a soft-landing policy towards North Korea in both domestic politics and Asian strategy.

3. Conclusion

Even after the US–North Korean nuclear deal in October 1994, security problems continued to plague the Korean peninsula. This chapter identified three cases that seem most responsible for military tensions during this period: South Korea's policy towards the North Korean food crisis, Pyongyang's provocations in the DMZ and Seoul's military and diplomatic responses, and the incursion of a North Korean submarine into Southern waters and the reactions of South Korea and the US. The subsequent discussion attempted to explain the motivations behind them, as well as evaluating the impact of each on relations. Three factors–the security dilemma, domestic politics, and the participation of the US–were suggested as possible explanations.

The security dilemma perspective examined Seoul's reluctance to provide food aid to North Korea in terms of its fear: the food aid could be used for military purposes, strengthening North Korea's war capacity. Whether such a concern was legitimate or not, this perspective stressed that South Korea's objection to food aid could have made the North feel even more insecure and hopeless, compelling it to consider a military solution. Pyongyang's wish to guarantee its security was suggested as a main motivation behind the military initiatives in the DMZ and the effort to nullify the armistice regime. Seoul's decision to upgrade WatchCon status was explained in terms of its concern about a weakening of the American military's commitment to defend South Korea. The security dilemma was also used to inform the heightened tensions surrounding the submarine incident.

The investigation of domestic politics highlighted the defeat of South Korea's ruling party in a local election as a main contributor to Seoul's hardened position on food aid to the North. It was also suggested that the South Korean military, following the instructions of its political leaders, deliberately exaggerated the seriousness of the North's DMZ provocation. Internal politics was likewise proposed as being responsible for the bizarre timing of North Korea's actions, positing the possibility of internal strife between hard-liners and pragmatists or implementation failure stemming from a lack of clear and coherent objectives. From this perspective, Seoul's response to the submarine incident was rooted in President Kim's desire to retain the capacity to govern during his last year in office by maintaining tension with North Korea.

The final explanation stressed the diverging perceptions of Seoul and Washington with regards to North Korea, and the influence of American policy. The Clinton administration's engagement of North Korea contributed to stabilising the food crisis and helped find a way out of the standoff between Seoul and Pyongyang. This perspective also looked at the Clinton administration's strategic and domestic interests regarding the Korean peninsula and Northeast Asia.

Though each focuses on different aspects, these three approaches seem to assist collectively in constructing a broad view. But what role did each play in developing the situation? Whereas US involvement mitigated tensions, security concerns and domestic politics both produced hard-line policies that played destructive roles. It is imperative, then, to investigate which of these two factors more decisively elevated tensions, and how extensive the positive impact of US involvement was in a situation where both the security dilemma and domestic politics played such a negative role.

On the relative importance in explaining South Korea's behaviour, domestic politics seems to have been a more decisive factor than the security dilemma. Security concerns appear to have been relevant in all three cases–the concern of food diversion for military purposes was not only raised in Seoul but also in Washington repeatedly among military officers and conservative congressmen, and behind Seoul's firm response to Pyongyang's provocations was certainly a genuine fear about its intentions. Nonetheless, Seoul's behaviours were exaggerated and sometimes inconsistent, uneasily explained by the security dilemma.

Firstly, although the concern of food diversion for military purposes was legitimate, such a claim was not raised among high-level officials until the fall of 1995, by which time the South Korean public felt betrayed and angry at the North's ingratitude.[182] In the case of the DMZ incident, the upgrade of WatchCon level can be interpreted, by and large, as excessive. The US did not agree with the South Korean government's decision, doubting the necessity of such a measure. Furthermore, an investigation conducted by the Kim Dae Jung administration showed that the Kim Young Sam administration had utilized security matters for domestic political purposes, though that enquiry may have itself been politically motivated. It was also suspected that political motivations lay behind South Korea's response to the submarine incident.[183] In all three cases, therefore, domestic political considerations were operating under heightened tensions. While the security dilemma might afford a broad background for Seoul's actions, domestic political motivations account for its more immediate actions. Without them, Seoul's behaviour could have been more controlled, contributing to a more stable and manageable situation.

With respect to North Korea's DMZ provocation, the security logic seems to offer a better explanation than do domestic political factors. Given Pyongyang's appeal for food assistance, some may point to the perplexing timing of such aggravations as proof of a lack of central control. It is also possible to interpret this behaviour as an example of 'antagonistic interdependence' between North and South Korea, because Pyongyang provoked Seoul right before its election, contributing to a victory for the conservative ruling party. However, as far as the North Korean regime's survival was concerned, a security guarantee from the US and a new peace mechanism were more critical than anything else. North Korea had consistently pressed for establishing a new treaty to replace the armistice regime, an effort which continued even in the midst of a deteriorating economy. In other words, exploiting the DMZ provocation to press for the neutralization of the armistice and a new peace treaty reflected the major concerns of the entire North Korean regime, not just factional interests of its military authorities or hard-liners. Pyongyang may thus have justified its behaviour as necessary to achieve a peace mechanism involving the US, even if it did jeopardize its appeal for food aid.

Furthermore, 'antagonistic interdependence' seems rather irrelevant in the DMZ case. According to North Korean defectors Ko Yong Hwan and Hyun Seong Il, Kim Jong Il simply chose a perfect time to attract American attention.[184] When North Korea undertook this provocation, President Clinton was visiting Japan and was scheduled to visit South Korea next. The South Korean election, they argue, held nowhere near the importance of building a new peace with the US.

Regarding the timing of the submarine incursion, 'implementation failure' appears to be the most satisfactory interpretation. Conducting a reconnaissance mission on enemy territory is part of the military's duties, and it is unlikely that the highest North Korean authorities gave specific approval for the timing of an infiltration mission. It can thus be inferred that contradictory actions–implementing a dangerous military mission and preparing for four-party talks and holding an economic forum–could be undertaken simultaneously.

Considering the hints of factional struggle within the North Korean power structure, another possible interpretation is that the hawks undertook measures to counteract the pragmatists' reforms. Unlike the provocation in the DMZ, however, the disturbance inflicted by the submarine incident did not result from the mission itself but from its failure, caused by an unexpected engine breakdown. It is hardly conceivable that the North Korean military had designed the mission to fail, sacrificing its soldiers and high-level officers, in order to disrupt the pragmatists' agenda. Moreover, given the significant changes in South Korean military facilities, the unusually large scale of the operation, and the unprecedented inclusion of a high-ranking officer among its crew, it seems plain that the North Korean military authorities took the mission very seriously. While the motivation to send a submarine can be explained by security logic, then, the strange timing and lack of governmental coordination can be understood in the context of implementation failure.

With both the security dilemma and domestic politics so negatively impacting relations, how are we to interpret the influence of the United States? Despite the initial dangerous and unyielding confrontations, all three of the cases treated in this chapter were resolved through American-assisted compromise. Does the resolution of these standoffs imply that US involvement was more influential than security concerns or domestic politics? Were the US's contributions more significant than security and political factors in the development of inter-Korean relations?

Despite the preference for confrontation exhibited in its security and domestic logic, it is obvious that Seoul could not simply write off Washington's position. The US constrained and moderated South Korea's instincts. However, this does not necessarily mean that the US was an exceptionally dominant or decisive factor in determining the course of events. Although the standoffs were resolved through Washington's involvement, they were accompanied by lengthy and heated confrontations. Security concerns and domestic politics may not have been completely under US control, but they were malleable to American demands after having attained their minimum requirements. For example, Seoul's acceptance of a diplomatic solution to the DMZ incident was not given until the upgrade in WatchCon status had already affected South Korean military preparedness and the ruling party's election strategy.[185] Similarly, President Kim's eventual acceptance of Northern 'regret' as an apology for the submarine infiltration was not until after he had successfully strengthened his control in South Korean politics.

In conclusion, the primary contributors to tensions during this period were North Korean provocations, stemming largely from security fears, and Seoul's hard-line responses, based largely on domestic political considerations. The US's engagement policy was the key impetus in resolving these tensions.

Notes

1. For an economic assessment, see Marcus Noland, 'The North Korean Economy', *Joint US–Korean Academic Studies, Economic and Regional Cooperation in Northeast Asia*, Korean Economic Institute, Washington, DC, vol. 6, 1996, pp. 127-78.
2. Samuel S. Kim, 'North Korea in 1995: The Crucible of Our Style Socialism', *Asian Survey*, 36, no. 1, January 1996, p. 65.
3. Philo Kim, 'The Social Impact of Food Crisis in North Korea', in Lim Gill-Chin and Chang Namsoo, ed., *Food Problems in North Korea: Current Situation and Possible Solutions*, (Seoul: ORUEM Publishing House, 2003), p. 152. On the other hand, defector Hwang Jang Yop claimed that 1.5 million people had already starved to death by the end of 1996. See *Munhwa Ilbo*, 21 May 1998.
4. Country Report: North Korea, *The US Committee for Refugees*, 2000, at http://www.refugees.org /world/countrypt/easia_pacific/north_korea.html.
5. Hwang Jang Yop, *Nanun yoksaui chili rul poattda [I have Witnessed Historical Truth]* (Seoul: Hanul, 1999), pp. 328-9.
6. Only a fourth of the respondents attributed the famine to natural disaster, Pyongyang's official explanation. See Andrew S. Natsios, *The Great North Korean Famine*, (Washington, DC: United States Institute of Peace Press, 2001), p. 219.
7. In the early 1990s, nearly 40 per cent of the country's 16 to 24 year-olds were in the military, and it was practically impossible to ensure that all military families were fed. See *ibid.*, p. 232; and for the data on North Korea's population see Nicholas Eberstadt and Judith Banister, *The Population of North Korea* (Berkeley: University of California Institute of East Asian Studies, 1992), pp. 20–4.
8. *Chosun Ilbo*, 29 May 1996.
9. *Chosun Ilbo*, 13 December 1995.
10. Samuel S. Kim, 'North Korea in 1995: The Crucible of Our Style Socialism', *Asian Survey*, 36, no. 1, January 1996, p. 71.
11. Asian Security 1996-97, p. 144.
12. The head of the Agency for National Security Planning (NSP), Kwon Yong Hae, said in his report to the Intelligence Committee of the National Assembly in December 1995 that the winter of 1995 through the spring of 1996 was the critical period for crisis management on the Korean peninsula. See *Chosun Ilbo*, 16 December 1995.
13. *Chosun Ilbo*, 23 December 1995.
14. *Dong-A Ilbo*, April 3, 1996.
15. Beginning in January 1995, Pyongyang appealed publicly to the outside world for food assistance, asking Japan and South Korea. It also turned to international organizations such as the UN Humanitarian Aid Agency, requesting nearly $500 million in flood relief and medical assistance
16. *Korea Newsreview*, 24 June 1995, pp. 4-5.
17. President Kim also said: 'It is a crime for North Korea to hope to receive aid while pouring all its national resources into maintaining its military power', quoted in *Korea Newsreview*, 13 January 1996, p. 7.
18. Park Kyung-Ae, 'Explaining North Korea's Negotiated Cooperation with the US', *Asian Survey*, 37, no. 7, July 1997, p. 625.
19. From June 1995 to October 2000, Japan provided 1 182 000 tons of food aid to North Korea. Most of aid was free of charge. See Samuel S. Kim, 'North Korea in 1995: The Crucible of Our Style Socialism', pp. 66-7; and Kim Hong Nack, 'Japanese-North Korean Relations after the 2002 Pyongyang Summit', *Korea and World Affairs*, vol. 28, no. 2 (Summer 2004), p. 185.

20. Kim Ilpyong J., 'China in North Korean Foreign Policy', in Samuel S. Kim, ed., *North Korean Foreign Relations In the Post-Cold War Era* (Oxford: Oxford University Press, 1998), p. 108; and Shin Sang-jin, 'Chŏllyaksang Yujitoenŭn Chung-Puk Tongmaeng Kwan'gye [Sino-North Korean alliance sustained based only on strategic reasons], *Chayukongnon [Free Public Opinion]* (November 1998), pp. 48-55.

21. The Ministry of Unification, *Unification White Paper 1997*, pp. 193-6.

22. *Korea Newsreview*, 25 May 1996, p. 6.

23. Oberdorfer, *The Two Koreas*, p. 374.

24. *Korea Newsreview*, 13 April 1996, p. 9; and Cheon Seongwhun, 'A Role Definition and Implementation Strategies for the Four-Party Peace Talks', *Korean Journal of National Unification*, vol. 6 (Seoul: Korea Institute for National Unification, 1997), p. 9.

25. Yonhap cited in *FBIS-EAS*, 5 April 1996, p. 31.

26. WatchCon 2 was designed for a situation wherein 'the enemy's threat and attack symptoms are substantial', while WatchCon 3 was for when 'national interests are at serious risk'. See Ministry of National Defence of Republic of Korea, *ROK – US Alliance and USFK*, (Seoul: Oh Sung Planning and Printing, 2003), p.55.

27. *Joong-Ang Ilbo*, 17 April 1996.

28. Cited in *Korea Newsreview*, 12 October 1996, p. 6.

29. To counter North Korea's armed provocation, Kim stressed that the government would 'place top priority on a policy re-evaluating the mobility and efficiency of our armed forces', expressing his commitment to the mobilization of the South Korean forces and its attendant budget increase. See *Korea Newsreview*, 5 October 1996, pp. 6-7.

30. *Korea Newsreview*, 12 October 1996, p. 7.

31. *Chosun Ilbo*, 3 October 1996.

32. In fact, South Korean workers were supposed to have begun work in November 1996 on the site of the reactors, but that had been postponed until the North apologized.

33. For the full statement of the UN Security Council, see *Korea Newsreview*, 19 October 1996, p. 7.

34. Michael A. Lev, 'N. Korea Issues A Rare Apology', *Chicago Tribune*, 30 December 1996, p. N3.

35. It also said that the North had stepped up its military activities, including manoeuvres and other suspicious exercises. See *Korea Newsreview*, 16 December 1995, p. 34.

36. Asked about the government's position on international rice aid to the North, he also stressed, 'The rice should be delivered to the civilians. It must be ensured that the food aid will not be used for military purpose'. See *Korea Newsreview*, 13 January 1996, pp. 9-10.

37. *Korea Newsreview*, 29 June 1996, p. 4.

38. Natsios, *The Great North Korean Famine*, p. 135.

39. For instance, several powerful members of the House of Representatives sent a letter in June 1997 to the Clinton administration against providing any substantial food aid to North Korea, unless it was confirmed that none of the food was diverted to the North Korea military. The letter was signed by the chairman of the House Foreign Affairs committee, Benjamin Gilman, along with the ranking Democrat on the committee, Lee Hamilton, as well as by Doug Beureter, who served as chairman of the House Committee on Agriculture. See Natsios, *The Great North Korean Famine*, pp. 143-4 and pp. 154-5.

40. See, for example, *Dong-A Ilbo* 9 and 20 January, 1996 in titles of 'The conditions of food aid' and 'The opposition of unconditional food assistance'.

41. See *Korea Newsreview*, 17 August 1996, p. 15.

42. Kim Dong Sup, 'There is enough rice stored for 170 days of war', *Weekly Chosun*, 27 June 1996. One academic dissertation even attempted to analyse the impact of South Korea's food assistance on North Korea's war-fighting capacity. See Kim Bong Gyu, 'A study on how the food shortage of North Korea would affect its battle achievement', (Master's Thesis, Chung-Ang University 1998).

43. Colonel Kim Sam Kon, an adviser to the Defence Minister from 1990 to 1997, claimed that South Korea's food aid was filling up the mostly empty food storages of North Korea. Interview with Colonel Kim, Seoul, 27 August 2002.

44. Emphasising that North Korea's stability was essential for achieving a gradual and harmonious unification, he declared: 'We do not wish a hasty and one-sided unification'. See *Korea Newsreview*, 20 May 1995, p. 6.

45. US ambassador James Laney made a similar point. According to Laney, President Kim was fully aware of the disastrous implications of a sudden North Korean collapse, though he did dream of making history by reunifying the country. See Oberdorfer, *The Two Koreas*, p. 373.

46. For the relations between these offensive and defensive motives in civil war cases, see Barbara F. Walter and Jack Snyder eds., *Civil Wars, Insecurity, and Intervention* (New York: Columbia University Press, 1999).

47. On preventive war see Richard Ned Lebow, 'Windows of Opportunity: Do States Jump through Them?', *International Security* 9, no. 1 (Summer 1984), pp. 147-86; Jack S. Levy, 'Declining Power and the Preventive Motivation for War', *World Politics* vol. 40, no. 1 (October 1987), pp. 82-107; and Thazhakuzhyil V. Paul, *Asymmetric Conflicts: war initiation by weaker powers* (Cambridge: Cambridge University Press, 1994).

48. As is the case in pre-emptive war, preventive war is not driven by expansionist aims, but by fear of the unavoidable consequences of 'doing nothing'. See Victor Cha, 'Is There Still a Rational North Korean Option for War?', *Security Dialogue*, vol. 29, no. 4 (December 1998), p. 479.

49. David Kang, 'Preventive War and North Korea', *Security Studies* 4, no. 2 (Winter 1994/95), p. 333. Furthermore, there is no factor that could ameliorate 'preventive war' situation in North Korea, such as liberal democracy and defensive military doctrines. See Randall Schweller, 'Domestic Structure and Preventive War', *World Politics*, vol. 44, no. 2, (January 1992), pp. 235-69.

50. Natsios, The Great North Korean Famine, pp. 136 and 217.

51. *Ibid.*, pp. 136-7.

52. Robert Burns, 'US Intelligence Sees Signs of Military Crackdown in Communist North Korea', *Associated Press*, 22 December 1995.

53. Mary Jordan, 'Speculation Grows on Demise of N. Korea', *Washington Post*, 6 April 1996, A11.

54. Selig S. Harrison, 'Promoting a Soft Landing in Korea', *Foreign Policy*, no. 106 (Spring 1997), p. 72.

55. Cited in David S. Maxwell, 'North Korea's Collapse and the US Response', *Sasang [Ideology]* (Fall 1997), p 12.

56. Oberdorfer, *The Two Koreas*, pp. 396-7.

57. According to a US intelligence report, China dismissed the possibility of Pyongyang attacking the South. This assessment was based on the serious oil shortage of the North, the non-intervention of Russia and China, and the North Korean leaders' fear that a war might precipitate the regime's loss of control over its people. See Maxwell, 'North Korea's Collapse and the US's Response', pp. 21-2.

58. He added that a few North Korean soldiers and civilians preferred war as a means to end their painful situation. *Korea Newsreview*, 21 October 1995, p. 11.

59. *Korea Newsreview*, 21 October 1995, p. 8.

60. See Whan Chun Chung, 'North Korea's Intention to Destroy the Truce Mechanism and the Current Situation on the Korean Peninsula', *East Asian Review*, vol. 8, no. 1 (Seoul: The Institute for East Asian Studies, Spring 1996), p. 31.

61. *Korea Newsreview*, 7 May 1994, p. 4. Under the armistice agreement, the MAC was established to supervise the implementation of the agreement and to settle any violations of the agreement.

62. Pyongyang's pressure on Beijing began as early as May 1994.

63. This did not mean unconditional approval of Pyongyang's new peace arrangement, however. The Xinhua News Agency, for example, quoted Tang Jiaxuan as saying that this decision 'was made at the request of North Korea', and also reported that China hoped all parties concerned would observe the Armistice Agreement until the new peace arrangement could be implemented. See Hideya Kurata, 'The International Context of North Korea's Proposal for a "New Peace Arrangement": Issues after the US–DPRK Nuclear Accord', *Korean Journal of Defense Analysis*, vol. VII, no. 1 (Summer 1995), pp. 264-5.

64. The mission of the NNSC is to carry out the functions of supervision, observation, inspections and investigations, and to report the results to the MAC. The NNSC was previously composed of delegates from Sweden and Switzerland on the UNC side and Poland and Czechoslovakia on the Communist side. But in April 1993, North Korea expelled the Czech delegation after Prague established diplomatic ties with Seoul in March. Afterwards, Polish soldiers were the only neutral observers on the North Korean side of the NNAC. *Korea Newsreview*, 14 May 1994, p. 6.

65. Pyongyang's proposal to make a bilateral peace treaty with Washington was not a new one. North Korea first proposed the signing of a peace pact in March 1974 in a letter to the US Congress. In it, Pyongyang called for the conclusion of a nonaggression pact, and the dissolution of the United Nations Command (UNC) stationed on the peninsula. Since then, the North had repeated similar proposals. Beginning in April of 1994, the issue became a much more serious matter in terms of intensity and character. In contrast to behaviour before the 1994 period, when the North had only made verbal claims, Pyongyang now undertook a series of unilateral actions to undermine the armistice mechanism.

66. In this sense, Lim Dong Won, National Security Adviser to President Kim Dae Jung, said: 'Only with the reversion of operational control will North Korea respect and fear the South. Unless the operational control is returned to us, the North will continue to confine its approaches to the United States alone and sidestep or bypass the South'. See Harrison, 'Promoting a Soft Landing in Korea', p. 72.

67. For example, one North Korean official said in an interview with Selig Harrison: 'If US troops pull out of Korea, Japan will rearm immediately. We will formally ask you to withdraw your troops, but we don't mean it'. See *ibid.*, p. 71.

68. *Ibid.*, p. 70.

69. The South Korean government did not believe these unofficial statements regarding American forces in Korea, dismissing them as Pyongyang's tactics to cause an estrangement between the US and South Korea. See Arms Control Bureau, the Ministry of National Defence, 'MND Measures for Four-Party Talks', p. 43; and interview with former Deputy Defence Minister Park Yong-ok, 25 August 2002.

70. Oberdorfer, *The Two Koreas*, p. 432.

71. Kim Il Yong and Cho Sung Ryul, *Chuhan Migun: yŏksa, Y isuwa Chŏnmang [The US Forces in Korea: History, issues, and Prospect]*. (Seoul: Hanwool Academy, 2003), pp. 264-5.

72. The same view can be found in Kwak Tae-Hwan, 'US Military-Security Policy toward the Korean Peninsula', *Korean Journal of Defence Analysis*, vol. 7, no. 2 (Winter 1995), pp. 257-9.

73. Whan, 'North Korea's Intention to Destroy the Truce Mechanism', p. 34.

74. White House spokesman Mike McCurry said: 'We haven't seen anything that indicates an offensive build-up that implies hostilities'. Terry Atlas, 'North Korea Vies for US Attention', *Chicago Tribune*, 9 April 1996, p. N3.

75. Given that any minor dissention between permanent members of the UN Security Council can greatly hinder the resolution process, the requirement of a new resolution could substantially restrict the swift involvement of UN-member countries in a Korean military conflict. See Kim and Cho, *Chuhan Migun [The US Forces in Korea]*, pp. 252-4.

76. Paik, 'Building a Peace Regime', pp. 71-3; and Whan, 'North Korea's Intention to Destroy the Truce Mechanism', pp. 37-8.

77. Arms Control Bureau, the Ministry of National Defence, *Kukpangbu Sajahoedam Choch'i Sahang [MND Measures for Four-Party Talks]*, p. 43.

78. For the general view in the South on the issue, see South Korean media's analyses in *FBIS-EAS*, 5 April 1996, p. 33.

79. Arms Control Bureau, the Ministry of National Defence, *Kukpangbu Sajahoedam Choch'i Sahang [MND Measures for Four-Party Talks]*, p. 43

80. *Ibid.*, p. 40. The US forces in Korea (USFK) and the United Nations Command (UNC) have totally different bases: while the UNC was formed according to the armistice agreement in 1953, the USFK are stationed under the US-ROK Mutual Defence Treaty in 1954. Thus, the dissolution of the UN Command or the termination of the armistice agreement has no direct impact on US forces in South Korea. To Seoul, however, the withdrawal of American forces and the transformation of the armistice into a new peace regime had been so strongly linked politically that Pyongyang's peace offensive was regarded as a disguised attempt to affect US troop withdrawal.

81. *Chosun Ilbo*, 21 September 1996.

82. Nicholas D. Kristof, 'How a Stalled Submarine Sank North Korea's Hopes', *New York Times*, 17 November 1996, p. 12.

83. Koh B.C., 'South Korea in 1996: Internal Strains and External Challenges', *Asian Survey*, 37, no. 1, January 1997, p. 7. This remark, however, might have been made in a situation where he was pressured to speak as the South Korean government wished.

84. *Joong-Ang Ilbo*, 23 September 1996.

85. Interview with an analysis officer at the Anti-Infiltration Intelligence Division, Seoul, 27 August 2002.

86. In an interview with the author, one intelligence analyst has said that the primary objective of the submarine incursion was a 'significant change' in an ROK military base at the time. Although he did not specify the 'change' due to its secret nature, he stressed the importance of the operation, referring to the inclusion of a colonel-level officer in the infiltration team for the first time, as well as the unusually large size of the team (twenty-five members). Interview with an intelligence officer, Seoul, 27 August 2002.

87. Calling for a sense of urgency, some experts on North Korea and military affairs argued that a North Korean attack on the South was imminent. See, for example, interview reports in *Dong-A Ilbo*, 21 September and 26 October 1996.

88. *Korea Newsreview*, 5 October 1996, p. 7.

89. *Joong-Ang Ilbo*, 30 September 1996.

90. Kim Ki Hun, 'Pŏlkŏpŏsŭn Kun [The naked military]', *Weekly Chosun*, 17 October 1996.

91. Nicholas D. Kristof, 'How a Stalled Submarine Sank North Korea's Hopes', *New York Times*, 17 November 1996, p. 12.

92. Ministry of National Defence of the Republic of Korea, ROK − US Alliance and USFK, (Seoul: Oh Sung Planning and Printing, 2003), p.54.

93. Stuart K. Masaki, 'The Korean Question: Assessing the Military Balance', *Security Studies* 4, no. 2 (Winter 1994/95) pp. 382-4.

94. This was the conclusion of the ROK Defence Ministry. Cited in *Joong Ang Ilbo*, 30 September 1996.

95. *Korea Newsreview*, 1 July 1995, p. 8.

96. *Korea Newsreview*, 8 July 1995, p. 34.

97. *Korea Newsreview*, 12 August 1995, p. 7.

98. Opinion leaders became critical about food aid negotiations with North Korea, calling on the South Korean government to maintain a tough position, even if it led to deterioration in inter-Korean relations. For one of those arguments, see *Dong-A Ilbo*, 3 October 1995.

99. *Korea Newsreview*, 13 January 1996, p. 8.

100. *Dong-A Ilbo*, 1 July 1995.

101. According to a survey conducted by *Joong-Ang Ilbo* the day after the election, the most important factor in the people's choice of candidates was the North's DMZ provocation. 30.2 per cent of people interviewed pointed out the DMZ incident as a main element in their decision. Economic issues, such as bankruptcy and economic decline, were the second most important factor, at 20.5 per cent. The government's financial scandal was listed only as 5.9 per cent. See *Joong-Ang Ilbo*, 13 April 1996.

102. There were as many as 38 places only in Seoul and the Kyong-ki province where the ruling party candidates won by a less than 10 per cent margin.

103. *Monthly Chosun*, June 1996.

104. It should be noted, however, that such an investigation may not be entirely reliable, as Kim Dae Jung had been a lifetime rival of Kim Young Sam and had suffered failure in the 1996 general election due to the ramifications of Pyongyang's actions.

105. Key figures involved in this political manipulation denied their involvement. However, Kim Dong Shin, Defence Minister at the time of investigation, had to resign because he was portrayed in the investigation report as one of the key persons in manipulating the situation.

106. Cited in Cho Seong Sik, 'Pukhan Wihyŏp Chojakŭn Itŏtda [Manipulation of the North's threat existed: A report of the presidential office on the DMZ incident]', *Monthly Sin Dong-A*, June 2000.

107. Cited in Cho, 'Pukhan Wihyŏp Chojakŭn Itŏtda [Manipulation of the North's threat existed]'.

108. Editorials in major newspapers called on the government to take a firm stance on North Korea, arguing that North Korea's war preparation was confirmed again through the submarine incursion. See, for example, *Chosun Ilbo*, 30 October 1996.

109. President Kim had just over a year left in office, and could not run again.

110. Nicholas D. Kristof, 'How a Stalled Submarine Sank North Korea's Hopes', *New York Times*, 17 November 1996, p. 12.

111. *Joong-Ang Ilbo*, 8 October 1996.

112. *Dong-A Ilbo*, 10 September 1996.

113. The National Assembly issued a supra-partisan resolution twice, in September and October, blaming North Korean provocations; the opposition party lost initiative during this 'security oriented' political climate. See *Chosun Ilbo*, 4 October 1996.

114. *Dong-A Ilbo*, 14 October 1996.

115. Sin Jun-yong, 'Tobalyinya P'yoryunya [Provocation or Drift?]', *Mal [Language]*, November, 1996, p. 59.

116. North Korean leaders also must have understood the simple fact that the major South Korean opposition party, the National Council for New Politics, led by Kim Dae Jung, a long-time advocate for inter-Korean reconciliation, was far more moderate and sympathetic towards North Korea than the Kim Young Sam administration.

117. Lim Hyung Kyun, 'Pukhanŭn Yŏdang P'yŏnyinga? [Is North Korea on the ruling party's side?]' *Weekly Chosun*, 18 April 1996.

118. Lee Jong-suk, *Hyŏndae Pukhanŭi Yihae [Understanding of Modern North Korea]* (Seoul: Yoksapipyongsa, 2000), p. 31. A similar concept to this 'asymmetric interdependence' is 'interface dynamics'. See Park Myong-lim, 'Pundan Chilsoŭi Kujowa Pyŏnhwa: Chŏktaewa Ŭichonŭi Taessangkwan'gyetonghak [Structure and Change of Division: Interface Dynamics of Hostility and Dependence]', *Kukka Chŏllyak [National Strategy]*, Vol. 3, No. 1 (Spring/Summer 1997), p. 44.

119. The Rajin – Sonbong area, 621 square kilometres close to the Chinese border, was declared by North Korea as a FETZ in December 1991, and it remained one of the most important North Korean experiments in pursuit of economic development with foreign investment. For a detailed explanation see James Cotton, 'The Rajin – Sonbong Free Trade Zone Experiment: North Korea in Pursuit of New International Linkage', in Samuel S. Kim, ed., *North Korean Foreign Relations In the Post-Cold War Era* (Oxford: Oxford University Press, 1998), pp. 212-34.

120. Im Ul Chul, 'Amch'oe Köllin Pukhanŭi Kaebang Sirhŏm [North Korea's opening-up experiment in quagmire]', *Hankyure 21*, 17 October 1996.

121. Cotton, 'The Rajin-Sonbong Free Trade Zone Experiment', p. 216.

122. In fact, one of the most important goals of the forum was to reassure foreign businessmen that the Korean peninsula was a stable and safe place to invest. It was reported that Chairman Kim Jong U and other North Korean officials repeatedly stressed this point. See Im Ul Chul, 'Amch'oe Köllin Pukhanŭi Kaebang Sirhŏm [North Korea's opening-up experiment in quagmire]', *Hankyure 21*, 17 October 1996.

123. Kim Jong U was the son of Kim Il Sung's father's sister and a classmate of Kim Jong Il from his days at Sungshil High School. See Cotton, 'The Rajin-Sonbong Free Trade Zone Experiment', p. 216.

124. Choi Kwang, the Minister of People's Armed Forces, was raised to No. 6 from 8 in 1996. Lee Eul Seoul, the KPA marshal and the director general of Security Service, Cho Myung Rok, the KPA vice martial and the director general of politburo, and Kim Young Chun, the chief of staff, were promoted to ranks from 11 to 13, equivalent to the status between a Central Committee member and a secondary member of Politburo. See Yoo Suk Yuel, 'Pukhan Kwŏllyŏksoyŏlŭi Pyŏnhwa Chŏngchaek Panghyang [Change of Power Hierarchy and Policy Direction of North Korea]', *Chuyŏ Kukchemunje Punsŏk [Analysis of Major International Issue]*, No. 1996~38 (October 1996), pp. 7-8.

125. Kim Chang Su, 'Paekbae Ch'ŏnbae Pobok Pŏt'ŭn Nuga Nurŭna [Who will press the button for 'a hundred or a thousand fold retaliation?]' *Weekly Chosun*, 17 October 1996.

126. *Chosun Ilbo*, 24 and 31 March 1996.

127. Oberdorfer, *The Two Koreas*, p. 375.

128. Kim Chang Su, 'Paekbae Ch'ŏnbae Pobok Pŏt'ŭn Nuga Nurŭna [Who will press the button for 'a hundred or a thousand fold retaliation?]' *Weekly Chosun*, 17 October 1996.

129. Kongdan Oh and Ralph C. Hassig, *North Korea Through the Looking Glass* (Washington, DC: Brookings Institution Press, 2000), p. 106.

130. In particular, Choe Kwang, a hard-line character, led the hijacking of the US intelligence vessel Pueblo, as well as the infiltration of armed guerrillas at Ul-Jin and Sam-chuck area in 1968. See Yoo, 'Pukhan Kwŏllyŏksoyŏlŭi Pyŏnhwa Chŏngchaek Panghyang [Change of Power Hierarchy and Policy Direction of North Korea]', p. 17.

131. For a critical view of Kim Il Sung-Kim Jong Il's over-determination on North Korean policy, see Suh Jae-jin, 'Policy direction after Kim Il Sung's death', KINU Seminar series 92-02; and Chang Dal Jung, 'Pukhan Chŏngch'aek Kyŏlchŏng Kujo Mit Kwachŏng [North Korea's policy-making structure and process]', *Social Science and Policy Studies*, Vol. 15, No. 2. (June 1993).

132. *Dong-A Ilbo*, 4 October 1996.

133. Morton H. Halperin, *Bureaucratic Politics and Foreign Policy* (Washington, DC: Brookings Institution, 1974), pp. 235-44.

134. *Ibid.*, pp. 235-6.

135. Koh Young-hwan, *Pyongyang Yisibosi [Pyongyang's Twenty Five Hours]*. (Seoul: Kyoryuone, 1992), p. 259.

136. Most notably, North Korean defectors Ko Young-hwan, Kang Myung-do, Hwang jang Yop, and Shin Sang-ok, a South Korean film director and his wife, the actress Choe Un-hui, who were abducted to North Korea on Kim Jong Il's order in 1978. See Oh and Hassig, *North Korea Through the Looking Glass*, pp. 91-3.

137. Oh and Hassig, *North Korea Through the Looking Glass*, pp. 96-98. The same point was made by Yoo Suk Yuel in his article, 'Pukhan Kwŏllyŏksoyŏlŭi Pyŏnhwa Chŏngchaek Panghyang [Change of Power Hierarchy and Policy Direction of North Korea]', pp. 9-10.

138. Oberdorfer, *The Two Koreas*, p. 376.

139. Beijing's positive but limited role can be seen in the four-party talks. Despite Washington's appeal for Chinese approval for the proposal, Beijing refused to put pressure on North Korea to accept it. Only after the talks got underway did China begin to play a special role by taking a neutral position between the Koreas. At the first round of preliminary talks in New York in August 1997, for example, China refused to support Pyongyang's position that the issue of US forces in Korea should be included on the agenda, while also opposing the joint US-ROK proposal that arms control issues should be addressed. On China's position on the four-party talks, see Samuel S. Kim, 'The Making of China's Korea Policy in the Era of Reform', in David M. Lampton, ed., *The Making of Chinese Foreign and Security Policy in the Era of Reform, 1978~2000* (Stanford: Stanford University Press, 2001), pp. 394-6; and Shin Sang-jin, 'Chŏllyaksang Yujitoenŭn Chung-Puk Tongmaeng Kwan'gye [Sino-North Korean alliance sustained based only on strategic reasons]', *Chayukongnon [Free Public Opinion]* (November 1998), pp. 48-55.

140. Victor Cha, 'Realism, Liberalism, and the Durability of the US – South Korean Alliance', *Asian Survey, 37*, no. 7, July 1997, pp. 609-22.

141. Nicholas D. Kristof, 'Tensions continue as both Koreas indulge in brinkmanship', *New York Times*, 17 November 1996; and Chung Yeon Ju, 'Wŏsingtŏnŭn Pulp'yŏnhada [Washington is uncomfortable with President Kim Young Sam]', *Hankyure 21*, 21 November 1996.

142. *BBC Summary*, Far East, No. 2504 (8 January 1996).

143. *Chosun Ilbo*, 26 January 1996.

144. Cited in Meki Cos, *Associated Press Worldstream*, 26 January 1996. Lord said before attending the Hawaii meeting that the Clinton administration wanted to give more food aid to North Korea.

145. R. Jeffrey Smith, 'US Calls Aid to N. Korea "Symbolic", *Washington Post*, 4 February 1996, A12.

146. Natsios, *The Great North Korean Famine*, pp. 134-5 and p. 151.

147. In May 1996, US Congressman Bill Richardson visited North Korea and with the approval of the NSC offered the North Koreans 1 million MT of food aid annually in exchange for Pyongyang's cooperation in the four-party talks and the return of the remains of US soldiers missing in action from the Korean War. However, Defence Department officials were irate when they learned of the offer, and the NSC told Richardson to withdraw the offer. See *ibid.*, pp. 143-6.

148. In the autumn of 1995 when the State Department official Quinones reported that a food crisis appeared to be under way after his visit to North Korea, the CIA and DIA described the State Department as being 'taken for a ride by the North Koreans'. See *ibid.*, p. 142.

149. *Chosun Ilbo*, 14 January 1996.

150. Cited in Nicholas D. Kristof, 'Tensions continue as both Koreas indulge in brinkmanship', *New York Times*, 17 November 1996.

151. Nicholas D. Kristof, 'How a Stalled Submarine Sank North Korea's Hopes', *New York Times*, 17 November 1996, p. 12.

152. Oberdorfer, *The Two Koreas*, pp. 382-3

153. *Ibid.*, p. 384.

154. Cited in Moon Chul, 'Sa Tang Chidobu Yuse Hyŏnjang [A scene from stumping tours by party leaders]', *Dong-A Ilbo*, 13 March 1996.

155. In addition, there was also Seoul's recognition that new developments in Washington-Pyongyang relations made it difficult to handle the Armistice issue in traditional ways. During the Cold War, the North's demand for a peace pact with the US had been rejected as nonsense. However, once South Korea normalized relations with its former opponents, the Soviet Union and China, the North's argument of transforming the Cold War structure on the peninsula into a permanent peace mechanism with the US could no longer be discounted as easily as before. See Paik, 'Building a Peace Regime on the Korean Peninsula', p. 64.

156. Oberdorfer, *The Two Koreas,* p. 390. Even after Christopher's call for restraint from 'all parties' angered Seoul, Defense Secretary Perry expressed a hope that 'both sides' would try not to aggravate the situation any further. While Seoul was still expecting unqualified American backing in security matters with Pyongyang, Washington was apparently taking a different step. Its new attitude towards North Korea created a sense of betrayal and anger in the South, which questioned the alliance's solidarity. In a phone call to an American Korean specialist working at the Heritage Foundation, a senior South Korean foreign official condemned the Clinton administration's policies towards the North as 'seriously flawed', amounting to 'appeasement'. Quoted in Daryl M. Plunk, 'No Way to Deal With North Korea', *Washington Post*, 29 September 1996, p. C2.

157. Lim Yool Chul, 'Mi-Puk Pukkyŏng Pimil Chŏpch'ok [The US~North Korea had secret contacts in Beijing]', *Hankyure 21*, 31 October 1996.

158. *BBC Summary,* Far East, No. 2753 (26 October 1996).

159. *BBC Summary,* Far East, No. 2756 (30 October 1996).

160. The official aim of Richardson's visit to Pyongyang was to release Evan Hunziker, who had been detained in North Korea. See *BBC Summary,* Far East, No. 2782 (29 November 1996).

161. *BBC Summary,* Far East, No. 2791 (10 December 1996).

162. Lim Yool Chul, 'Nambuk Kwan'gye Hanp'a Kkŭnanda [Cold inter-Korean relationship ends]', *Hankyuree 21*, 28 November 1996.

163. Michael A. Lev, 'N. Korea Issues A Rare Apology', *Chicago Tribune*, 30 December 1996, N3.

164. 'North Korea's New Message', *New York Times*, 1 January 1997, p. 38.

165. Washington wanted to move ahead with its policy of bringing North Korea out of isolation, despite Seoul's reluctance to cooperate. In the face of the continuing standoff between North and South Korea due to the submarine incident, US Ambassador James Laney said: 'We all have too much at stake to get hung up here'. See Nicholas D. Kristof, 'Tensions continue as both Koreas indulge in brinkmanship', *New York Times*, 17 November 1996.

166. North Korea tested its Scud-missile ranging 300-500km in the 1980s, and developed the 1,300km-range Rodong missile in 1993. Furthermore, in August 1998, it test-launched the long-range Daepodong missile with a range from 1500-2000km. Encountering the improved missiles capability of North Korea, the US initiated negotiations to halt the North's missile development in April 1994. After five rounds of discussions, the two countries reached a tentative agreement in September 1999 to freeze temporarily the test-launching of long-range missiles. In return, the US announced a partial removal of economic sanctions against North Korea. See Centre for Non-proliferation Studies, Chronology of North Korea's Missile Trade and Development (http://cns.miis.edu/research/korea/chron2.htm).

167. Robert Manning, for example, argued in a seminar in Seoul that 'The Agreed Framework is likely to prove unsustainable unless it is embedded in a larger policy of North – South reconciliation'.

168. Cheon Seongwhun, 'A Role Definition and Implementation Strategies for the Four-Party Peace Talks', *Korean Journal of National Unification,* vol. 6 (Seoul: Korea Institute for National Unification, 1997).

169. *Chosun Ilbo*, 17 January 1996.

170. James Laney, 'North and South Korea: Beyond Deterrence', Speech at the Asia Society, 11 May 1996.

171. It has often been said that President Clinton was too busy and disinclined to sort out contradictory recommendations from his staff on China policy until there was a crisis. Whereas the Bush administration had been prepared to fight Congress in pursuit of a defined China policy, Clinton did not want to squander Capitol Hill votes that he would need for domestic issues. See David M. Lampton, *Same Bed, Different Dreams: Managing US–China Relations, 1989–2000* (Berkeley, Los Angeles, London: University of California Press, 2001), pp.34-7.

172. In particular, the visit of Taiwan President Lee Teng-hui to the US in June 1995 and the following military demonstrations of China and the US in the Taiwan Strait were serious sources of tensions in Sino–US relations. See Jonathan D. Pollack, 'The United States and Asia in 1995: The Case of the Missing President', *Asian Survey*, 36, no. 1, January 1996, pp. 1-12.

173. Furthermore, the arrest of American soldiers in September 1995 for involvement in the rape of an Okinawa schoolgirl unleashed widespread public outrage in Japan. See Pollack, 'The United States and Asia in 1995', pp. 8-9.

174. David M. Lampton, 'China and Clinton's America: Have They Learned Anything?' *Asian Survey*, 37, no. 12, December 1997, pp.1102-3.

175. Judith F. Kornberg, 'Comprehensive Engagement: New Frameworks for Sino-American Relations', *Journal of East Asian Affairs*, vol. 10, no. 1, Winter/Spring 1996, pp. 13-44. In an address in New York City on 17 May 1996, Secretary of State Christopher provided the China policy framework for the remainder of the first Clinton term and the entirety of the second. By stressing 'overall strategic relationship', he said, 'Our focus must be on the long term and we must seek to resolve our differences through engagement, not confrontation...' See Lampton, *Same Bed, Different Dreams*, pp. 54.

176. Jonathan D. Pollack, 'The United States and Asia in 1996: Under Renovation, but Open for Business', *Asian Survey*, 37, no. 1, January 1997, pp. 101-3.

178. The White House, *A National Security Strategy of Engagement and Enlargement* (February 1996) at http://www.fas.org/spp/military/docops/national/1996stra.htm.

179. The engagement policy was officially adopted by National Security Adviser Anthony Lake in September 1993, although it was not fully implemented until circa 1996, late in Bill Clinton's first term. See Anthony Lake, 'From Containment to Enlargement', US Department of State, Bureau of Public Affairs, *Dispatch*, vol. 4, no. 39, September 1993.

180. Daryl M. Plunk, 'No Way to Deal With North Korea', *Washington Post*, 29 September 1996, p. C2. In the Democratic Party's presidential primaries in August 1996, Clinton himself mentioned the Agreed Framework as one of his major foreign policy accomplishment.

181. Park Doo Sik, 'Hanmi HyŏpCho Purhyŏp Hwaŭm [Discord in the ROK-US cooperation]', *Weekly Chosun*, 17 October 1996.

182. 'Sakangŭi Tu Moksori [Two voices of four powers on the North's food shortage]', *Weekly Chosun*, 18 January 1996.

183. The concern of food diversion to the military began to appear in the fall of 1995, after the North's detention of a South Korean rice ship in July.

184. Among other things, President Kim's appraisal of the situation as a 'real possibility of war' was hard to justify.

185. Kim Dong Sup, 'Pukhanŭn Kŭllintŏn Chesŏnŭl Topgo Itda [North Korea is helping Clinton to be re-elected]', *Weekly Chosun*, 9 May 1996, pp. 28-9.

186. Furthermore, given that the geo-strategic condition of the Korean peninsula reflects an ameliorated security dilemma, the security dilemma logic would not have demanded Seoul to adopt such extreme measures.

7. Conclusion

When the Berlin Wall fell in 1989, it was hoped that the fears and legacies associated with the Cold War would disappear. The movement towards German reunification suggested that the same would soon happen on the Korean peninsula. The US removed its tactical nuclear weapons from South Korea in 1991, and called off 'Team Spirit', the major joint military exercise which had long been criticized by Pyongyang on the grounds that it represented preparation for an attack. Seoul established diplomatic ties with a number of eastern European countries, normalizing relations with Russia in 1990 and China in 1992, and prime ministers from both Koreas signed an important agreement calling for mutual respect and prohibition of armed provocations in December 1992. However, such positive developments were not sustained, and military tensions and perils of war have continued to cast their shadows over the peninsula. Diplomatic relations have yet to be established between North Korea, the US and Japan, while conventional military confrontation has persisted. Pyongyang's nuclear weapons programme has further increased military and political tensions, and the possibility of war has frequently been considered. After an initial settlement of the nuclear issue in 1994, inter-Korean relations were again agitated by a series of aggressive North Korean actions, including military demonstrations along the Military Demarcation Line and the submarine infiltration incident in 1996.

Although world politics has entered the post-Cold War era, the Korean peninsula has not. Analysts have asserted different reasons for the continuing tension on the Korean peninsula: 1) the aggressive and the irrational disposition of the North Korean regime, 2) the South Korean government's offensive strategy and mismanagement of dealings vis-à-vis Northern insecurity, 3) domestic politics in the two Koreas, and 4) American dominance of Korean security issues.

While previous accounts rightly point to contributing factors in the recurrent tensions, they do not adequately explain which factors matter most under what circumstances and how the factors are related to one another. Hence, the aim of this thesis has been to examine a set of factors that give a more balanced understanding of the causes: the security dilemma,[1] domestic politics, and the influence of international actors, particularly the US, and the IAEA and China, and peripherally Japan and Russia.

Several prominent cases critical to tension in inter-Korean relations from

1988 to 1997 have been examined.[2] They have encompassed the following: the failure to normalize US–North Korea and Japan-North Korea relations; the lack of progress in conventional arms control between the two Koreas; the dispute over challenge inspections and the Team Spirit exercise; the North's declaration of withdrawal from the NPT; the mounting nuclear crisis and the danger of war; North Korea's food shortages; increased military tension in the DMZ; and the submarine infiltration incident. The main concern of this study has been why cooperation is so difficult to sustain on the Korean peninsula, and why high tension and crises continue to erupt. What roles have the above factors–the security dilemma, domestic politics and external actors–played in creating and resolving hostilities? The findings are summarized in the table below.

Examination of the above cases suggests a number of findings and implications. First, the security dilemma aggravated relations by stimulating a sense of insecurity in both Koreas. Former analyses have stressed the North's aggressive and forceful reunification policy or the South's attempts to expedite the collapse of the North Korean regime as the main reasons for increased tension on the peninsula. Based on assumptions of Pyongyang's antagonism, deterrence has been a dominant element of strategic thinking in Washington and Seoul for the last half century. Utilizing the security dilemma theory, this study has proposed that the belligerent behaviours of both Koreas have, in fact, often been primarily rooted in defensive motivations.[3] The strategic environment of the peninsula leaves defensive and offensive actions hardly distinguishable, and, as was illustrated in the case of both the Team Spirit exercise and conventional arms control talks, the structural security dilemma may have been further complicated by cognitive error. Each side might have misinterpreted the other's motivations, misapprehending the opponent's evaluations.

This is not to suggest, however, that deterrence became irrelevant on the peninsula in the post-Cold War era. Vehement debate continues over the North's intentions and goals; even scholars advocating engagement disagree over whether the North has fundamentally changed.[4] In other words, it is impossible to rule out that North Korea is a potentially revisionist nation. If North Korea recaptures some of its strength in the future, it may be accompanied by increasing ambition. Moreover, not all its actions may have been driven by purely defensive motivations. A combination of defensive motives and a desire to exploit the South have probably prompted the North's behaviour.[5] Its demand for the withdrawal of US forces from the South, for example, may have stemmed from fear, but it may also have represented Pyongyang's opportunistic desire to reunify Korea by force. As Thomas Christensen argues, if one deals with a potential revisionist that has both a security fear and an ambition to exploit, the security dilemma and deterrence models can go hand in hand, suggesting a combination of assurance and threats as a policy recommendation.[6]

Nonetheless, the deterrence model is not in and of itself a satisfactory

Table 7.1 Summary of the Findings

Factors Cases	Security Dilemma (negative influence)	Domestic Politics (negative influence)	International Actors
III. Limitations and shortcomings : 1988.January-1991.December			
Diplomatic talks between the US and NK	**SK: relevant** - US troops withdrawal	**SK: relevant** - president's reputation	**The US: relevant** (negative) - preoccupation with Europe
Normalization talks between Japan and NK	**SK: less relevant**	**SK: relevant** - president's reputation	**The US: relevant** (negative) - pressure to slow down talks
Conventional arms control	**NK: relevant** - fear of being exploited	**NK: less relevant**	Not visible
	SK: relevant - fear of being exploited - misperception	**SK: relevant** - military–industrial complex	
IV. From accommodation to crisis (NPT Withdrawal) : 1992.January-1993.March			
Dispute over challenge (special) inspections	**NK: relevant** - negotiation strategy - fear of exposure	**NK: less relevant**	**The US: relevant** (negative) - intelligence failure in Iraq
	SK: relevant - nuclear transparency	**SK: relevant**	**IAEA: relevant** (negative)
SK's resumption of the Team Spirit	**SK: relevant** - military readiness - misperception	**SK: less relevant** - electoral politics - bureaucratic politics	**The US: less relevant** (positive) - distraction with domestic issues
NK's response (NPT withdrawal announcement)	**NK: relevant** - fear about the exercise - misperception	**NK: relevant** - power succession - the rise of the military	- interregnum politics
V. Dramatic reversal at the brink of a Collision : 1993.March-1994.Octobers			
A long delayed package solution (The Agreed Framework)	**SK: relevant** - fear of estrangement with the US - concern about nuclear transparency	**SK: less relevant** - president's determination not to be sidelined - bureaucratic politics	**The US: relevant** (positive) **China: relevant** (positive) - indirect influence on the US&NK **IAEA: relevant** (negative) - legalistic approach

VI. Recurrent hostilities : 1994.October-1997.December

SK's reluctance in food aid to NK	**SK: less relevant** - food diversion concern	**SK: relevant** - defeat in election	**The US: relevant** (positive)
NK's provocations in the DMZ and SK's hard-line response	**NK: relevant** - peace treaty offensive **SK: less relevant**	**NK: less relevant** **SK: relevant** - electoral politics	**The US: relevant** (positive) -soft-landing policy
Submarine incident	**NK: relevant** - intelligence gap **SK: less relevant**	**NK: less relevant** In terms of timing, relevant **SK: relevant** - protection of lame duck	**The US: relevant** (positive) -soft-landing policy

analytical tool to understand the source of tension on the peninsula since the end of the Cold War. While successful in explaining how war was avoided, it is unable to provide a sufficient reason as to why tension continued to mount.[7] Hence, what deterrence theory explains–prevention of war–is too narrow, since threats to peace and stability on the peninsula should not simply be equated with a second major war.[8] On the other hand, security dilemma theory can explain various forms and degrees of violence and tension, recognising insecurity as a source of spiral interactions between the two Koreas.

Another finding of this study is that North Korea's foreign policy, despite the reputation of its dictatorial regime, was decided mainly by security concerns, while domestic political motivations were merely part of the political landscape. Security motivations were the impetus for almost every North Korean action except its withdrawal from the NPT following the resumption of Team Spirit. Few cases suggest that domestic politics critically influenced Pyongyang's actions.[9] The rise of military authority and the goal of stability during the transition of power were worth considering as the bases of North Korea's policy. It was determined, however, that these factors did not have a direct causal relationship with North Korea's hard-line policy. The lack of such a link indicates that North Korean leadership was more calculating and rational than it appeared to be. The fact that security factors were more critical than domestic politics in Pyongyang's foreign policy may also suggest that their urgency in security did not allow North Korean leaders to manipulate them for domestic political purposes. However, this may reflect the intrinsic difficulty in learning about domestic political motivations in North Korea due to the limited access about the closed regime. It might be possible to find many cases where North Korean domestic politics played a major role if the time period of research were extended, more cases were selected for analysis, or internal documents and testimonies of North Korean defectors became available.

Additionally, this study did not discover any direct causal relationship between the North Korea's actions and the 'Juche' ideology so often considered a precursor to its irrational behaviour.[10] For instance, North Korea's negotiation with the 'American imperialists' over the nuclear issue can be considered practical, given its calculated and consistent strategy to gain maximum benefits from the US. Pyongyang also worked towards establishing diplomatic relations with Japan, despite its prior colonization of the Korean peninsula. North Korea's adoption of such policies shows that 'Juche' is not an absolute ideology that constrains and defines North Korean behaviour. Furthermore, even though North Korea's actions might appear irrational and unpredictable, such as its abrupt announcement of withdrawal from the NPT in 1993, they can be understood in the context of the security dilemma.[11] As Kongdan Oh and Ralph Hassig argue, 'Juche' seems to be better understood as a flexible concept that has evolved over time, addressing various concerns of the North Korean leadership, rather than as a fixed ideology dictating Pyongyang's foreign policy directions.[12]

This study has also found that South Korea's domestic politics undermined sustained progress in inter-Korean relations. In other words, the primary impetus for South Korea's hard-line policy towards the North at critical moments arose from electoral politics targeting conservative votes, the bureaucratic interests of conservatives and military authorities, and political leaders' personal interests. The fact that such matters aggravated inter-Korean relations has to do with the asymmetrical impact of positive and negative inter-Korean incidents on South Korean domestic politics. In other words, while positive events, such as a deal on conventional arms control talks or the nuclear issue, have rarely rewarded leaders with political benefits, negative events and hard-line policy have often greatly contributed to consolidating the position of the party in power.[13]

Hence, both the security dilemma and domestic politics were important factors in triggering military tensions on the peninsula vis-à-vis South Korea. However, it is hard to tell which played a greater role. Of the nine cases selected pertaining to South Korean behaviour for this study, it has been concluded that both were equally influential in three cases, while domestic politics proved relatively dominant in four cases, and the security dilemma was more significant in the remaining two cases.[14] The security dilemma dominating cases, such as inspection of North Korea's nuclear programme and the package solution of the nuclear issue, related more closely to the core of South Korea's security concerns than cases where domestic politics played a greater role, such as food aid to the North and the submarine incident. This implies that policy-makers had a relatively informed understanding of the characteristics and seriousness of security issues, whereas the public was vulnerable to the leaders' exploitation of them for political reasons.

Regarding external actors, it has been demonstrated that they played roles, to differing degrees, in heightening and resolving tensions on the peninsula. Not surprisingly, the US's part was the most significant in shaping the situation. The US was visible and its influence was substantial in most cases affecting its interests on the peninsula and in the region. It eased tensions created by Pyongyang's provocation of and Seoul's tough response to the military demonstration in the DMZ and the submarine incursion in 1996. In addition, the 1994 nuclear deal with North Korea can be mainly credited to Washington's diplomatic efforts. In a few cases, however, such as the issue of the 1993 Team Spirit exercise, the positive role of the US was limited by Seoul's hard-line position. Moreover, when the US was preoccupied with other international issues or its own domestic problems, diplomatic breakthroughs on the normalization of relations with North Korea were not realized, despite Pyongyang's concerted efforts to that end. But not all cases in which the US was involved had a positive outcome. At the initial stage of nuclear negotiations with the North, for example, the US, with the IAEA and South Korea, strongly insisted on rigorous inspections, and contributed in shifting these nuclear talks towards a deadlock.

China was capable of playing a mediating role between the US and North Korea, as its cautious and balanced approach towards the two Koreas helped it maintain influence on Pyongyang. While constraining Washington's hard-line behaviour towards Pyongyang, such as its sanctions strategy in 1993, Beijing often indirectly and secretly persuaded Pyongyang to adopt a more accommodating position. Examples include Pyongyang's cooperative stance towards Washington's nuclear diplomacy in 1992, inter-Korean prime-ministerial contacts, and the joint admission of UN membership.

Moscow, however, was not very visible in Korean affairs. In the midst of the dissolution of the Soviet bloc and internal economic and political troubles, it did not have any role in the North's 1994 nuclear crisis other than failed attempts to call for an international conference.[15] Russia was also excluded from a multilateral international forum called the four-party talks, in which the US, China and the two Koreas began to participate in 1996.[16] After Andrei Kozyrev was replaced by Yevgeny Primakov as Foreign Minister in January 1996, Russia showed a greater interest in Asia and the Pacific, and in improving relations with North Korea. Unlike the Western-focused Andrei Kozyrev, who had been under attack for his neglect of Russian interests in Asia, Primakov placed greater interest in the East, aiming to build a strategic partnership with China, expand relations with Japan and re-establish Russian ties with North Korea.[17] Nevertheless, Russia's status on the Korean peninsula remained far from its Cold-War levels.

Japan also failed to play a substantial role in promoting progress on the peninsula. Despite its enhanced status as a country capable of helping Pyongyang overcome economic hardship and diplomatic isolation, Japan's foreign policy during this period represented a passive tendency to follow US leadership. Constrained by pressure from Washington and Seoul, as well as bureaucratic disagreement, Japan slowed its normalization talks with Pyongyang, and failed to influence the direction of Korean security.

In addition to these national states, the IAEA played an important role in the North's nuclear issues. Although the agency shared a basic interest with other international actors in preventing the North from going nuclear, it had a different priority and approach to the issue. Throughout the negotiations, the IAEA maintained a tough position, sometimes rejecting progress made between the US and North Korea when the agency believed it to be insufficient.[18] Behind this tough position was a concern within the agency about its mission and reputation, particularly given its failure in Iraq.[19] Combined with Pyongyang's strategy of dealing only with the US and its disregard of the agency, the IAEA's determination to ensure non-proliferation complicated the diplomatic process.

How, then, can we understand the interrelationship between the three explanatory factors? The security dilemma and domestic politics tended to aggravate matters in a similar way except in a few cases, leaving it difficult to weigh their relative importance. The interaction of internal factors (the security dilemma and domestic politics) and external elements is more complicated. When Washington's attention to the Korean peninsula was distracted by other pressing issues, little diplomatic progress was made and sometimes serious crises followed. Soon after the Cold War ended, for example, the Bush administration was preoccupied with Europe and the Gulf area, and constrained by a bureaucratic dispute over how to respond to the North Korean issue. The US's policy was mainly reactive and incremental, inhibiting an upgrade in diplomatic relations with North Korea. Moreover, the moderate American position regarding the resumption of the Team Spirit was overruled by Seoul's strong hard-line position in the fall of 1992. Faced with political pressure to pay more attention to the economy before the upcoming presidential election, the first Bush administration was reluctant to get into a dispute with South Korea over security issues. The new Clinton administration, whose President had little confidence and interest in foreign affairs, found it difficult to rescind the decision, and the exercise was resumed.[20] Pyongyang then abruptly announced its withdrawal from the NPT, and nuclear crisis followed.

By contrast, when Washington actively engaged, it played a key role in resolving tensions in spite of South Korean opposition.[21] Despite the way Seoul's hard-line position frequently heightened tensions in such cases as the DMZ military provocation and the submarine incident, the 'soft-landing' policy of the Clinton administration prevailed in the end. In addition, Washington's diplomatic efforts led to a compromise resolution of the North's nuclear problems in October 1994. In the face of American resolve, the South Korean government had to adjust its initial hard-line position due to the asymmetrical nature of the power relationship between the US and South Korea.[22] China likewise played a role in sustaining the diplomatic efforts by restricting hard-line

American initiatives like economic sanctions against North Korea. In this light, Washington's decision to adopt and maintain a diplomatic approach towards North Korea was made under consideration of Beijing's role in protecting Pyongyang from international pressure.

Despite the significant influence of foreign players on the eventual outcome of various phases in inter-Korean relations, the security dilemma and domestic political factors in South Korea played an important role in escalating or prolonging tensions even when Washington put its energy into achieving diplomatic progress. For example, the agreed nuclear package deal was substantially delayed by opposition from the South Korean government all the while heightening the peril of war. In addition, although the Clinton administration's determination for a soft-landing policy was significant in the resolution of the DMZ and submarine infiltration incidents, the hard-line position of the South Korean government substantially increased military tension until they were resolved. In other words, the US's engagement policy did not entirely suppress Seoul's opposition, and inter-Korean relations were inevitably influenced by the South's hard-line policy to some extent. In sum, South Korea's security dilemma and domestic politics influenced the evolution of these kinds of situations, heightening the tension until matters were resolved by American intervention. China's role was to press the US into adopting or maintaining this engagement approach, all the while exercising its influence on North Korea to facilitate compromise.

In conclusion, the findings in this research suggest that the security dilemma in both North and South Korea and the domestic politics of the South were responsible for aggravating inter-Korean relations, while a direct and significant correlation between Pyongyang's domestic politics and its external behaviour is hard to support. Such a conclusion implies that the US and South Korea should understand the calculating and rational aspects of Pyongyang's behaviour in the context of its security concerns. Additionally, although the tensions and crises cited in this study were ultimately resolved, in most cases through US involvement and Chinese moderation, it nonetheless demonstrates the potential of the security dilemma in both Koreas and domestic politics in the South to escalate or prolong tensions.

Since the late 1990s, considerable changes have occurred in Korean security. The Republican Party led by President George W. Bush came into power in 2001, and the new US administration appears to be more sceptical about cooperation with Pyongyang than its predecessor. In Seoul, more liberal and reform-minded political groups led by former President Kim Dae Jung and current President Roh Moo Hyun have begun to pursue a resolute and consistent engagement policy towards North Korea. Such a change represents new thinking about North Korea among the younger generation and new political leaders in Seoul. Further research would be necessary to determine the limitations and relevance of this study's findings in such a changed climate. Nevertheless, it is possible to speculate on the prospects of a pending security issue, such as 'the six party talks' for the North's nuclear issue, to see if the implications of this study offer any guidance.[23]

It is almost impossible to predict the future of the nuclear talks with any accuracy, given their complexity and the domestic and international uncertainties surrounding the parties involved. Based on the findings of this study, it is possible to speculate that a diplomatic solution will eventually be likely, but the process will probably include North Korean provocations and international pressure for sanctions. Focused on its objective of so-called 'Complete, Verifiable, and Irreversible Dismantlement (CVID)', the US does not seem to be prepared to make a fundamental compromise. Moreover, many key officials in the Bush administration believe that Washington should adopt a strategy of containment and isolation, rather than reward Pyongyang for its behaviour, and prefer changing the Kim Jong Il regime.

If negotiations stall and the prospects of a diplomatic solution become dark, the voice for sanctions against the North, particularly on the part of the US, is expected to strengthen. If North Korea refuses to cooperate, Japan would probably support US-led economic sanctions. Tokyo has been playing a far more prominent role this time compared with the first nuclear crisis of 1993–4. Invited as an official participant, Japan is attending the six-party talks and has actively consulted the other participants on various occasions, including the preliminary three-party talks with the US and South Korea. Although Japanese–North Korean negotiations appeared to reach a breakthrough after Prime Minister Koizumi's historic visit to Pyongyang on 17 September 2002, relations deteriorated due to the abduction of eight Japanese citizens and a clandestine nuclear enrichment programme.[24] Japan has since hardened its position and decided to cooperate fully with the US.[25]

Even the South Korean government's emphasis on diplomacy can be absorbed into a US-initiated sanctions strategy. Despite changes in the ruling elite and their new perception of North Korea, conservatives and many other Koreans, still apprehensive about the North's intentions as well as its military capabilities, urge a tough-line policy towards North Korea. Thus, the security dilemma can compel the South Korean government to follow the US-led economic sanctions, if it is faced with a continuing stalemate and the North's provocations.

Although an American sanctions strategy would face Chinese opposition, the suggestion itself would lead to a dangerous escalation of tension. An increase of pressure on the North by the international community would only strengthen the preventive logic on which Pyongyang operates. In other words, if faced with intimidation or pressure, the North may conclude that undertaking threatening behaviour, like reprocessing nuclear material or testing missiles, is better than doing nothing, as the status quo will be perceived as an unbearable and losing situation.[26] Pyongyang's provocations, in turn, will strengthen the Bush administration's temptation to undertake a surgical strike against the North's nuclear facilities, as the Clinton administration had contemplated in 1993 and 1994.[27] On the other hand, North Korea might be compelled to consider acting pre-emptively, if it concludes that a US attack is imminent and inevitable.[28] Clearly, such an escalation of tension involves a real danger of military action.

Nevertheless, a diplomatic breakthrough is still possible. Despite North Korea's apparently unpredictable and risk-prone behaviour, this study has shown that North Korea is, in fact, calculating and rational in dealing with its security issues. However attractive the nuclear option might be, Pyongyang is well aware that nuclear deterrence cannot guarantee its survival–the threat to the regime stems not only from its military disadvantage, but from its collapsing economy and diplomatic isolation. Political and economic benefits need to be acquired in order to sustain the regime; otherwise, playing its nuclear card can only hasten the collapse of the regime.

In addition, China will work to prevent tension from reaching dangerous heights. In contrast to its lukewarm and protective stance during the nuclear crisis of 1993–4, China has been far more active since October 2002. Although Beijing has reiterated that it possesses limited influence over Pyongyang and that the US should play an active role in resolving the problem, some discernible changes have taken place. In February 2003, for example, Wang Yi, China's Deputy Foreign Minister, met North Korea's Foreign Minister Paik Nam-soon in Pyongyang and reportedly made a straightforward plea that North Korea end its nuclear brinkmanship.[29] Furthermore, in late February 2003, the oil pipelines from China to North Korea were shut down for almost three days. While the official explanation for this unprecedented event was 'technical difficulties', many observers speculated that it was a warning signal from Beijing to Pyongyang.[30] Two months later, when China offered to host a three-party talk (the US, North Korea and China), North Korea changed its position and accepted the invitation. Coupled with the pressure of high-level official visits to Pyongyang, the pipelines incident seems to have contributed to the materialization of the three-party talk in April.[31] Given Beijing's activeness regarding the six-party talks, it seems likely that it will continue its efforts to effect North Korean cooperation, especially when relations between the US and North Korea appear to be heading towards a clash that would likely prove disastrous for China.

While pressing North Korea to compromise, China will also constrain Washington from adopting hard-line options. Above all, the US will have a difficult time enlisting international support for political and economic pressure if it cannot demonstrate that it has exhausted diplomatic efforts. Moreover, a preventive attack is a far less attractive option for the US on the Korean peninsula than it was with Iraq. Given the North's formidable retaliatory power, war in Korea would be much more devastating, and stretch the American military even more than Iraq. Aside from the military challenge, a strike on the North would face strong opposition from China and South Korea, damaging the US–ROK alliance irrevocably.[32] Both the US and North Korea, then, have little choice but to compromise, however reluctant they might be.[33] Given such limited options for both countries, a diplomatic solution appears possible, although the process might involve dangerous periods of stalemate and crisis.

North Korea's nuclear problem is not the only issue which needs to be addressed. The core issues dealt with in this study–Pyongyang's unsuccessful attempts to establish diplomatic relations with the US and Japan, the lack of conventional arms control between North and South Korea, the replacement of the armistice regime, Pyongyang's maritime provocations, and North Korea's food shortage and its destabilising implications for the region–remain unresolved. In dealing with those issues, the three explanatory factors employed in this essay–the influence of international actors, the security dilemma, and domestic politics–will continue to offer valuable perspectives on security relations on the Korean peninsula.[34]

Notes

1. This study has questioned the argument that the North's aggressive approach and its irrational demeanour have been sources of trouble, and instead explored the idea of a security dilemma.
2. Chapter 2 deals with the limited but positive diplomatic progress of the early 1990s — including US diplomatic initiatives, Pyongyang's signing of the nuclear safeguards agreement with the IAEA, and inter-Korean prime ministerial talks — in order to provide readers with a sufficient background against which to examine how the three explanatory factors have operated in halting or disrupting positive developments.
3. The motivation to protect South Korea's security vis-à-vis a potential North Korean threat was an important factor in five out of the nine cases involving South Korea: US — North Korea diplomatic contacts, inter-Korean arms control, the Team Spirit exercise, special inspections, and a nuclear deal between the US and North Korea. On the other hand, a desire to enhance its security under isolated and weakening diplomatic and economic conditions appears to be behind all five of the cases involving North Korea.
4. David Kang, for example, believes that the North's intentions have shifted in the direction of reform and away from revisionism. On the other hand, Victor Cha sees the North's accommodating behaviour as tactical actions aimed at improving the short-term situation. See Victor Cha, 'Why We Must Pursue Hawk Engagement', in Cha and Kang, *Nuclear North Korea: A Debate on Engagement Strategies* (New York: Columbia University Press, 2003), p. 81.
5. This interaction of defensive and offensive motives is well analysed vis-à-vis civil wars in Barbara F. Walter and Jack Snyder eds, *Civil Wars, Insecurity, and Intervention* (New York: Columbia University Press, 1999).
6. For a critical review of the relationship between deterrence and spiral models, see Thomas J. Christensen, 'The Contemporary Security Dilemma: Deterring a Taiwan Conflict', *Washington Quarterly*, vol. 25, no. 4 (Autumn 2002), pp. 7-21.
7. In some respects, confrontation after the Cold War appears to be even more dangerous and destabilising than during the Cold War, when the standoff between the Koreas had been managed within the harsh but stable framework of the US — USSR. polarity.
8. Victor Cha, 'Why We Must Pursue Hawk Engagement', p. 71.
9. Even in the case of the North's decision to withdraw from the NPT in the spring of 1993, both domestic politics and the security logic were considered.
10. Adrian Buzo argues that 'Juche' ideology has been the chief impediment for North Korea positively entering conversations with the US and Japan, since Kim Il Sung's world view identified 'US imperialism and Japanese militarism as immutable, sworn enemies of the Korean revolution'. See Adrian Buzo, *The Guerrilla Dynasty: Politics and Leadership in North Korea*, (London and New York: I.B. Tauris Publishers, 1999), p. 190.
11. Responding to the North's announcement of NPT withdrawal, South Korean Foreign Minister Han Sung Joo said: 'from the North's perspective, the move had an element of rationality and calculation', while Makoto Sakuma, a senior Japanese military officer, called North Korea 'an extremely peculiar nation'. Cited in interview with Han Sung Joo by KBS, 13 March 1993; and 'SDF Head Opposes Foreign Pressure on DPRK', *Kyodo News*, March 18, 1993.
12. Kongdan Oh and Ralph C. Hassig, *North Korea through the Looking Glass* (Washington, DC: Brookings Institution Press, 2000). Or it could be understood that the principles of Juche, such as economic self-sustenance and self-reliance in national defence, are recessed because of the economic hardship and diplomatic isolation faced by the regime after the end of the Cold War.
13. For a historical review of the asymmetrical impact of inter-Korean events on the domestic politics of South Korea, see Lee Jong-suk, *Pundansidaeŭi T'ong'ilhak [The Study of Reunification in the Divided Era]* (Seoul: Hanul, 1999), pp. 45-6.
14. The security dilemma and domestic political factors were equally influential in the following three cases – its opposition to the North's attempt to normalize relations with the US, its

lukewarm attitude in conventional arms control, and the resumption of the Team Spirit exercise. On the other hand, domestic politics seem to have been more critical than security concerns in the following four instances – opposition to the normalization of diplomatic relations between North Korea and Japan, passive attitude towards food aid to the North, and the hard-line stance on the DMZ and submarine infiltration incidents. Finally, the security dilemma seems to have been a primary factor, despite the partial impact of domestic politics, for the remaining two cases: Seoul's strong opposition to the 'challenge inspections' and the package deal.

15. As the Soviet Union substantially curtailed economic assistance to North Korea and abruptly established diplomatic relations with Seoul in 1990, Moscow's influence on Pyongyang quickly became minimal.

16. Russia was unhappy to be excluded from the proposed talks. One Russian Foreign Ministry spokesman said: 'The problem of the Korean peninsula should be settled on a multilateral basis, taking into account the interests of all the parties involved'. Apart from expressing its disapproval of the four-party proposal, however, Moscow did not play a very meaningful role in negotiations. See *Korea Herald*, April 17, 1996.

17. Herbert J. Ellison, 'Russia, Korea, and Northeast Asia', in Eberstadt and Ellings. eds, *Korea's Future and the Great Powers*. Seattle: University of Washington Press, 2001, pp. 164-84.

18. Sigal, *Disarming Strangers*, pp. 95-108.

19. Reese, *The Prospects for North Korea's Survival*, pp. 47-8.

20. The role of the US was not visible in cases such as inter-Korean prime ministerial talks and conventional arms control probably because issues initiated by the two Koreas were not grave enough to attract Washington's attention.

21. As mentioned earlier, the US sometimes maintained a hard-line position, such as its insistence on rigorous nuclear inspections in the summer of 1992. The American factor, the security dilemma and the domestic politics of South Korea all aggravated the situation in this case.

22. The low intensity of the security dilemma may also explain why Seoul abandoned its tough line towards Pyongyang in the face of Washington's engagement policy. The security dilemma operates because offence and defence are indistinguishable under the strategic and geographic conditions of the peninsula. However, the retaliatory power of both North and South Korea has made defence more effective, and the security dilemma does not operate as strongly as it would if offensive strategies were dominant. Hence, the security dilemma on the peninsula is somewhat ameliorated. In other words, although the offensive actions of one side might threaten the security of the other, that threat is limited because it does not pose an imminent menace.

23. The Six Party Talks were established in August 2003 to deal with North Korea's nuclear issue (involving the US, North and South Korea, China, Japan and Russia), as the Agreed Framework came to crisis and tensions followed.

24. As a result of Koizumi's visit to Pyongyang, Japan and North Korea resumed normalized talks, making progress on some key issues. Kim Jong Il promised to comply with 'all related international agreements', including the 1994 Agreed Framework, and confessed to the charge of abduction of the Japanese citizens. However, circumstances deteriorated when North Korea failed to provide satisfactory explanations regarding the deaths of the eight abducted Japanese. The revelation of a clandestine nuclear enrichment programme in October 2003 became another blocking issue for the talks. For more on current Japanese-North Korean relations, see Kim Hong Nack, 'Japanese-North Korean Relations after the 2002 Pyongyang Summit', *Korea and World Affairs*, vol. 28, no. 2 (Summer 2004), pp. 163-97.

25. In this sober climate, Bush and Koizumi declared at the US-Japan summit meeting in late May 2003 that they were determined not to tolerate North Korea's nuclear ambition. See *Dong-A Ilbo*, May 26, 2003.

26. Victor Cha, 'Weak But Still Threatening', in *Nuclear North Korea*, p. 34.

27. Aidan Foster-Carter, 'Kim's nuclear deceit makes it harder to negotiate this time', *Daily Times*, April 23, 2005.
28. In contrast to the traditional view that war will break out only in the case of failure to deter North Korea's aggression, the Korean peninsula now faces different kinds of danger: the US's counter-proliferation strategy and North Korea's preventive or pre-emptive provocations.
29. David M. Lampton, 'China: Fed up with North Korea', *Washington Post*, June 4, 2003.
30. Charles Hutzler and Gordon Fairclough, 'The Koreas: China Breaks with Its Wartime Past', *Far Eastern Economic Review*, 7 August, 2003.
31. Another high-level visit by a Chinese official preceded Pyongyang's decision to participate in multilateral nuclear negotiations. Dai Bingguo travelled to North Korea in July 2003, and it appears that his visit facilitated the first six-party talk in August. See Chung Jae Ho, 'China's Korea Policy Under the New Leadership: Stealth Changes in the Making?', *Journal of East Asian Affairs*, vol. 18, no. 1 (Spring/Summer 2004), pp. 1-18.
32. This is not to say that a military clash is improbable. As mentioned earlier, a prolonged stalemate and increasing international pressure would escalate tensions, stimulating North Korea's sense of insecurity and pre-emptive logic. The point is that an unintended military clash in the midst of escalating tension is more likely than a pre-planned American attack.
33. In addition, the gap between the American and North Korean positions does not appear to be insurmountable, though it is wide. All parties agree that any agreement will involve a staged or sequenced approach of coordinated steps. The difference is mainly timing and sequencing-what reciprocal steps should be exchanged at which stage. For example, while North Korea wants the US to lift economic sanctions and resume oil shipments in exchange for freezing nuclear activities, the US is not inclined to reward North Korea for restoring a freeze that it had broken in the first place.
34. New understanding about North Korea seems to moderate the security dilemma factor in South Korea, since it can be mitigated by altering how Northern behaviour is interpreted. That is why the current Roh Moo Hyun administration has advocated an engagement policy even in the face of the North's nuclear challenge, whereas the Kim Young Sam administration had often called for a hard-line strategy in dealing with the issue. But many conservatives in the South, including the major opposition party and major media institutions, still hold a traditional view of North Korea as a dangerous enemy who has not given up its goal of communising the entire peninsula. Thus, the security dilemma is still operative in the minds of many South Korean people, and it may strongly influence the South Korean government's policy again, if the ruling elite changes in the 2007 presidential election. See Robert Jervis, 'From Balance to Concert: A study of international security cooperation', World Politics, vol. 38 (October 1985), pp. 58-79.

Bibliography

PRIMARY SOURCES

1. Interviews

Ahn, Kwang-chan, Major General, former Deputy Chief of Staff of the ROK~US Combined Forces Command (CFC), Seoul, ROK, 10 September 2002.

Chung, Jong Wook, National Security Adviser to President Kim Young Sam, Suwon, ROK, 17 September 2002.

Han, Yong-sup, Former Director of Arms Control Division of Defense Ministry, Seoul, ROK, 5 September 2002.

Kim, Chong Whi, National Security Adviser to President Roh Tae Woo, Seoul, ROK, 26 August 2002.

Kim, Sam Kon, Colonel, Adviser to the Defense Ministers from 1990 to 1997, Seoul, ROK, 27 August 2002.

Lee, Bu-jik, Major General, former South Korean delegate to the Joint Nuclear Control Committee (JNCC), Seoul, ROK, 21 August 2002.

Lee, Sang-ok, Foreign Minister during the Roh Tae Woo administration, Seoul, ROK, 12 August 2002.

Park, Yong-ok, Former General Director of Arms Control Bureau of the Defense Ministry, Seoul, ROK, 25 August 2002.

Samore, Gary, Former Director of the Office of Regional Non-Proliferation Affairs of the US State Department, London, UK, 3 July 2002.

2. Published official documents

Kim, Il Sung (1979), *On the Juche Idea,* Pyongyang: Foreign Languages Publishing House.

Kim, Il Sung (1980–93), *Kim Il Sung Works,* 38, Pyongyang: Foreign Languages Publishing House.

Kim, Jong Il (1992–93), *Kim Jong Il: Selected Works,* 1-2, Pyongyang: Foreign Languages Publishing House.

Kim, Jong Il (1997), *Kim Jong Il Seonjip 9-11 [Kim Jong Il: Selected Works 9-11],* Pyongyang: Chosun Nodongdang Chulpansa.

IAEA (1997), *Arms Control and Verification: Safeguards in a Changing World,* Bulletin 39 (3).

International Institute for Strategic Studies (2004), *North Korea's Weapons Programmes: A Net Assessment,* An IISS Strategic Dossier.

Perry, William (1999), *Review of United States Policy toward North Korea: Findings and Recommendations.* Unclassified Report to the President and the Secretary of State, Washington, DC

ROK Ministry of Foreign Affairs and Trade (1999), *Gunch'uk Bihwaksan Pyunram [Overview of Disarmament and Non-proliferation].*

ROK Ministry of National Defense (1988–98), *Defense White Paper.*

ROK Ministry of National Defense (2003), *ROK-US Alliance and USFK,* Seoul: Oh Sung Planning and Printing.

ROK Ministry of National Unification (1988–98), *Peace and Cooperation: White Paper on Korean Unification.*

ROK Ministry of National Unification (2000–01), *Tongil Paeksŏ [White Paper on Korean Unification].*

ROK National Unification Board (1992), *Nambuk Gibonhapŭisŏ Haesŏl [The Interpretation of the Basic Agreement].*

ROK Office of Arms Control of MND (1990–2000), *Hanbando Gunbitongje [Arms Control on the Korean Peninsula].*

US Defense Intelligence Agency (1995), *North Korea: The Foundations for Military Strength,* Washington, DC: DIA.

US Department of Defense (1990), *A Strategic Framework for the Asian Pacific Rim: Looking toward the 21st Century.*

US Department of Defense (1995, 1998), *The United States Security Strategy for the East Asia − Pacific Region.*

White House (1996), *A National Security Strategy of Engagement and Enlargement.*

3. News sources

English

Agence France Presse
Asahi News Service
BBC Monitoring Reports, Summary of World Broadcasts
Central News Agency (Taiwan)
Chicago Tribune
Daily Yomiuri
FBIS Daily Report-EAS (Foreign Broadcast Information Service, East Asia)
Financial Times (London)
Independent (London)
Japan Economic Newswire
Kyodo News
Los Angeles Times
New York Times
Wall Street Journal
Washington Post

Korean

Chosun Ilbo
Dong-A Ilbo
Hankyure Shinmun
Hankyure 21
Joong-Ang Ilbo
Korea Herald
Korea Newsreview
Mal
Monthly Chosun
Monthly Sin Dong-A
Munhwa Ilbo
North Korea News
SISA Journal
Weekly Chosun

SECONDARY WORKS

1. Books

English

Albright, David and Kevin O'Neill (eds) (2000), *Solving the North Korean Nuclear Puzzle,* Washington: Institute for Science and International Security Press.

Allison, Graham (1971), *Essence of Decision: Explaining the Cuban Missile Crisis,* Boston: Little Brown.

Art, Robert J. and Robert Jervis (1992), *International Politics: Enduring Concepts and Contemporary Issues,* New York: HarperCollins Publishers.

Axelrod, R. (ed.) (1976), *Structure of Decision,* Princeton, NJ: Princeton University Press.

Bandow, Doug (1996), *Tripwire: Korea and US Foreign Policy in a Changed World,* Washington, DC: CATO Institute.

Bermudez, Joseph S. Jr. (2001), *The Armed Forces of North Korea,* London: I.B. Tauris.

Brennan, Donald G. (ed.) (1961), *Arms Control, Disarmament, and National Security,* New York: Georgy Braziller.

Brown, Michael E. et al. (2000), *The Rise of China,* Cambridge: MIT Press.

Butterfield, Herbert (1951), *History and Human Relations,* London: Collins.

Buzo, Adrian (1999), *The Guerrilla Dynasty: Politics and Leadership in North Korea,* Boulder, C: Westview Press.

Carter, Ashton B. and William J. Perry (1999), *Preventive Defense: A New Security Strategy for America,* Washington, DC: Brookings Institution Press.

Cha, Victor D. and David C. Kang (2003), *Nuclear North Korea: A Debate on Engagement Strategies,* New York: Columbia University Press.

Cimbala, Stephen J. (1996), *Clinton and post-Cold War defense,* Westport, C: Praeger.

Clough, Ralph N. (1976), *Deterrence and Defense in Korea: The Role of US Forces,* Washington, DC: Brookings Institution.

Cotton, James (ed.) (1993), *Korea under Roh Tae-Woo: Democratisation, Northern Policy and Inter-Korean Relations,* Allen & Unwin.

Cumings, Bruce (200), *North Korea: Another Country,* New York: New Press.

Downs, Chuck (1999), *Over the Line: North Korea's Negotiating Strategy,* Washington: AEI Press.

Eberstadt, Nicholas and Judith Banister (1992), *The Population of North Korea,* Berkeley: University of California Institute of East Asian Studies.

Eberstadt, Nicholas and Judith Banister and Richard J. Ellings (eds) (2001), *Korea's Future and the Great Powers,* Seattle: University of Washington Press.

Foot, Rosemary (1995), *The Practice of Power: US Relations with China since 1949,* Oxford: Oxford University Press.

Gallagher, Nancy W. (ed.) (1998), *Arms Control: New Approaches to Theory and Policy,* London: Frank Cass.

Goldstein, Judith and Robert Keohane (eds) (1993), *Ideas and Foreign Policy: Beliefs, Institutions, and Political Change,* Ithaca and London: Cornell University Press.

Gordon, Andrew (ed.) (1993), *Postwar Japan as History,* Berkeley: University of California Press.

Green, Michael J. (2003), *Japan's Reluctant Realism: foreign policy challenges in an era of uncertain power,* New York: Palgrave.

Halperin, Morton H. (1974), *Bureaucratic Politics and Foreign Policy,* Washington, DC: Brookings Institution.

Ham, Taik-young (1999), *Arming the Two Koreas: State, Capital and Military Power,* London and New York: Routledge.

Harding, Harry (1992), *A Fragile Relationship: The United States and China since 1972,* Washington, DC: Brookings Institution.

Harrison, Selig S. (2002), *Korean Endgame: A Strategy for Reunification and US Disengagement,* Princeton: Princeton University Press.

Hart-Landsberg, Martin (1998), *Korea: Division, Reunification, and US Foreign Policy,* New York: Monthly Review Press.

Hayes, Peter (1991), *Pacific Powderkeg: American Nuclear Dilemmas in Korea,* Lexington: Lexington Books.

Henriksen, Thomas H. (1996), *Clinton's Foreign Policy in Somalia, Bosnia, Haiti, and North Korea,* Stanford: Hoover Institution on War, Revolution and Peace.

Herrnson, Paul S. and Dilys M. Hill (eds) (1999), *The Clinton Presidency: The First Term, 1992~96,* London: Macmillan Press.

Hilsman, Roger (1990), *The Politics of Policy Making in Defense and Foreign Affairs: Conceptual Models and Bureaucratic Politics,* Englewood Cliffs, NJ: Prentice-Hall.

Hook, Glenn D. et al. (2001), *Japan's International Relations: politics, economics, and security,* London: Routledge.

Hughes, Christopher W. (2004), *Japan's Security Agenda: military, economic, and environmental dimensions,* Boulder, CO: Lynne Rienner Publishers.

Hyland, William G. (1999), *Clinton's World: Remaking American Foreign Policy,* London: Praeger.

Ikenberry, John G. and Michael Mastanduno (eds) (2003), *International Relations Theory and the Asia~Pacific,* New York: Columbia University Press.

Jervis, Robert (1976), *Perception and Misperception in International Politics,* Princeton: Princeton University Press.

Kegley, Charles W. and Eugene R. Wittkopf (eds) (1988), *The Domestic Sources of American Foreign Policy: Insights and Evidence,* New York: St. Martin's.

Khong, Yuen Foong (1992), *Analogies at War: Korea, Munich, Dien Bien Phu, and the Vietnam Decisions of 1965,* Princeton, New Jersey: Princeton University press.

Kim, Ilpyong J. (ed) (1998), *Two Koreas In Transition: Implications for US Policy,* Rockville, MD: InDepth Books.

Kim, Samuel S. (ed.) (1998), *North Korean Foreign Relations In the Post-Cold War Era,* Oxford: Oxford University Press.

Kim, Samuel S. (ed.) (1998), *China and the World: Chinese Foreign Policy Faces the New Millennium,* Boulder, CO: Westview Press.

Kim, Samuel S. (ed.) (2004), *The International Relations of Northeast Asia,* Lanham: Rownan & Littlefield Publishers.

Kim, Samuel S. (ed.) (2004), *Inter-Korean Relations: Problems and Prospects,* Basingstoke: Palgrave Macmillan.

Kwak, Tae-Hwan and Edward A. Olsen (eds) (1996), *The Major Powers of Northeast Asia,* London: Lynne Rienner Publishers.

Lampton, David M. (2001), *Same Bed, Different Dreams: Managing US~China Relations, 1989~2000,* Berkeley, Los Angeles, London: University of California Press.

Lampton, David M. (ed.) (2001), *The Making of Chinese Foreign and Security Policy in the Ear of Reform, 1978~2000,* Stanford: Stanford University Press.

Larson, Deborah Welch (1985), *Origins of Containment: A Psychological Explanation,* Princeton: Princeton University Press.

Lee, Manwoo (1990), *The Odyssey of Korean Democracy: Korean Politics, 1987~1990,* New York: Praeger Publishers.

Lee, Manwoo and Richard W. Mansbach (eds) (1993), *The Changing Order in Northeast Asia and the Korean Peninsula,* Seoul: Institute for Far Eastern Studies, Kyungnam University.

Lee, Such-Ho (1989), *Party-Military Relations in North Korea: A Comparative Analysis,* Seoul: Research Center for Peace and Unification of Korea.

Lim, Gill-Chin and Namsoo Chang (ed.) (2003), *Food Problems in North Korea: Current Situation and Possible Solutions,* Seoul: ORUEM Publishing House.

Litwak, Robert S. (2000), *Rogue States and US Foreign Policy: Containment after the Cold War,* Washington, DC: Woodrow Wilson Center Press.

Little, Richard and Steve Smith (eds) (1988), *Belief Systems and International Relations,* Oxford: Blackwell.

Mazarr, Michael J. (1995), *North Korea and the Bomb: a Case Study in Non-proliferation,* Basingstoke: Macmillan.

Mearsheimer, John (1983), *Conventional Deterrence,* Ithaca, NY: Cornell University Press.

Mercer, Jonathan (1996), *Reputation and International Politics,* Ithaca, NY: Cornell University Press.

Moltz, James Clay and Alexandre Y. Mansourov (eds) (2000), *The North Korean Nuclear Program: Security, Strategy, and New Perspectives from Russia,* New York: Routledge.

Moon, Chung-in (1996), *Arms Control on the Korean Peninsula: Domestic Perceptions, Regional Dynamics, International Penetrations,* Seoul: Yonsei University Press.

Moon, Chung-in. et al. (eds) (2000), *The Perry Report, the Missile Quagmire, and the North Korean Question: The Quest of New Alternatives,* Seoul: Yonsei University Press.

Natsios, Andrew S. (2001), *The Great North Korean Famine,* Washington, DC: United States Institute of Peace Press.

Nisbett, Richard and Lee Ross (1980), *Human Inference: Strategies and Shortcomings of Social Judgment,* Englewood Cliffs, New Jersey: Prentice-Hall.

Noland, Marcus (2000), *Avoiding the Apocalypse: The Future of the Two Koreas,* Washington: Institute for International Economics.

Oberdorfer, Don (1998), *The Two Koreas, A Contemporary History,* New York: Addison-Wesley.

Oh, Kongdan and Ralph C. Hassig (2000), *North Korea Through the Looking Glass,* Washington, DC: Brookings Institution Press.

O'Hanlon, Michael and Mike Mochizuki (2003), *Crisis on the Korean Peninsula: How to Deal with a Nuclear North Korea,* New York: McGraw-Hill.

Oye. Kenneth A. (ed.) (1986), *Cooperation Under Anarchy,* Princeton: Princeton University Press.

Paul, Thazhakuzhyil V. (1994), *Asymmetric Conflicts: War Initiation by Weaker Powers,* Cambridge: Cambridge University Press.

Park, Han S. (eds) (1996), *North Korea: Ideology, Politics, Economy,* New Jersey: Prentice Hall.

Park, Han S. (2002), *North Korea: The Politics of Unconventional Wisdom,* Boulder, Co: Lynne Reiner.

Rosegrant, Susan (1995), *Carrots, Sticks, and Question Marks: Negotiating the North Korean Nuclear Crisis,* Boston: Harvard University, John F. Kennedy School of Government.

Reese, David (1998), *The Prospects for North Korea's Survival,* Oxford: Oxford University Press.

Schelling, Thomas (1966), *Arms and Influence,* New Haven: Yale University Press.

Schelling, Thomas and Morton H. Halperin (1961), *Strategy and Arms Control,* New York: A Pergaman-Brasseys Classic.

Sigal, Leon (1998), *Disarming Strangers: Nuclear Diplomacy with North Korea,* Princeton, NJ: Princeton University Press.

Skidmore, David and Valerie M. Hudson (eds) (1993), *The Limits of State Autonomy: Societal Groups and Foreign Policy Formulation,* Boulder, CO: Westview Press.

Snyder, Glenn (1960), *Deterrence and Defense,* Princeton: Princeton University Press.

Stockwin, J.A.A. (James Arthur Ainscow) (1999), *Governing Japan: Divided Politics in a Major Economy,* Malden, Ma.: Blackwell.

Suh, Dae-Sook (1988), *Kim Il Sung: The North Korean Leader,* New York: Columbia University Press.

Suh, Dae-Sook and Chae-Jin Lee (eds) (1998), *North Korea After Kim Il Sung,* London: Lynne Rienner Publishers.

Sullivan, John and Roberta Foss (eds) (1987), *Two Koreas – One Future?* Lanham: University Press of America.

Taylor, Wlliam, Young-koo Cha and John Blodgett (eds) (1990), *The Korean Peninsula: Prospects for Arms Reduction under Global Détente,* Boulder: Westview.

Thomas, Raju G.C. (ed.) (1998), *The Nuclear Non-Proliferation Regime: Prospects for the 21st Century,* London: Macmillan Press.

Walter, Barbara F. and Jack Snyder (eds) (1999), *Civil Wars, Insecurity, and Intervention,* New York: Columbia University Press.

Wit, Joel S, Daniel B. Poneman and Robert L. Gallucci (2004), *Going Critical: The First North Korean Nuclear Crisis,* Washington, DC: Brookings Institution Press.

Yahuda, Michael (1996), *The International Politics of the Asia-Pacific, 1945~1995,* London: Routledge.

Yang, Sung Chul (1999), *The North and South Korean Political Systems: A Comparative Analysis,* Revised Edition, New Jersey: Hollym.

Korean

Choe, Yong-chol (1993), *T'ong'il-ro Makhimyŏn Tolasŏ Kacha [Let's go around if the road to unification is blocked],* Seoul: T'ong'il Ponyong Yonguwon.

Chung, Ok-nim (1995), *Bukhaek 588il [588 days of North Korean nuclear bombs],* Seoul: Seoul Press.

Ham, Taik-young et al. (1992), *Nanbukhan Gunbi Gyungjaenggwa Gunch'uk [North~South Korean Arms Race and Arms],* Seoul: Kyoungnam University Press.

Hwang, Jang Yop (1999), *Nanŭn Yŏksaŭi Chilli rul Poattda [I have Witnessed Historical Truth],* Seoul: Hanul.

Hwang, Jin Hwoan (1998), *Kunsaryuk Kŏnsŏl gwa Kunbitongjei eŭ Hyoyuljeok Johwa Pangan [The Measures for Balancing between Military Build-Up and Arms Control],* Seoul: The Army Military Academy Press.

Kim, Gye-Dong (2002), *Pukhanŭi Oekyo Chŏngch'ek [Foreign Policy of North Korea],* Seoul: Baiksan Publishing House.

Kim, Jae-hong (2000), *Kimdaejung Chŏngbuŭi Nampuk Hwahaejeongch'ekgwa Chŏngch'icommunication [Kim Dae-jung Government's Policy of Inter-Korean Reconciliation and Political Communication],* Seoul: Sejong Institute.

Kim, Il Yong and Sung Ryul Cho (2003), *Chuhan Migun: yŏksa, Y isuwa Chŏnmang [The US Forces in Korea: History, issues, and Prospect],* Seoul: Hanwool Academy.

Kim, Young Sam (2001), *Kim Young Sam Taet'ongnyŏng Hoegorok: Minjujuuirul Wihan Naŭi T'ujaeng [President Kim Young Sam Memoir: My Struggle for Democracy],* Seoul: Chosun Ilbo Press.

Koh, Young-hwan (1992), *Pyongyang Yisibosi [Pyongyang's Twenty Five Hours],* Seoul: Kyoryuone.

Kwak, Tae-Hwan et al. (1997), *Pukhan eu Hyupsang Jeonryuk gwa Nampukhan Kwangye [North Korea's Negotiation Strategy and the South-North Relationship],* Seoul: Kyoungnam University Press.

Lee, Jong-suk (1999), *Pundansidaeŭi T'ong'ilhak [The Study of Reunification in the Divided Era],* Seoul: Hanul.

Lee, Jong-suk (2000), *Hyŏndae Pukhanŭi Yihae [Understanding of Modern North Korea],* Seoul: Yoksapipyongsa.

Lee, Jong-suk (2000), *Pukhan-Chungguk Kwan'gye [North Korea-China Relations: 1945~2000],* Seoul: Chungsim.

Lee, Ju-chol (2000), *Kim Jong Il eu Saenggak Ilkgi [Understanding of Kim Jong Il's Mind],* Seoul: Jisikgongjakso.

Lee, Kyo-duk (1997), *Pukilsukyowa Nampukhan Kwan'gye [North Korea~Japan normalisation and Inter-Korean Relations],* Seoul: Minjokt'ong'il Yonguwon.

Lee, Sam-sung (1994), *Hanbando Haekmunjewa Migukyoekyo [The Nuclear Question and US Policy on the Korean Peninsula],* Seoul: Hangil Publishing.

Park, Hak Soon and Chang Soo Jin (eds) (1999), *Pukhanmunjeui Kukchechŏk Chengchŏm [International Ramifications of the 'North Korean P0roblem'],* Seoul: Sejong Institute.

Park, Jae-Kyu et al. (1983), *Pukhan Kunsa Chŏngch'ek Ron [A Study of North Korean Military Policy],* Seoul: Kyoungnam University Press.

Quinones, Kenneth (2000), *Hanbando Unmyŏng: Pukpokyinya Hyŏpsangyinya [North Korea's nuclear threat 'off the record' memories],* Seoul: Jongang M&B.

Sin, Ji-Ho (2000), *Pukhanŭi Kaehyok Kaebang: Kwagŏ, Hyŏnhwang, Chŏnmang [North Korea's Reform and Open-Door Policy: past, present, and the prospect],* Seoul: Hanul Academy.

Yi, Chan-haeng (1994), *Ingan Kim Jong Il, Suryong Kim Jong Il: Kuui Sidae wa Pukhan Sahoe [Kim Jong Il as a Person and as the Supreme Leader: His Times and North Korean Society,* Seoul: Yollin Sesang.

2. Articles

Ahn, Byung-joon (1994), 'The Man Who Would Be Kim', *Foreign Affairs, 73* (6).

Albright, David (1993), 'North Korea Drops Out', *The Bulletin of the Atomic Scientists.*

Bazhanov, Eugene (1992), 'Soviet Policy toward South Korea under Gorbachev', in Il Yung Chung (ed.), *Korea and Russia: Toward the 21st Century,* Seoul: Sejong Institute.

Bermudez Jr, Joseph S. (1996), 'North Korea's Nuclear Arsenal', *Jane's Intelligence Review.*

Bracken, Paul (1995), 'Risks and Promises in the Two Koreas', *Orbis, 39* (1).

Calder, Kent (1989), 'The Reactive State: Japanese Foreign Policy', *World Politics, 40* (4).

Cha, Victor D. (1997), 'Realism, Liberalism, and the Durability of the US – South Korean Alliance', *Asian Survey, 37* (7).

Cha, Victor D. (1998), 'Is there still a rational North Korea option for war?', *Security Dialogue, 29* (4).

Cha, Victor D. (2000), 'Engaging North Korea Credibly', *Survival, 42* (2).

Cha, Victor D. (2003), 'Why We Must Pursue Hawk Engagement', in Victor D. Cha and David C. Kang, *Nuclear North Korea: A Debate on Engagement Strategies,* New York: Columbia University Press.

Chang, Dal Jung (1993), 'Pukhan Chŏngch'aek Kyŏlchŏng Kujo Mit Kwachŏng [North Korea's policy-making structure and process]', *Sŏultae Sahoe Kwahakkwa Chŏngchaek Yŏn'gu [Social Science and Policy Studies, Seoul National University], 15* (2).

Cheon, Seongwhun (1997), 'A Role Definition and Implementation Strategies for the Four-Party Peace Talks', *The Korean Journal of National Unification, 6.*

Christensen, Thomas J. (1999), 'China, the US – Japan Alliance, and the Security Dilemma in East Asia', *International Security 23* (4).

Christensen, Thomas J. (2002), 'The Contemporary Security Dilemma: Deterring a Taiwan Conflict', *Washington Quarterly, 25* (4).

Chung, Jae Ho (2004), 'China's Korea Policy Under the New Leadership: Stealth Changes in the Making?', *Journal of East Asian Affairs, 18* (1).

Cotton, James (1998), 'The Rajin-Sonbong Free Trade Zone Experiment: North Korea in Pursuit of New International Linkage', in Samuel S. Kim (ed.), *North Korean Foreign Relations In the Post-Cold War Era,* Oxford: Oxford University Press.

Crowe, William Jr. and Alan D. Romberg (1991), 'Rethinking Security in the Pacific', *Foreign Affairs, 70* (2).

Cumings, Bruce (1998), 'Nuclear Imbalance of Terror: The American Surveillance Regime and North Korea's Nuclear Programme', in Raju G.C. Thomas (ed.), *The Nuclear Non-Proliferation Regime: Prospects for the 21st Century,* London: Macmillan Press.

Dembinski, Matthias (1995), 'North Korea, IAEA Special Inspections, and the Future of the Nonproliferation Regime', *The Nonproliferation Review.*

Dower, John (1993), 'Peace and Democracy in Two systems', in Andrew Gordon (ed.), *Postwar Japan as History,* Berkeley: University of California Press.

Eberstadt, Nicholas and Richard J. Ellings (2001), 'Assessing Interests and Objectives of Major Actors in the Korean Drama', in Eberstadt and Ellings (eds), *Korea's Future and the Great Powers,* Seattle: University of Washington Press.

Ellison, Herbert J. (2001), 'Russia, Korea, and Northeast Asia', in Eberstadt and Ellings (eds), *Korea's Future and the Great Powers,* Seattle: University of Washington Press.

Foot, Rosemary J. (1988), 'Nuclear Coercion and the Ending of the Korean Conflict', *International Security 13* (3).

Foster-Carter, Aidan (2001), 'Dove Myths: No Better Than Hawk Myths', *Nautilus Institute Policy Forum Online (PFO)* 01–02D.

Glaser, Charles L. (1997), 'The Security Dilemma Revisited', *World Politics, 50.*

Goldstein, Judith and Robert Keohane (1993), 'Ideas and Foreign Policy', in Judith Goldstein and Robert Keohane (eds), *Ideas and Foreign Policy: Beliefs, Institutions, and Political Change,* Ithaca and London: Cornell University Press.

Goose, Stephen (1987), 'The Military Situation on the Korean Peninsula', in John Sullivan and Roberta Foss (eds), *Two Koreas – One Future?,* Lanham: University Press of America.

Halloran, Richard (1998), 'North Korean Relations with Japan', in Dae-Sook Suh and Chae-Jin Lee (eds), *North Korea After Kim Il Sung,* London: Lynne Rienner Publishers.

Hames, Tim (1999), 'Foreign Policy', in Paul S. Herrnson and Dilys M. Hill (eds), *The Clinton Presidency: The First Term, 1992-6,* London: Macmillan Press.

Harnisch, Sebastian (2002), 'US – North Korean Relations Under the Bush Administration: From "Slow Go" to "No Go"', *Asian Survey, XLII* (6).

Harrison, Selig S. (1997), 'Promoting a Soft Landing in Korea', *Foreign Policy, 106.*

Harrison, Selig S. (1998), 'US Policy Toward North Korea', in Dae-Sook Suh and Chae-Jin Lee (ed.), *North Korea After Kim Il Sung,* London: Lynne Rienner Publishers.

Herman, Tamar (1993), 'Grassroots Activism as a Factor in Foreign Policy-Making: The Case of the Israeli Peace Movement', in David Skidmore and Valerie M. Hudson (eds), *The Limits of State Autonomy: Societal Groups and Foreign Policy Formulation,* Boulder, Co.: Westview Press.

Herz, John H. (1950), 'Idealist Internationalism and the Security Dilemma', *World Politics, 2.*

Holsti, Ole R. (1976), 'Foreign policy formation viewed cognitively', in R. Axelrod (ed.), *Structure of Decision,* Princeton, NJ: Princeton University Press.

Jervis, Robert (1968), 'Hypotheses on Misperception', *World Politics, 20* (3).

Jervis, Robert (1985), 'From Balance to Concert: A Study of International Security Cooperation', *World Politics, 38.*

Jervis, Robert (1988), 'Realism, Game Theory, and Cooperation', *World Politics, 40.*

Jervis, Robert (1992), 'Offence, Defense, and the Security Dilemma', in Robert J. Art and Robert Jervis, *International Politics: Enduring Concepts and Contemporary Issues,* New York: HarperCollins Publishers.

Jin, Chang Soo (1999), 'Pukil Kwan'gye: Kukkyo Sulibŭi Chŏngch'ichŏk Yoin' [North Korea–Japan Relations: political factors of normalisation.], in Hak Soon Park and Chang Soo Jin (eds), *Pukhanmunjeui Kukchechŏk Chengchŏm [International Ramifications of the 'North Korean Problem'],* Seoul: Sejong Institute.

Kang, David (1994), 'Preventive War and North Korea', *Security Studies 4* (2).

Kang, David (1998), 'North Korea's Military and Security Policy', in Samuel Kim (ed.), *North Korean Foreign Relations In the Post-Cold War Era,* Oxford: Oxford University Press.

Kang, David (2003), 'Threatening, but Deterrence Works', in Victor D. Cha and David C. Kang, *Nuclear North Korea: A Debate on Engagement Strategies,* New York: Columbia University Press.

Kanwisher, Nancy (1989), 'Cognitive Heuristics and American Security Policy', *Journal of Conflict Resolution, 33.*

Kim, Hak-Joon (1993), 'The Republic of Korea's Northern Policy: Origin, Development, and Prospects', in James Cotton (ed.), *Korea under Roh Tae-Woo: Democratisation, Northern Policy and Inter-Korean Relations,* Allen & Unwin.

Kim, Hong Nack (2004), 'Japanese–North Korean Relations after the 2002 Pyongyang Summit', *Korea and World Affairs, 28* (2).

Kim, Ilpyong J. (1998), 'China in North Korean Foreign Policy', in Samuel Kim (ed.), *North Korean Foreign Relations In the Post-Cold War Era,* Oxford: Oxford University Press.

Kim, Philo (2003), 'The Social Impact of Food Crisis in North Korea', in Gill-Chin Lim and Namsoo Chang (eds), *Food Problems in North Korea: Current Situation and Possible Solutions,* Seoul: ORUEM Publishing House.

Kim, Samuel S. (1996), 'North Korea in 1995: The Crucible of 'Our Style Socialism', *Asian Survey, 36* (1).

Kim, Samuel S. (2001), 'The Making of China's Korea Policy in the Era of Reform', in David M. Lampton (ed.), *The Making of Chinese Foreign and Security Policy in the Era of Reform, 1978-2000,* Stanford: Stanford University Press.

Kim, Young C. (1989), 'The Politics of Arms Control in Korea', *Korean Journal of Defense Analysis, 1* (1).

Koh, B.C. (1997), 'South Korea in 1996: Internal Strains and External Challenges', *Asian Survey, 37* (1).

Koh, B.C. (1988), 'North Korea's Unification Policy after the Seoul Olympics', *Korea Observer, 19* (4).

Kornberg, Judith F. (1996), 'Comprehensive Engagement: New Frameworks for Sino-American Relations', *Journal of East Asian Affairs, 10* (1).

Krasner, Stephen D. (1988), 'Are Bureaucracies Important? A Re-examination of Accounts of the Cuban Missile Crisis', in Charles W. Kegley and Eugene R. Wittkopf (eds), *The Domestic Sources of American Foreign Policy: Insights and Evidence,* New York: St. Martin's.

Kreisberg, Paul H. (1990), 'The US and Asia in 1989: Mounting Dilemmas', *Asian Survey, 30* (1).

Kristof, Nicholas D. (1993), 'The Rise of China', *Foreign Affairs, 72* (5).

Kurata, Hideya (1995), 'The International Context of North Korea's Proposal for a 'New Peace Arrangement': Issues after the US – DPRK Nuclear Accord', *Korean Journal of Defense Analysis, 7* (1).

Kwak, Tae-Hwan (1995), 'US Military-Security Policy toward the Korean Peninsula in the 1990s', *Korean Journal of Defense Analysis, 7* (2).

Lake, Anthony (1993), 'From Containment to Enlargement', US Department of State, Bureau of Public Affairs, *Dispatch, 4* (3).

Lampton, David M. (1997), 'China and Clinton's America: Have They Learned Anything?' *Asian Survey, 37* (12).

Lebow, Richard Ned (1984), 'Windows of Opportunity: Do States Jump through Them?', *International Security, 9* (1).

Lee, Manwoo (1993), 'Changes in South Korea and Inter-Korean relations', *Pacific Focus.*

Lee, Tonghun (1993), 'Pukhan Kunsa Chŏngch'aek Kyŏlchŏngkujo Mit Kwachŏngkwa Kunbi T'ongjaeŭi Munje' [The Structure and Process of Military Policy Making of North Korea and Arms Control Issues], *Sŏultae Sahoe Kwahakkwa Chŏngchaek Yŏn'gu [Social Science and Policy Studies, Seoul National University]*, 15 (2).

Levy, Jack S. (1987), 'Declining Power and the Preventive Motivation for War', *World Politics, 40* (1).

Lim, Dongwon (1993), 'Inter-Korean Relations Oriented Toward Reconciliation and Cooperation', in James Cotton (ed.), *Korea under Roh Tae-Woo: Democratisation, Northern Policy and Inter-Korean Relations,* Allen & Unwin.

Livsey, W. (1985), 'US and ROK Readiness', *Asia-Pacific Defense Forum, 10* (1).

Mansfield, Edward and Jack Snyder (1995), 'Democratization and the Danger of War', *International Security, 20* (1).

Masaki, Stuart K. (1994), 'The Korean Question: Assessing the Military Balance', *Security Studies, 4* (2).

Maxwell, David S. (1997), 'North Korea's Collapse and the US Response', *Sasang [Ideology]*.

Moon, Chung-in (1991), 'The Political Economy of Defense Industrialization in South Korea: Constraints, Opportunities, and Prospects', *The Journal of East Asian Affairs, 5* (2).

Moon, Chung-in and Won K. Paik (1998), 'The Post-Cold War Environment, Democratization, and National Security in South Korea', in Ilpyong J. Kim (eds), *Two Koreas In Transition: Implications for US Policy,* Rockville, MD: InDepth Books.

Noland, Marcus (1996), 'The North Korean Economy', *Joint US~Korean Academic Studies, Economic and Regional Cooperation in Northeast Asia, 6.*

Oh, Kong Dan (1990), 'North Korea in 1989: Touched by Winds of Change?', *Asian Survey, 30* (1).

O'Hanlon, Michael (1998), 'Stopping a North Korean Invasion: Why Defending South Korea Is Easier than The Pentagon Thinks', *International Security, 22* (4).

Okonogi, Masao (1993), 'Japan–North Korean Negotiations for Normalization: An Overview', in Manwoo Lee and Richard W. Mansbach (eds), *The Changing Order in Northeast Asia and the Korean Peninsula,* Seoul: Institute for Far Eastern Studies, Kyungnam University.

Olsen, Edward A. (1986), 'The Arms Race on the Korean Peninsula', *Asian Survey, 26* (8).

Oye, Kenneth A. (1986), 'Explaining Cooperation Under Anarchy: Hypotheses and Strategies', in Kenneth A. Oye (eds), *Cooperation Under Anarchy,* Princeton: Princeton University Press.

Park, Han S. (1998), 'The Nature and Evolution of Juche', in Ilpyong J. Kim (eds), *Two Koreas In Transition: Implications for US Policy,* Rockville, MD: InDepth Books.

Park, Jin (1990), 'Political Change in South Korea: the challenge of the conservative alliance', *Asian Survey, 30* (12).

Park, Kyung-Ae (1997), 'Explaining North Korea's Negotiated Cooperation with the U.S.', *Asian Survey, 37* (7).

Park, Myong-lim (1997), 'Pundan Chilsoŭi Kujowa Pyŏnhwa: Chŏktaewa Ŭichonŭi Taessangkwan'gyetonghak' [Structure and Change of Division: Interface Dynamics of Hostility and Dependence], *Kukka Chŏllyak [National Strategy], 3* (1).

Park, Tong-whan (1992), 'Issues of Arms Control Between the two Koreas', *Asian Survey, 32* (4).

Phipps, John (1991), 'North Korea – Will it be the "Great Leader's" Turn Next?', *Government and Opposition.*

Pollack, Jonathan D. (1996), 'The United States and Asia in 1995: The Case of the Missing President', *Asian Survey, 36* (1).

Pollack, Jonathan D. (1997), 'The United States and Asia in 1996: Under Renovation, but Open for Business', *Asian Survey, 37* (1).

Putnam, Robert D. (1998), 'Diplomacy and Domestic Politics: The Logic of Two-Level Games', *International Organization, 42* (3).

Rhee, Sang-woo (1991), 'North Korea in 1990: Lonesome Struggle to Keep Juche', *Asian Survey, 31* (1).

Risse-Kappen, Thomas (1991), 'Public Opinion, Domestic Structures, and Foreign Policy in Liberal Democracies', *World Politics, 43* (4).

Roberts, Brad (1993), 'From Nonproliferation to Antiproliferation', *International Security, 18* (1).

Roy, Denny (1988), 'North Korea's Relations with Japan: The Legacy of War', *Asian Survey, 28* (12).

Roy, Denny (1994), 'North Korea and Madman Theory', *Security Dialogue,* 25 (3).

Scalapino, Robert A. (2001), 'China and Korean Reunification – A Neighbor's Concerns', in Eberstadt and Ellings (eds), *Korea's Future and the Great Powers,* Seattle: University of Washington Press.

Schweller, Randall (1992), 'Domestic Structure and Preventive War', *World Politics, 44* (2).

Segal, Gerald (1999), 'Does China Matter?' *Foreign Affairs, 78* (5).

Shambaugh, David (1992), 'China in 1991: Living Cautiously', *Asian Survey, 32* (1).

Sigal, Leon V. (2001), 'US-DPRK Relations and Military Issues on the Korean Peninsula', *KNDU Review, 6* (2).

Shin, Sang-jin (1998), 'Chŏllyaksang Yujitoenŭn Chung-Puk Tongmaeng Kwan'gye [Sino-North Korean alliance sustained based only on strategic reasons]', *Chayukongnon [Free Public Opinion].*

Smith, Steve (1988), 'Belief Systems and the Study of International Relations', in Richard Little and Steve Smith (eds), *Belief Systems and International Relations,* Oxford: Blackwell.

Snyder, Jack L. (1985), 'Perceptions of the Security Dilemma in 1914', in Robert Jervis, Ned Lebow and Janice G. Stein (eds), *Psychology and Deterrence,* Baltimore: Johns Hopkins University Press.

Son, Sung Young (1991), 'The Korean Nuclear Issue', *Korea and World Affairs,* 15 (3).

Spector, Leonard and Jacqueline Smith (1991), 'North Korea: The Next Nuclear Nightmare?', *Arms Control Today, 21* (2).

Suh, Dae-Sook (1998), 'North Korea: The Present and the Future', *Korean Journal of Defense Analysis, 9* (2).

Suh, Dae-Sook (1998), 'Kim Jong Il and New Leadership in North Korea', in Dae-Sook Suh and Chae-Jin Lee (eds), *North Korea After Kim Il Sung,* London: Lynne Rienner Publishers.

Suh, Jae-jin (1992), 'Policy direction after Kim Il Sung's death', *KINU Seminar series* 92– 02.

Taylor, William J. and Michael J. Mazarr (1992), 'US– Korean Security Relations: Post-Reunification', *Korean Journal of Defense Analysis 4* (1).

Totten, George O. (1985), 'Japan's Policy Toward North Korea', *Korea Observer, 16* (2).

Tow, William (1991), 'Reassessing Deterrence on the Korean peninsula', *Korean Journal of Defense Analysis, 3* (1).

Wang, Jianwei and Zhimin Lin (1992), 'Chinese Perceptions in the Post-Cold War Era: Three Images of the United States', *Asian Survey, 32* (10).

Whan, Chun Chung (1996), 'North Korea's Intention to Destroy the Truce Mechanism and the Current Situation on the Korean Peninsula', *East Asian Review, 8* (1).

Yoo, Suk Yuel (1996), 'Pukhan Kwŏllyŏksoyŏlŭi Pyŏnhwa *Chŏngchaek* Panghyang [Change of Power Hierarchy and Policy Direction of North Korea]', Chuyŏ Kukchemunje Punsŏk [*Analysis of Major International Issue*], 1996– 38.

Zacek, Jane Shapiro (1998), 'Russia in North Korean Foreign Policy', in Samuel S. Kim (ed.), *North Korean Foreign Relations In the Post-Cold War Era,* Oxford: Oxford University Press.

3. Dissertations

Hong, Yong-Pyo (1995), 'State Security and Regime Security: The security policy of South Korea under the Syngman Rhee government', D.Phil. Dissertation, Oxford University.

Lee, Jung-Yong (2002), 'North Korea's Arms Control Policy and the Challenge of South Korea's Sunshine Policy', D.Phil. Dissertation, Aberdeen University.

Lho, Cholsoo (1999), 'The Transformation of South Korea's Foreign Policy 1988–1993: Nordpolitik, Moscow and the Road to Pyongyang', D.Phil. Dissertation, Oxford University.

Kim, Bong Gyu (1998), 'A study on how the food shortage of North Korea would affect its battle achievement', Master's Dissertation, Chung-Ang University.

4. Unpublished speech

Laney, James (1996), 'North and South Korea: Beyond Deterrence', Speech at the Asia Society, 11 May 1996.

Index